D0561547

Bloom's Modern Critical Views

Bloom's Modern Critical Views

Bloom's Modern Critical Views

JAY WRIGHT

Edited and with an introduction by
Harold Bloom
Sterling Professor of the Humanities
Yale University

CHELSEA HOUSE
PUBLISHERS
A Haights Cross Communications Company

Philadelphia

Bruton Memorial Library
Plant City, Florida 33563

©2004 by Chelsea House Publishers, a subsidiary of
Haights Cross Communications.

A Haights Cross Communications ✦ Company

Introduction © 2004 by Harold Bloom.

All rights reserved. No part of this publication may be
reproduced or transmitted in any form or by any means
without the written permission of the publisher.

Printed and bound in the United States of America.
10 9 8 7 6 5 4 3 2 1

Library of Congress Cataloging-in-Publication Data

Jay Wright / edited and with an introduction by Harold Bloom.
      p. cm. -- (Bloom's modern critical views)
Includes bibliographical references and index.
   ISBN: 0-7910-7661-X
 1. Wright, Jay, 1935---Criticism and interpretation. I. Bloom,
Harold. II. Title III. Series.
   PS3583.R5364Z74 2003
   811'.54--dc22
                                        2003012273

Chelsea House Publishers
1974 Sproul Road, Suite 400
Broomall, PA 19008-0914

http://www.chelseahouse.com

Contributing Editor: Aaron Tillman

Cover designed by Terry Mallon

Cover: © Don J. Usner

Layout by EJB Publishing Services

Contents

Editor's Note

My Introduction was first published in 1998 in an edition of 110 copies designed, printed, and bound by Ken Botnick for Washington University Library Special Collections, St. Louis, under the title, *Jay Wright: The American Sublime Ode; the Black Limbo.*

Darryl Pinckney, confessing that he is at sea, is washed away by Jay Wright's difficult and pungent *The Double Invention of Komo.*

African religion and myth, central to Wright, is accurately viewed by Gerald Barrax, who judges Wright's first five books to be essentially religious poetry, while Robert B. Stepto lucidly introduces all of Wright's work as an ongoing process of making us whole.

Wright's leading scholar, Vera M. Kutzinski, analyzes the superb early poem, "Benjamin Banneker Helps to Build a City."

A very useful interview with the poet is conducted by Charles H. Rowell, after which Vera M. Kutzinski returns with an exposition of Jay Wright's poetics.

Robert B. Shaw confesses himself defeated by the *Selected Poems,* while Isidore Okpewho bravely sketches some of the complexities of Dogon and Bambara mythology that are crucial to apprehending Jay Wright.

In an appreciation, Ron Welburn focuses upon Wright's poetic voice, after which Paul Christiansen struggles with the poet's spiritual stances.

Poet-critic John Hollander, reviewing the collected poems, *Transfigurations,* cogently emphasizes Wright's relationship to late Romantic poetry, including the work of Robert Hayden and Hart Crane.

In the finest and most advanced criticism yet devoted to Jay Wright, Steven Meyer concludes this book by praising this great poet's mastery of an authentic, inventive formalism.

HAROLD BLOOM

Introduction

One central image in Jay Wright's poetry is creation-by-twinning, in which a poem becomes a limbo dance, a gateway out of the Middle Passage of the slave trade, a gateway that is also a logbook, and so a poem for passage. The limbo is a West Indian dance performed under a gradually lowered bar, until the dancer is a spider-man, spread-eagling his arms and legs. Interpreters refer the limbo to the terrible Middle Passage, the route of slave ships from Africa to America, during which the slaves were crowded into so little space that they contorted themselves into human spiders. In Jay Wright's art, the limbo is a metaphor for this poet's aesthetic project, a quest for a gateway out of the Middle Passage by making "a log for passage." This logbook offers initiation by twinning, a mode of divine creation in the Dogon mythology of West Africa. There Amma or Yahweh twins himself hermetically as Nommo or Adam, a forerunner for the Black Son of God, who will be the gateway for everyone out of a universal Middle Passage. In his poem, "The Albuquerque Graveyard," Wright had returned to the burial place of early friends and associates:

> I am going back
> to the Black limbo,
> an unwritten history
> of our own tensions.
> The dead lie here
> in a hierarchy of small defeats.
>   [*Selected Poems* 62]

A somewhat later poem, "The Abstract of Knowledge / The First Test," has an intricate passage adumbrating this image of the limbo, at

1

once Dante's place outside of Hell, Purgatory, and Heaven, and a dance ironically commemorating bondage:

> If you go from the certainty of oneness
> into solitude and return,
> I must divest you of your double
> and twin you in love's seclusion.
> My instruments toll you into limbo;
> > [*Selected Poems* 180]

Dogon mythology teaches that every being, indeed every object, has its own language, which is its twin or double, its Nommo or Adam. Western Hermetism has roughly the same teaching, which influenced Symbolist poetry, both in Rimbaud and in Hart Crane. Jakob Boehme's grand phrase for this doubling was "the signature of all things." In many respects, Jay Wright's poetry attempts to read the signatures of all things, a daunting project for any poet, but one peculiarly fraught with hazards for an African-American writer in our America after the Millennium. The extra-literary pressures placed upon the late Ralph Ellison were excruciating, and doubtless had their effect in seeing to it that *Invisible Man* remained a solitary achievement. Ellison once wryly remarked to me that only internal pressures could be fecund; the evidence for his proud truthtelling can be found all about us, in all the clamors of Resentment, emanating as they do from every possible ideology. What Ellison is to the African-American novel, Jay Wright is to black poetry in the United States. It is not accidental that Wright has become the Invisible Man: reclusive, isolated, and ceaselessly meditating in a remote part of Vermont, alone with his wife. What other context does our self-betrayed culture afford him? But I have cried out upon these matters too often, and I am so wearied by Resenters who urge historicizing and politicizing upon me, that for now I will just forget them, and will analyze and appreciate Jay Wright's poetry as it sets him in company of his peers: Rilke, Hölderlin, Hart Crane, Robert Hayden, Paul Celan, and Luis Cernuda, the marvelous Spanish poet of the Sublime who fled Franco and died by his own hand in Mexico. My love for Wright's poetry goes back a quarter-century to *The Homecoming Singer* (1971), and has been heightened with each subsequent volume, culminating with *Boleros* (1991). There has been no book by Wright these last five years, but I will quote and discuss one of his most recent poems. At sixty-one, Wright is one of the handful of major American poets that we have alive among us, but alas he is the least read and studied of them all. Partly this is caused by the authentic cognitive and imaginative difficulties that his work presents, but partly the neglect of his poetry comes from nearly everyone's wrong-headed expectations of an African-American poet. Wright is a protest poet only as Dante was. A visionary poet, whether William Blake or Hart Crane or Jay Wright, has an agenda that an age of politicized criticism cannot apprehend. Wright is a great religious poet, whose spirituality is a syncretic weave of African, American, and European strands. The American component in this weaving is New Mexican and Mexican, the European is Dantesque, the African most often Dogon. We have little capacity for apprehending so complex and original a spiritual vision, which enhances Jay Wright's poetic difficulty for us. Yet I am speaking of a central American poet, one fully comparable to John Ashbery, A. R. Ammons, and only a handful of others now living among us. That so remarkable and capacious a poet is neglected is another, terrible symptom of our current cultural decay.

The American Sublime, however we mock it, remains the crucial mode of our poetry, from Emerson, Whitman and Dickinson through Wallace Stevens and Hart Crane on to James Merrill, Ammons, and Jay Wright. By the Sublime I intend the Longinian sense of being upon the heights, a transcendental and agonistic mode of aesthetic experience, and one that is highly consonant with extraordinary learning. Learned poets are not infrequent, in all the great poetic traditions. Jay Wright legitimately participates in so many strong traditions that inevitably he is an immensely learned poet. The difficulties presented to the reader are different neither in degree nor in kind from those we have to confront in John Milton or in William Blake. I have expressed my critical conviction that only Wright is of Ralph Ellison's eminence among all African-American creators of imaginative literature, up to this present time. But *Invisible Man* is a post-Faulknerian novel, and has much the same relation to *Light in August* or *Absalom, Absalom!* as these books have to Joseph Conrad's principal fictions. Modern poetry, however, is bewilderingly multiform in its relation to anterior poetry, and Wright is syncretic and diverse to an extraordinary degree. If you compare him to an exact contemporary like the admirable Mark Strand, one of your first conclusions will be that Strand has an intense relation to only a few precursors, Wallace Stevens and Elizabeth Bishop in particular. Strand's *Dark Harbor*, a book-length sequence of marvelous eloquence and poignancy, relies upon its intricate evasions of Stevens's influence, at once embraced without ambivalence, yet also warded-off, lest Strand drown in

Stevens. Wright seems to me closest to Hart Crane among American poets, but neither Crane nor the Crane-influenced Robert Hayden are as central to Wright's art as Stevens is to Strand's. Sometimes, particularly in *The Double Invention of Komo*, Wright seems as haunted by T.S. Eliot's *Four Quartets* as Crane was by *The Waste Land*. It can be a touch disconcerting to hear Eliot's voice in Wright's St. Augustine:

> This is the dance of the changeless
> and the changing,
> the spirit's intensity
> for the world's endurance.
> Knowledge is motion in twilight,
> a state of falling into sight;
> one by one,
> the spirit's eyes touch and grow.
> *Peregrinus*, the tense spirit
> tenses and returns to its
> own understanding.
> There is always the going forth
> and the returning;
> there is always the act,
> the slow fusion of being.
> All things,
> by the strength of being joined,
> will continue;
> the sin is to turn away;
> ignorance is inattention ...
> [*Double Invention* 51]

In his "Afterword" to *The Double Invention of Komo*, Wright comments upon poetic voicing and its relation to ritual:

> In ritual, one does not step back from vision; one follows
> it. My poem risks ritual's arrogance. It presents a dominant
> voice, that of the initiate undergoing Komo's rigorous
> formalities ... [*Double Invention* 114]

The "dominant voice" of the poem is certainly Wright's own, though it fascinates me as to just why the later Eliot continues to break in, usurping the celebrant of Bambara ritual. I take the Eliotic intrusions, here and elsewhere in Wright, to be a sign that anthropology and poetry do not necessarily dwell together so comfortably as Wright insists they do. It is well worth remarking that Wright is a poet of the Sublime; he is not an anthropologist, a cultural historian, or a revivalist of archaic African religions. Yes, he is a soothsayer and reads omens, but primarily as a path to writing his own poems. So fiercely fused are his gifts, at their best, that he transforms ritual into poetry, but never poetry into ritual, the prime flaw of Eliot in the *Quartets*. I learn something about African spirituality by reading Wright, and by following up his references to crucial scholarship upon this matter, but after all one can read his sources without reading him. In a review of Wright's *Selected Poems*, a not unsympathetic poet-critic, Robert B. Shaw, called the author of *The Double Invention of Komo* and *Dimensions of History* "a belated High Modernist," and lamented that readers uneducated in the relevant anthropological sources would require commentaries before they could judge the question of value in Wright's work. Yet, like T.S. Eliot and Hart Crane, Jay Wright at his most appealing is an incantatory writer whose initial impact transcends the necessity of commentary. Pindar is an immensely difficult poet, dense with mythological allusiveness, but his passionate pride in his own agonistic poetic prowess eloquently goes beyond his intricate ecstasies of mythic counterpoint. The high song more than sustains its difficulties, and Pindar always asks and answers the triple-question of the Sublime: more than? less than? or equal to? Excellence in the range and reach of the spirit is always the burden of the Sublime—in Pindar, Hölderlin, Shelley, Hart Crane, and very much in the major phase of Jay Wright.

It is one of the central ironies of our poetry that the major African-American poet, one of whose prime tropes being what he calls "the black limbo," should be our crucial composer of the American sublime ode as we begin the Millennium. There are a few living poets of Jay Wright's eminence among us—John Ashbery and A. R. Ammons in particular—but their recent work has turned in other directions. If you define the modern Sublime mode with historical precision, then its central characteristic has to be an ambition of transcendence. The American Sublime, though Wallace Stevens nervously mocked it, is nevertheless well defined by the marvelous conclusion of his "The Idea of Order at Key West":

> The maker's rage to order words of the sea,
> Words of the fragrant portals, dimly-starred,
> And of ourselves and of our origins,
> In ghostlier demarcations, keener sounds.

Wright, neither a poet of the sea nor of those Keatsian portals, labors incessantly to order words of ourselves and of our origins in ways that will render the demarcations ghostlier, the sounds keener. Yet his sense of our origins, and his own, is so multiform and complex, that he gives a new and fuller meaning to the descriptive term "African-American." I scarcely can think of another American poet who has so astonishingly adumbrated that particular hyphen.

Wright's poetry is so large and varied, in scope and design, that I will center now, in some detail, upon my personal favorites among all his published work to date, the sequence of five grand odes that conclude his superb volume, *Elaine's Book* (1988; Elaine being the sister of his wife, Lois). These five poems—"The Anatomy of Resonance," "Journey to the Place of Ghosts," "Saltos," "The Power of Reeds," "Desire's Persistence"—are exalted in tone and stance, and attempt to mount the high places of the spirit. They remind us that Wright, like Hölderlin and Hart Crane, is a secular religious poet. Crane rather wistfully called himself a "Pindar of the Machine Age," while Wright should be termed a "Pindar of the Chaotic Age," for that is where we are now, drifting as we do towards a new Theocratic Age. Perhaps most of our current poets who matter—from A. R. Ammons to Jorie Graham—quest for their authentic spiritual ancestors, a search that is essential to the high, Pindaric mode of invocation and celebration. But no other major poet now writing among us carries out this mission with the urgency and intensity of Jay Wright.

The literary context of Wright's sequence of odes is provided by a startlingly effective blend of Hölderlin and Paul Celan, on the one side, and Aztec poetry, on the other. What allies the two visionary modes, in Wright's implicit interpretation, is a kind of despairing transcendence, a triumph of the Negative over the pseudo-spiritualities of much received religious tradition. In a sense, Wright returns to the argument of his long poem, *Dimensions of History*, where Aztec mythology was employed as an intricate instance of mingled creation and destruction in the world-cycles commemorated by the huge pyramid-temples that still survive. But a mythic history of the contending forces of the Aztec versions of Venus and Mars, for all its brazen power, had to be tempered if Wright was to achieve a subtler and more articulated vision than that of *Dimensions of History*. Hölderlin and Celan are played off by Wright against the Aztec splendor, which he knows was in its way as barbaric as the cruel Catholicism of the Spanish invaders who destroyed the Aztec culture. The suicidal intensity of Hölderlin and of Celan retains a personalism that is alien to the Aztec clash of gods and historical cycles, and Jay Wright's heroic insistence upon the individuality of the poet draws much of its authority from the examples of Hölderlin and Celan.

"The Anatomy of Resistance," the first of Wright's cycle of five odes, takes its epigraph from Hölderlin:

> And the bird of the night whirs
>> Down, so close that you shield your eyes.

Baudelaire wrote of the wing of madness coming so close that it brushed his ear; Hölderlin records a similar immediacy, so that both poets express the terrible cost of imaginative vision. Wright is concerned, not with the cost, but rather with "the anatomy of resonance," the analysis of that close whirring down that makes the poet apotropaically shield his eyes against his own vision. Seven stages mark this resonance, each headed by a crucial word in Hölderlin's sublime, composite metaphor: *The Bird, Night, Whirs, Down, Close, Shield, Eyes.* I rather should say Wright's revision of Hölderlin's trope, since here is the German original, "Die Kürze," written by Hölderlin in 1798:

> «Warum bist du so kurz? liebst du, wie vormals, denn
>> «Nun nicht mehr den Gesang? fandst du, als Jüngling,
> doch,
>> «In den Tagen der Hoffnung,
>>> «Wenn du sangest, das Ende nie!»
> Wie mein Glück, ist mein Lied.— Willst du im Abenrot
>> Froh dich baden? hinweg ists! und die Erd' ist kalt,
>>> Und der Vogel der Nacht schwirrt
>>> Unbequem vor das Auge dir.
>>>> [*Selected Verse,* 15–16]

The title is generally translated as "Brevity," and here is the most literal translation that I can give:

> "Why are you so brief? Do you love singing less than you did formerly? since, as a young man, in the days of hope, when you sang, there was no end to your singing!"
>
> As is my fortune, so is my song. Would you bathe happily in the evening redness? It has vanished! And the earth is cold, and the bird of night whirs uncomfortably down towards your eyes.

Unbequem, "uncomfortably," is taken by Wright as "so close that you shield," the eyes being more than uncomfortable with the whirring that threatens to brush them. Hölderlin laments the end of an early poetic joyousness, a primal exuberance that has yielded to a supposedly more limited, or at least less celebratory art. Adroitly, Wright's first movement, *Bird*, has nothing in it of Hölderlin's "theology of existence":

BIRD

There must be an atmosphere,
or an evergreen,
or the green shading into the red-yellow
                brown of earth, for the eye,
surely,
some choir in which the ornamented arms
might tune themselves
          to the absolute A of air.
Creatures given to this air
shape their own suspension,
         a process of weight,
thrust away from the body's substance,
and the depths of a woman's body,
         of maple and ash,
hold the arc of another substance,
a memory of unrealized absence.
There is a river here,
where the white heron fastens its claws
to the flat blue surface,
as though it stood in a flowing altar
         to call into the dense grove
of arrested light around the water.
Look and you will see the plume of communion,
a possible intention that arises only here.
It seems that the river has been clay
         for feather and bone,
for the elastic tissue of the bird's voice.
And the ...
words that begin a theology of existence,
a political history of flight,
an interrupted dream of being definite.
         [*Elaine's Book* 68–9]

"The absolute A of air" recalls the last of the "Logbook of Judgments" section in *Dimensions of History*, "Meta-A and the A of Absolutes" (available now in *Selected Poems of Jay Wright*):

I am good when I know the darkness of all light,
and accept the darkness, not as a sign, but as my body.
This is the A of absolutes,
the logbook of judgments,
the good sign.
[*Selected Poems* 176]

This has been Wright's mature poetics, the Dogon insistence that each being (even an object) has its own language which is its own Adam, its Nommo, the Adamic twin or double, frequently antithetical to the being or object. So "the darkness of all light," an emergence from Plato's cave, is also a log for passage, an emergence from the Middle Passage, the black limbo of bondage. *That* is where we are in the first movement of "The Anatomy of Resonance," in the A of absolutes, the absolute A of air, a purged epiphany or moment of vision, an atmosphere tuned for the poetic eye, which then would require no shielding. And so Wright replaces the bird of the night with the Yeatsian (or even Sarah Orne Jewettian) white heron, for whose voice "the river has been clay / for feather and bone," the clay intimating the red clay out of which Adam or Nommo, antithetical double and twin, has been formed. Therefore Wright characterizes his epigraph, *And the bird of the night whirs / Down, so close that you shield your eyes*, as a theology of existence, and even as "a political history of flight," where "political" takes on the shade of "politic," meaning "prudential" and even "artful," as befits a dweller in the city of poetry. And that is why this epiphany is "an interrupted dream of being definite," since the interruption is the whirring of Hölderlin's bird of night, which now distracts Wright from his absolute A of air, his authentic poetic dream of definite being.

Night, the second movement, rewrites the history of darkness, invoking Cuzco, the ancient Incan capital, rebuilt by the conquering Spaniards upon the ruins of the old, streets of the dead. Cuzco here, in "The Anatomy of Resonance," recalls the destroyed cities of *Dimensions of History*, the Mayan capital Labna, and the Aztec capital Tenochtitlán, upon whose remnants Mexico City is built. Wright's "pecked cross" is not Catholic but Aztec, described in a note to *Dimensions of History* as representing the "four points of the compass," and so as an emblem of the wind and the rain, "pecked" because beaked in Aztec bird symbolism. Out of the absence of light, in a poetically reclaimed lost city of the Americas, a radiant voice rises, in an antiphony with the despairing voice of the Old World Hölderlin, visionary of unredeemed loss. Wright, humbly cognizant that he cannot be Pindar or Hölderlin, nevertheless enters the agon that is the Sublime mode by affirming his African and New Mexican heritages, by again asserting his spiritual ancestry in the splendors that the invading Europeans only could ruin. Beautifully modulated, *Night* is a negative epiphany twinning the serenity of *The Bird*.

Taken together, these first two movements define Wright's swerve away from the tradition of the Sublime, in an intricate irony or allegory reliant upon the Dogon mythology of Anima (Yahweh) and the Seventh Nommo (the Christ or Redeemer) that is always central to Wright's mature poetry. *Whirs*, the third movement, attempts instead an antithetical completion of Hölderlin's whirring resonance, by way of the "devastating hum of the jackal's song":

WHIRS

The jackal has learned to sing in the ash,
a severe chanty in praise of the cock and the fish,
of the aureole balm of evening.
When the moment arrives for singing,
palm leaves that are heavy with windlessness
           vibrate to a star's breath,
and the ear, attuned to all the harmonies of neglect,
lifts the soteriological wisdom of loss
           from its parish bed.
There is a moment when the boy comes out of the wood,
his feet slippered with a bee sound, his face
turned to the bull roar following his flight.
The boy carries an apple sound in his head,
something to enhance the dissonant eruption
           of his new morning.
Now, mother night has dressed herself
to dance to the dulcimer of his spring.
Father now to the boy,
she will lock his arms, and twirl him,
and fill his body with the deep
and devastating hum of the jackal's song.
           [*Elaine's Book* 70]

A mothering night that transforms to fatherhood centers this stately lyric in which sound prevails, from the jackal's singing its severe chanty of what sustains it through the stellar vibration of palms, sounds of bee, bull, and apple, and the dissonance of the boy's own advent. His spring is a dulcimer, and his dance twirls his body into the resonance of the jackal's chanty. Wright gives us here one of the staples of the Sublime ode, the incarnation of the Poetic Character in the poet's younger self, akin to the sensibility of song's abundance that Hölderlin elegizes as his own first phase. Yet brevity is not Wright's burden; his complex ancestry has its saving strand neither in the Old World nor in the New, but in the indigenous spiritualities of Africa, which is why the *Whirs* movement celebrates "the soteriological wisdom of loss," in opposition to Hölderlin's Sublime grandeur of loss. Soteriology, in Christianity, is the theological doctrine of deliverance by Jesus, a salvation dependent upon a unique biography, both in and out of time. Wright intimates again, here as elsewhere, a different wisdom of loss, the sacrifice of the Nommo figured in the African jackal, a forager who has learned to sing in the ash of his foraging, and whose song is a cyclic repetition. Amma made love to the earth, which first brought forth a jackal, who in turn violated the earth his mother, all evil subsequently proceeding out of that mismatch. Wisdom is in the cycle, and not in the single manifestation of a savior as much out of time as in it, and so not even in the Seventh Nommo.

Down, the fourth movement, returns to another of Wright's geographies, Scotland, where he lived for a year that has been deeply impressed upon all his subsequent poetry, a North Sea vision playing off against Africa, Old and New Mexico, and upper New England. In *Down*, Wright experiences an emptying-out of the poetic self, a defensive movement of the spirit resting from the Sublime:

DOWN

Under the rock, in the hollow,
there are stones the color of cats' eyes.
Old women who have seen these eyes
know that the body should be eiderdown
and bathed with the water of holy wells
and mineral springs, a blue water
with just the hint of hardness
          a slight taste of sulfur.
So the sinistra side of that other body
would drift to the North Sea,

and come down in its emerald armor,
to be welcomed in a Latin wood,
where a crescent moon peeks over
                    the empty seawall.
My dunum and dum boots quiver
on the qui vive,
                    anxious
to enlist water again
        to unruffle and fix
the mystery of buried stone.
                    [*Elaine's Book* 70–1]

The supposed Scottish legend here is a variant upon the Celtic myth
of Arthur, and "the other body ... in its emerald armor" becomes, in
Wright's vision, not the return of a warrior-king but of a poetic vision
reconfirmed by the marvelous lyric, *Close*, the next in "The Anatomy of
Resonance":

CLOSE

Time and the deductive season
teach an intimacy, reason
enough to set sail under seal,
a tenaciously secret keel
of abbeys and cathedrals, found
in the strictest boroughs, the round
plot of land dense with unicorns;
as in a soul's tapestry, horns
flagellate the air. Now confined
near an emerald sun, defined
by my spirit's strictest account,
I cling to my dole, and dismount.
I have filled my bowl with the rose
smoke of ecstasy in a close.

This intricate little Eliotic poem, with its internal and slant rhymes,
is itself a miniature of the daemonic Sublime, fusing the Celtic "emerald
sun," the warrior-king returned, with the famous unicorn tapestry,
Hermetic record of an emblazoned reality unexpectedly regained. Ecstasy,
a close only in the sense of an enclosure, leads downwards to the undoing
movement, *Shield*:

SHIELD

Skewed, perhaps,
the heart's road bends sinister,
not out of skin and hide,
        owing nothing
to the combustible partition
            crowning
those trees
    a doe's leap away.
Maude had it right—
John would be closer to love's blossom.
She had been given nothing,
and had only a desire to see
down the dextrous avenue of self.
Clearly, Maude knew
      who would be impaled,
who would sit on an order's collar,
what weight the father would bear
         against his own kind.
Kindness,
     or call it the valor of salvation,
         roots in a shell,
scaled to catch the rattle of friendship
      and war heat alliance.
We are stretched over the heart's house,
to defend such kindness as remains,
when the sun, strawberry red,
dips itself into the lime green water
      that flows endlessly home.
         [*Elaine's Book* 72]

Maude is Mary Magdalene, John is the Beloved Disciple, and the account of the "impaling" of Christ has a Gnostic flavoring, as Wright again subtly rejects a Western image of salvation not in accord with the Akan doctrine of God, of Amma who would not bear a weight against his own kind, as the Christian God certainly does in the sacrifice of Jesus. Before he turns to *Eyes*, the final movement, Wright gives us a remarkable epigraph from Paul Celan's *Schneebett* (Snowbed): "Augen, weltblind, in Sterbegeklüft ...," rendered here as "Eyes, worldblind, in the lode-break of dying." *Sterbegeklüft* is a tough word, presumably one of Celan's coinages,

and perhaps should be translated as "the fissure (or cleft) of dying."
Wright wants the fissure to be a break in a vein of ore, as though dying is
itself a wealth:

EYES

Old light, at this depth, knows
the veil of deception, the water valley
through which it leaps and divides.
So here, as the south wind alerts the body
to the season's change, the scarlet poplar
leaf runs, from point through point,
a topsy-turvy body to be fixed
                    in a different mirror.
An eye, such as this, may be worldblind
in the lode-break of dying. An eye, such as this,
may be no more than a peacock's tail,
the infant bud in a cutting, or the different
curve of a voice in the earth.
There is a market town in Suffolk,
where the bones and Roman urns and coins
mark a sacred ground with the sound of vision.
Time must tell us everything about sensation
and the way we have come to terms
                    with our failure
to see anything but the blue point of desire
                    that leads us home.
[*Elaine's Book* 73]

This is the Return of the Dead, of Hölderlin and of Celan, in
Wright's own great ode, and confronts the challenge of answering
Hölderlin's despairing vision: "And the bird of the night whirs / Down, so
close that you shield your eyes." Wright employs his interpretation of
Celan to exalt a rekindled poetic eye, one that transcends: "Old light" and
the "veil of deception." To be "worldblind, in the lode-break of dying,"
whatever it meant to Celan, becomes in Jay Wright a marvelously hopeful
image for a fresh poetic beginning. It is a loving critique of the Western
Sublime of Hölderlin (and of Celan) that Wright presents, yet a critique
nevertheless. The American Sublime, in Wright, becomes identical with
the black limbo, the dance that takes slaves out of the Middle Passage.

Remembering a market town in Suffolk, where the sound of vision
rose for him from a different curve, or dimension of history in the earth,

Wright reaffirms the possibility of his own "The Eye of God, The Soul's First Vision," the opening poem of his epic of poetic incarnation, *Dimensions of History*. There Wright combined Dogon and Aztec symbolism in a riddle of initiation that is very different from the poetic election of Hölderlin's Greco-German Sublime. Implicit in the final movement of "The Anatomy of Resonance" is Wright's African mode of twinning, of election-by-substitution, as here at the start of *Dimensions of History*:

Where did I learn to present myself
to the cut of some other voice,
substitute in a mime
my body breaks to contain?

There is Wright's own intricate balance, poised between "the signs of understanding / that I assert, but cannot reach alone," and the solitary eye of Hölderlin and Celan, agonistic and isolate. Time, which for the African-American Wright, is purely a dimension of history, has to tell us everything about the sensation of confronting the whirring bird of the night, a sensation that for Hölderlin is inviolate and single. The Western Sublime mode, which includes the American Sublime before Ralph Ellison and Jay Wright, is indeed a strenuous way of coming to terms with our tendency to see only "the blue point of desire / that leads us home." With reverence for Hölderlin, Wright dialectically terms that kind of transcendence a failure, one that he has come to seal by bringing us an African-Aztec poetic vision as a saving balance. Such an assertion is audacious, yet "The Anatomy of Resonance" goes a good distance towards sustaining it.

"Desire's Persistence," the last of Wright's five odes, will take us back to that home-seeking, High Romantic "blue point of desire," in another poem as elaborate as "The Anatomy of Resonance." Between come three odes, simpler but no less magnificent, all addressing the poetic vocation. "Journey to the Place of Ghosts" takes another epigraph from Celan, yet is almost entirely African in its setting and emphasis. I pass over it here, except to note that its ritual descent to the dead yields a rekindling of the poetic self, but at the expense of a psychic cost more harrowing than any other I recall in Wright's work. "Saltos," with its title hinting at the need to become a spiritual acrobat, follows and again I must neglect its splendors, though the poignance of being "awakened by a sun I will never see" testifies to Wright's awareness that his Africa is purely a vision, and not an empirical experience. "The Power of Reeds," the fourth ode, retrieves lost connections, in a characteristic Wrightian uncovering of the weave that analogizes ancient Greek, African and Mexican Indian visionary songs and singing. This too, though it is the most powerful of these three middle odes, I set aside while noting that again the African strand is the strongest in the weave. Wright, who is sublimely above the vulgar cultural politics of our academies and our journalists, is far more devoted to African culture and scholarship than are the entire camp of Resenters and cultural nationalists.

"The Anatomy of Resonance," by any rational standards of aesthetic eminence is a great poem, but "Desire's Persistence" seems to me even stronger, and is one of the double handful of Sublime achievements by poets of Jay Wright's own American generation. I return therefore to a rather close reading because Wright, as I reiterate, is a legitimately difficult poet who requires exegesis. I am sufficiently unregenerate so that I regard this as a merit, rather than a flaw, of his poetry. The ultimate archetype of the poet for Wright is Dante. Hart Crane, a difficult poet and a strong rhetorical influence upon the young Jay Wright, was drawn to Dante precisely as Wright is, seeking a paradigm for the poet's relation to his own poetry. In some sense, all of Wright's poetry to date constitutes his *Vita Nuova* and his *canzoni*. Though *Dimensions of History* and *The Double Invention of Komo* are epics in the Pound–Eliot mode, both were composed a little early in Wright's career. His work-in-progress, *Transformations*, consists of extended, meditative lyrics, wisdom literature, rather than the celebratory and lamenting odes of *Elaine's Book* and *Boleros*. Unlike Crane, who suffered a death by water at thirty-two, Wright is at the start of his sixties, and I am moved to prophesy that an African-American Dante may yet be revealed to us.

"Desire's Persistence" is indeed as beautiful as it is difficult. Its title comes from the Aztec, as does the line that Wright quarries for the name of the individual movements: "I lift the red flower of winter into the wind." But before we go to the sequence of *I, Lift, Red, Flower, Winter, Wind*, Wright allows the narrator, Desire, to speak:

> In the region of rain and cloud,
> I live in shade,
> under the moss mat of days bruised
>   purple with desire.
> My dominion is a song in the wide ring of water.
> There, I run to and fro,

braiding the logical act
    in the birth of an Ear of Corn,
polychromatic story I will now tell
in the weaving, power's form in motion,
a devotion to the unstressed.
Once, I wreathed around a king,
became a fishing-net, a maze,
    "a deadly wealth of robe."
Mothers who have heard me sing take heart;
I always prick them into power.
     [*Elaine's Book* 82]

The chanter, Desire, takes on the ambivalent guise of "a fishing-net, a maze / 'a deadly wealth of robe,'" that last presumably an allusion to the shirt of the centaur Nessus that became a fire to consume Heracles. Whether the dangerous desire, "power's form in motion," can be transfigured wholly from a destructive force to a transcending charisma is unclear, even when the chanter, the *I* section, becomes the astral body of resurrection and so an augmented Hamlet, "Dane of Degrees." Yet even the first section ends on the image of fresh life, and this gives a particular aura to "I lift the red flower of winter into the wind." Whatever that meant in its ancient Mexican context, here it carries the burden of vitalization, the blessing of more life, even though the *I* section rocks back and forth between images of rising and descents to the sepulchre:

Out of the ninth circle,
a Phoenician boat rocks upward into light
and the warmth of a name—given to heaven—
that arises in the ninth realm.
Earth's realm discloses the Egyptian
on the point of invention,
       deprived of life and death,
heart deep in the soul's hawk,
a thymos shadow knapping the tombed body.
Some one or thing is always heaven bound.
Some flowered log doubles my bones.
The spirit of Toltec turtledoves escapes.
A sharp, metaphorical cry sends me
      into the adorned sepulchre,
and the thing that decays learns

how to speak its name.
[*Elaine's Book* 83]

John Hollander has compared Wright to Geoffrey Hill, since they share "a secularized religious power that keeps them questing among the chapels of ruined tropes," though Hollander rightly adds that Hill contends mostly with English poetic history, while Wright's agon gives "a unique relational profundity to the hyphenation itself in 'African-American.'" The dimensions of Wright's personal history, those of an African-American born in Albuquerque and educated in California, have helped him to so uncover the weave of our country's cultural heritages as to make him our only authentic multi-cultural poet of aesthetic eminence, though there are younger poets who follow already on the new roads he has broken. Generally I wince at the term "multi-cultural," because it is a cant term of those who would destroy literary study in the name of what purports to be social justice, but in fact is merely a networking cabal of resentful academic commissars who feel guilty because their teachers (my exhausted self included) once taught them to love poetry for its own sake. Now I protect myself, because when someone says "multiculturalism" to me, I immediately say: "Ah, yes, you mean the poetry of Jay Wright, at once Hispanic, African, German, Italian, and above all Indic-American and African-American." By then the rabblement have retreated because while they have read Foucault and Lacan, they have read no poems by Jay Wright, fully the peer of John Ashbery and A. R. Ammons and Geoffrey Hill, and so one of the most exalted poets still alive.

My excursus over, I return to "Desire's Persistence," where "the thing that decays learns / how to speak its name." That thing *can* be the resurrected body, returning to an awareness, whether in the ninth Hell or the ninth Heaven of Dante. All of culture, Wright shrewdly implies, shares in a common shamanism, together uttering "a sharp, metaphorical cry," since Wright, like so many heterodox religious poets, locates us in the imaginal world, midway between empiricist reduction and transcendental intensities likely to seem ghostly to many among us. *Lift* concludes with the arcane or astral body and Hamlet's strangely transcendent death, both of which are removed from Wright, yet he himself is curiously removed throughout this movement. His estrangement, more imagined than personal, is enhanced in the brief, reverberating movement called *Red*.

RED

The heart, catalectic though it be, does glow,
responds to every midnight bell within you.
This is a discourse on reading heat,
the flushed char of burned moments one sees
after the sexton's lamp flows
over the body's dark book.
There is suspicion
here that violet
traces of
sacrifice
stand
bare.

[*Elaine's Book* 84–5]

What syllables does the poet's heart lack? Presumably those that toll the midnight bells of the psyche, intimations of mortality. In the variations of redness—the glowing of the heart, the reading of heat, flushed char, burned moments, flowering lamplight, the violet traces of sacrifice—this masterly, brief lyric reads the body's dark book by the illumination of the majestic Aztec trope: *I lift the red flower of winter into the wind*. We come to see that winter's red flower is an image of resurrection-through-sacrifice, another evidence of the persistence of desire, a persistence at the center of the next movement *Flower*:

FLOWER

This marble dust recalls that sunset
with the best burgundy, and the way,
after the charm of it, the peacocks
escaped their cages on the green.
I would now embellish the flame
that ornaments you,
even as it once in that moment
                                    did.

I carry you blossomed,
cream and salt of a high crown.
You *must* flare,
        stream forth,
blister and scale me,
even as you structure the enveloping kiss,

sporophore of our highest loss.
    [*Elaine's Book* 85]

The flame, now of sexual passion, flaming forth, is an extension of
the Aztec flower's redness of resurrection. But between comes the *Winter*
movement of our decline, an intimation of mortality that prompts one of
Jay Wright's triumph in the Sublime mode:

WINTER

Under the evergreens,
the grouse have gone under the snow.
Women who follow their fall flight
tell us that, if you listen, you can hear
their dove's voices ridge the air,
a singing that follows us to a bourne
                    released from its heat sleep.
We have come to an imagined line,
                    celestial,
that binds us to the burr of a sheltered thing
and rings us with a fire that will not dance,
        in a horn that will not sound.
We have learned, like these birds,
to publish our decline,
when over knotted apples and straw-crisp leaves,
the slanted sun welcomes us once again
to the arrested music in the earth's divided embrace.
    [*Elaine's Book* 85–6]

This intricate music, eloquently arrested and divided, conveys a
northern New England ambiance, the poet's most persistent context in
these mature years of his solitude. What matters most about this Winter
chant is its astonishingly achieved high style, its hushed yet piercingly
pitched voice altogether Wright's own. The birds' singing yields to the
now soundless, stationary image of desire's flame, a desire paradoxically
kept constant by its temporal awareness both of cyclic renewal and of
cyclic decline. Since the organizing Aztec metaphor relates to sacrifice and
its transformations, we ought not to be startled that the concluding *Wind*
movement shifts shamanistically to a woman's identity, desire speaking
with a radically altered voice:

WIND

Through winter,
harmattan blacks the air.
My body fat with oil,
I become another star at noon,
when the vatic insistence
of the dog star's breath clings to me.
Though I am a woman,
I turn south,
toward the fire,
and hear the spirits in the bush.
But this is my conceit:
water will come from the west,
and I will have my trance,

          be reborn,

perhaps in a Mediterranean air,
the Rhone delta's contention
with the eastern side of rain.
In all these disguises,
I follow the aroma of power.
So I am charged in my own field,
to give birth to the solar wind,
particles spiraling around the line
          of my body,
moving toward the disruption,
the moment when the oil of my star at noon
          is a new dawn.
   [*Elaine's Book* 86–7]

Giving birth to the solar wind renews the Aztec sense of desire's persistence, but this shamaness is an African woman, since the harmattan is a dust-laden wind on the Atlantic coast of Africa. Turned towards the flames, she enters her spirit-trance and is reborn, perhaps where the Rhone comes down to the Mediterranean, in a Latin culture. With his reincarnation assigned to her, the poet accepts immolation, joining the finished Tolteca singers, whose work was subsumed by the Aztecs:

3

I shall go away, I shall disappear,
I shall be stretched on a bed of yellow roses

and the old women will cry for me.
So the Toltecas wrote: their books are finished,
but your heart has become perfect.
                [*Elaine's Book* 87]

The Toltec bed of yellow roses goes back to the powerful dramatic monologue, "Zapata and the Egúngún Mask," which comes earlier in *Elaine's Book*. There Zapata cries out:

When there is no more flesh for the thorn,
how can I nurture this yellow rose of love between us?
                [*Elaine's Book* 23]

The yellow rose yields to the Aztec red flower of winter, and Wright's book is finished even as those of the Toltecas are concluded. Yet, addressing himself, he can assert a Sublime consultation: "But your heart has become perfect." Perfect returns to its origin in *perfectus*, complete or finished, fashioned as a carpenter of the spirit might have fashioned it "in the region of rain and cloud."

The step beyond the namings of the Sublime odes in *Elaine's Book* was taken by Wright in his next volume, *Boleros* (1988). Boleros are, in the first place, stately Spanish dances marked by sharp turns, punctuated by foot-stamping, and most dramatically by sudden gestured pauses, when the dancer holds one arm arched over the head. Jay Wright's *Boleros* are intricately interlaced odes, lyrics, and meditations, most of them paced with a deliberate slowness, and many with their own sharp punctuations, positioned and poised archings. Some of the poems are among Wright's finest, and almost all contain astonishing touches of grace and grandeur. Of the forty separate pieces, the central work is the fifth, a three-part ode celebrating and lamenting names and naming, in an American tradition strongest in its founders—Emerson, Whitman, Dickinson—and in their great inheritor, Wallace Stevens. Jay Wright, both more Spanish (by way of New Mexico), and more African in his culture, handles naming and unnaming very differently than did Stevens and his precursors. Take as representative Emersonian unnaming the penultimate section of "The Man With the Blue Guitar":

Throw away the lights, the definitions,
And say of what you see in the dark

That it is this or that it is that,
But do not use the rotted names.

The fifth *Bolero* opens with the rather categorical line: "all names are invocations, or curses," and proceeds to the namelessness of a particular child who never came forth. It is not clear whether the poet laments his own unborn child, or a generic one of

those who were impeached for unspeakable desire,
even as they lay in mothers' cave hollow wombs,
speechless, eyeless, days away from the lyrics of light
                              and a naming.
         [*Boleros* 9]

A lyrical second movement of the poem returns to the images of loss and of the child:

These are memory's accoutrements, reason to have searched
a flowered place with a name that fits,
where love's every echo is a child's loss.
              [*Boleros* 10]

Presumably the name that fits invokes the flowered place, and the child's loss is part of the curse of namelessness. Yet the poem's wonderful concluding movement refuses names, whether as invocations or as curses:

All names are false.
The soothsaying leaves call winter a paradox—
a northern traveler on a southern wind.
The ice on a weather-broken barn recalls May poppies.
I would have you recall the exhilaration
of reading broken sonnets, on cinnamon-
scented nights, in a tiled room,
while the charity doctors disputed their loves
              on the cobblestones below.
I enter again the bells and traces of desire,
call and recall, the pacing of love stalking us.
What is love's form when the body fails,
or fails to appear? What is love's habitation
but a fable of boundaries, lovers passing

athwart all limits toward a crux ansata?
I have carried your name on velvet,
knowing you are free, having never suffered the
heartache of patience that love and naming
that this our divided world requires.
                    [*Boleros* 10–11]

This returns to the Sublime arena of the great ode, "Desire's Persistence," for the "bells and traces" surely include that poem. A superb meditation that is part of the work-in-progress, *Transformations*, resumes the quest for desire's persistence, under the highly appropriate title, "The Cradle Logic of Autumn":

> *En mi país el otoño nace de una flor seca, de algunos pájaros ...*
> *o del vaho penetrante de ciertos ríos de la llanura.*
> > > *Molinari, "Oda a una larga tristeza"*

Each instant comes with a price, the blue-edged bill
on the draft of a bird almost incarnadine,
the shanked ochre of an inn that sits as still
as the beavertail cactus it guards (the fine
rose of that flower gone as bronze as sand),
the river's chalky white insistence as it
moves past the gray afternoon toward sunset.
Autumn feels the chill of a late summer lit
only by goldenrod and a misplaced strand
of blackberries; deplores all such sleight-of-hand;
turns sullen, selfish, envious, full of regret.

Someone more adept would mute its voice. The spill
of its truncated experience would shine
less bravely and, out of the dust and dunghill
of this existence (call it hope, in decline),
as here the blue light of autumn falls, command
what is left of exhilaration and fit
this season's unfolding to the alphabet
of turn and counterturn, all that implicit
arc of a heart searching for a place to stand.
Yet even that diminished voice can withstand
the currying of its spirit. Here lies—not yet.

If, and only if, the leafless rose he sees,
or thinks he sees, flowered a moment ago,
this endangered heart flows with the river that flees
the plain, and listens with eye raised to the slow
revelation of cloud, hoping to approve
himself, or to admonish the rose for slight
transgressions of the past, this the ecstatic
ethos, a logic that seems set to reprove
his facility with unsettling delight.
Autumn might be only desire, a Twelfth-night
gone awry, a gift almost too emphatic.

At sixty, the poet rehearses the season's cradle logic, this sense that what begins anew each autumn, in a blue light, is the prospect of a "diminished voice." What to make of a diminished thing, the Frostian project, suits only Wright's Vermont landscape, but not the persistence of the Sublime in his spirit. He counts the price, instant by instant, tallying what Emerson would have called his cost of confirmation. It is high enough to make him cast out his mythologies; this meditation is remarkably direct and poignant. Or perhaps the mythologies—Dogon, Bambara, Aztec, Romantic Sublime—are held just barely in abeyance in this latest Jay Wright, who beholds no celestial birds, such as Toltec turtledoves, but rather "a bird almost incarnadine." As Wright well knows, you hardly can use the word "incarnadine" without evoking Macbeth's "this my hand will rather / The multitudinous seas incarnadine." Deftly allusive as this is, we are cautioned by it to see that the poet struggles to keep desire's persistence from becoming mere ambition's survival, lest he follow Shakespeare's most imaginative villain and fall "into the sear, the yellow leaf." Autumn's cradle logic finally (and very subtly) is repudiated, since what persists in it is not the desire that will lift the red flower of winter into the wind. *That* desire, more truly Jay Wright's, retains an element of sacrifice, rather than the emphatic persistence of "a Twelfth-night / gone awry."

When Ralph Ellison's *Invisible Man*, nameless and yet at last all-knowing, concluded by going down and living underground, he asserted that he spoke for us, whoever we were. I can trace Ellison's spirit in Jay Wright's poetry, partly because, on a higher frequency, I find that Wright speaks for me. West African religion seems to me the likeliest point-of-origin of our American gnosis, our sense that there is a little man or woman inside the big man or woman. That little being is the true self, the

Gnostic spark or *pneuma* that has access to the Seventh Nommo, the black Christ. Twinning or doubling, as we have seen (by glimpses only) is Wright's preferred mode of troping, his downward path to wisdom. Without the power of Wright's metaphors, he could not aid us in our struggle against the jackal who mates with the earth, and who brings forth from the earth the bad verse and worst prose of the counter-culture. Multiculturalism, in our literary journalism and in our ruined literary education, is the ideology that says: our bad writers are no worse than your bad writers. [...] Without standards—aesthetic, cognitive, and imaginative—we will all perish, indeed are perishing already. In one of his better moments, T.S. Eliot spoke of the spirit as "unappeasable and peregrine." I can locate few such spirits among us now: I have to wait for them to locate me. Jay Wright's poetry first found me a quarter century ago, and has not abandoned me since.

DARRYL PINCKNEY

You're in the Army Now

A critic who is young and not confident in his scholarship should not
write about poetry, particularly if he—or she—dislikes the work under
consideration. It does not help the young critic to go about knocking poets
who take themselves seriously. It does not help poetry—not that poetry
needs help from anyone. If, however, a critic has chosen a subject—Afro-
American literature, for example—perhaps he might discover something
in thinking about the works of Jay Wright and Etheridge Knight, two
American poets who are also black men.

An Afterword is appended to Jay Wright's *The Double Invention of
Komo*, a free-verse work of over 100 pages. This Afterword provides no
clues and therefore no relief. There is little discussion of Bambara culture
or the cult of Komo, which is a pity: few readers of poetry in America are
familiar with these things. But Wright does not intend to inform the
reader about ritual in a concrete way: this a poem of daunting abstraction.

Wright does name some of the texts that inspired him. The poem is
dedicated to the memory of Maurice Griaule, the tireless anthropologist
who studied the Dogon in French West Africa. Griaule's work interested
Wright in Dogon and Bambara cosmologies. Several medieval and
Renaissance scholars are cited. "Frances Yates continues to inform me
about various renaissances." Soyinka is mentioned. We even get Gerald

From *Parnassus: Poetry in Review* 9, no. 1 (Spring/Summer 1981) © 1983 by Darryl Pinckney.

Holton's *Thematic Origins of Scientific Thought* and A. d'Abro's *The Rise of the New Physics*. "The reader will, of course, recognize the claims of Goethe, Augustine (as a dual citizen), Dante, Duns Scotus, and the renaissances on my poem." Yes, of course. (Caveat emptor.) There are quotes from Hölderlin, Karl Barth, and Coltrane stitched into the poem as well. It is swollen with allusion, down to Martha's lament about Lazarus.

The Afterword contains many assertions concerning Wright's intent. The poem, he states, is "a contribution to a well-known cultural process, and uses the Komo initiation rite among the Bambara to open an exploration into the fact of history." This exploration, as it turns out, is a very private journey, one not quite worth the arduous trek for others. Wright has a quarrel with clarity. "My poem risks ritual's arrogance." That is scarcely the half of it. Pretension is a word that comes easily to mind. He who understands it would be able to add another story to the Tower of Babel, indeed.

Much of what is widely admired in modern poetry is difficult in one sense or another. But there is a kind of obscurity that repels, one that has to do with deceit or delusion. Every poem has its strategic laws, and unraveling them is part of the joy of reading. Then why is it hard to care truly whether one can or cannot breathe the thin, piercing air of Wright's lofty levels of meaning? The incredible monotony of this poem betrays the strain of the idea. It does not have much convincing speculative force, and for all the intricacies of its surface, the language of this poem does not speak to the ear with any urgency, intimacy, or power.

This is a poem about escape, rebirth, consciousness, discovery, framed by stages of an initiation rite. It begins "This is the language of desire/ *bana yiri kqrq* ..." and ends "You present me to sacred things./ I am reborn into a new life./ My eyes open to Komo" in the same key, in the same tone, part of the aggressive complacency of enlightenment or religious feeling. Throughout, there is a discourse with history, both general and private, and about modes of perception, dulled by an utter opacity, which may be a form of shrewdness. The lack of drama slows the movement of the poem, though voices call out from a wood, from a village, from Paris, from Los Angeles, Berlin, Rome, Florence, Venice, Bad Nauheim, Albuquerque, Mexico City. Perhaps this is a poem about naming things, identifying with things, becoming things, the thingness of things, oneness, or "coming into the word"—large abstractions broken into steps that are meant to correspond to the process of acquiring knowledge. The initiate is a pilgrim, a *peregrinus*, insistent on what might pass for the classical mood. But what is discovered seems predetermined.

This initiate has no need for humility, awe, or passion. He can, after all, follow Dante into exile—"Let sister Florence/ truss herself in virtue"— and not contract malaria.

The poem's sections have titles such as "The Invocation" or "The Opening of the Ceremony/the Coming Out of Komo." There is much talk of stairs, ladders, altars, pools, eggs, *donu* birds, instruments, tests, and signs throughout. (The "Komo signs" are printed alongside the text.) But these symbols do not, somehow, accumulate, or make for a compelling system.

> Now, if I,
> initiate, enter,
> under air,
> and under
> the thunderstone,
> I hear the pool in the wind.
> Water will dock the spirit's light
> along my body.
> Now, by the light's fall,
> I assemble an aggregation
> of fact, and appoint
> the body's wisdom to its place.
> I oppose earth's figure and ground
> to the divisions of my person.
> My eye's bell alerts me to the kapok and the palm.
> My ear pins the fern's dance in the wind
> to a singer's voice.
> I brace my arm under the moon of my shoulder blade,
> where memory's book resides.
> My fingers dampen the bird's flight.
> My spine is set to penetrate the tomb's resolve.

Page after page of the merely declarative, very prose-like, passage after passage of symbols mercilessly recapitulated, of lines that do not form true images. "As your initiate's agent on creation's knife/ I open the membrane of my celebrant's voice." Or: "There is a tree that is divine./ Its scalar leaves reveal/ a scapulary mother at its base." It might not be to the point to ask to understand the lines but the inner landscape Wright, apparently, is trying to open isn't very evocative or intriguing. Surrealism, if anything, has made it difficult for the surreal to move us.

The choice of archaic words and sometimes the odd syntax are meant, perhaps, to lend a primitive quality to the poem and also a certain formal elegance, the dignity of the primordial. Some phrases are striking, but, inevitably, they are weakened by an ambiguous resolution of line.

My monody impels you to the shore,
where I enroll among the thorns
clutched in the rocks.
I will, by my heart's hunker-down
hazard, examine your twilight eyes
and will.

Sukodyi.
The dead leather their mourning bells
about your hucklebones.
Like flame, these cannon chants
provoke you to a dance along the shore.
Gold darkness, mist,
and April,
a jade tree,
the white woman in blood
on the blue bottom's bed,
my violet trembling,
near the pool's pulpit,
you, star raked and scorched,
play in a rainbow of desire.

You shuttle your hands in the sand,
believe it my grave,
listen for my breath's clock
to arrange me on your loom.
Because I am thorned to endure,
a bearded little boy,
I sword the rocks aside.
I see you in what seems like a prayer
over a body that will not come.

You inhale.
You bellow.

You undo the smallest grain.
Your breath shapes a red clavicle.
    I am beside you.
     I am in you.

What does this long meditation mean and how can one penetrate the obedient, rigid regiments of sentences that collapse so short of the hoped-for sublime? It is hard to follow who is speaking, hard to appreciate the few shifts in cadence, hard to wade through the metaphors, through the barren terrain. "I have been trying to create a language/ to return what you have lost/ and what you have abandoned,/ a language to return you to yourself,/ to return to you." Perhaps "the vital, arrogant, fatal, dominant X" has vanquished yet another.

The poetry of Etheridge Knight presents a problem that is the exact opposite of *The Double Invention of Komo*. The poems brought together in *Born of a Woman* are, for the most part, simple to the point of being facile, even crude.

> Poets are naturally meddlers. They meddle in other people's lives and they meddle in their own, always searching and loving and questioning and digging into this or that. Poets meddle with whores—they meddle with politicians, zen, the church, god, and children; they meddle with monkeys, freaks, soft warm lovers, flowers, whiskey, dope and other artists— especially jive–assed doctors.

Knight takes a very funky posture in his Preface and this posture is the depressing thing about this collection. Knight's subjects include the loneliness of prison cells, women leaving, trying to kick drugs, black musicians, family feeling, Malcolm X, politics—a wide range of experience and admirable concerns. That is not the problem. Anything can be the occasion for a poem. But not just anything on the page makes for a poem. Etheridge Knight writes in a loose, funky style associated with the Sixties and black militancy, a period that was loud and noisy with talk against the tyranny of so-called white poetics.

Dudley Randall, in his Introduction to the anthology *The Black Poets* (1971), spoke of the black poets of the Fifties and Sixties as having "absorbed the techniques of the masters," and rejected them in order to go in new directions. Addison Gayle, Jr., a self-appointed architect of the

"Black Aesthetic," also wrote about the struggle to end cultural hegemony. None of this was new. Alain Locke, in the 1920s, recognized the need for blacks to speak for themselves. The history of literature is a quest for new forms. But many, since the Sixties, seemed to use the call for a new aesthetic as an apologia for the unrendered. Discussions of the oral tradition became popular, as if the oral, in black culture, acquitted the black poet of his—or her—responsibility to the language. Anyone who has heard Robert Hayden's "Runagate Runagate" or Sterling Brown's "The Strong Men" knows that the written and the spoken abide by the same unnameable rules. Those who feel that poetry, in essence, is a performance art ought to join a circus.

The world Knight portrays in his poems is often harsh and brutal. He aspires to a language that will remain true to these experiences, words that will not give any falsifying distance. It makes for a very vigorous and immediate style that is often successful. "The Idea of Ancestry":

> I walked barefooted in my grandmother's backyard/ I smelled the
>   old
> land and the woods/ I sipped cornwhiskey from fruit jars with the
>   men/
> I flirted with the women/ I had a ball till the caps ran out
> and my habit came down. That night I looked at my grandmother
> and split/ my guts were screaming for junk/ but I was almost
> contented/ I had almost caught up with me.
> (The next day in Memphis I cracked a croaker's crib for a fix.)

Far too often, however, the poems evince that uninteresting tendency to feel that a *rap* is all that need be offered. "A Poem for 3rd World Brothers":

> or they will send their lackeys to kill for them.
> and if those negroes fail
> white/ america will whip out her boss okie doke:
> make miss ann lift the hem of her mystic skirt
> and flash white thighs in your eye to blind you....

A rap is not enough, however true, politically, the message is taken. Raps that are trying to pass for poems have a strange redundant quality: we feel we know all this already and not much is going on in the poem to make us see or feel this in a new way. The ordinariness of the imagery makes the poems degenerate into sentimentality, which is a disservice to Knight's capacity for tender expression. "Our love is a rock against the wind,/ Not soft like silk or lace." Another danger of the rap is that it dates quickly. There are some poems in which Knight is embarrassingly on the wrong side, such as "Love Song to Idi Amin:"

> The white/ men/ are
> Boiling poison in
> A big/ black/ pot, are
> Shouting out
> Omens
> By satellites, are/ out
> To kill you, man, ...
>
> You, love/ singer,
> Skinning and grinning
> In the African sun—
> You/ have/ already/ won
> The war.

Several thousand Africans in Uganda lost under Amin.

Knight seems to have a fondness for the haiku, which is an acquired taste even when written well.

> Under moon shadows
> A tall boy flashes knife and
> Slices star bright ice.

Or:

> Beyond the brown hill
> Above the silent cedars,
> Blackbirds flee April rains.

He is also given to a not very sophisticated use of internal rhyme.

> And, we must not forget
> that Flukum was paid well to let the Red
> Blood. And sin? If Flukum ever thought about sin
> or Hell for squashing the yellow men, the good Chaplain

(Holy by God and by Congree) pointed out with
Devilish skill that to kill the colored men was not
altogether a sin.
Flukum marched back from the war, straight and tall,
and with presents for all ....

There are moments of painful formal constraint: "Apology for Apostasy?":

Soft songs, like birds, die in poison air
So my song cannot now be candy.
Anger rots the oak and elm; roses are rare,
Seldom seen through blind despair.

Clumsily deployed rhymes or metrics do not enhance the playfulness or irony of his poems and are disastrous when he is reaching toward the poignant. Knight is best in the more open, rapid, darting poems, such as "A Conversation with Myself:"

What am I
            doing here
    in these missouri hills
hitch/ hiking these hi/ ways
                    where farmers
    fondle their guns
    and eye my back
    the cars zoom by
                zoom zoom zoom....

The freer movement of line is a better way of expressing his humor and sense of life.

Knight's *Poems from Prison* brought him recognition when it appeared in 1968, and it is easy to understand why his radical message and comfortable style were so well received. Though Knight has not renounced his interest in investigating the consequences of racism, it is disappointing that the new poems do not indicate much artistic growth. They seem rather tame and conventional. Some of Jay Wright's earlier poems—"Death as History" or "A Plea for the Politic Man"—shared in the rebellious mood of the Sixties. Wright's work since then, such as the long poem, *Dimensions of History*, revealed a change in direction, an attempt to fuse aspects of varied cultures. *The Double Invention of Komo* is a more ambitious experiment and, unfortunately, not a very engaging one.

What can the young critic discover? Only what has always been true and so general that it can hardly count as an insight: the black experience, however real, does not by itself make poetry; it must be turned into art, like everything else. Erudition or mere feeling will not make poetry; African myth or familiarity with prison is, weirdly, not enough. It does not matter that a poet is black. The tradition and demands of the language— in this case, English—matter. A work of art can only be correct in the political sense when it is first correct in the literary sense, Walter Benjamin wrote. Black poets must be judged by the same standards as for any other poets. Any other considerations are racist. There is no need for a minority admissions program into the canon of literature. Vision and mastery of form are the bootstraps that lift.

GERALD BARRAX

The Early Poetry of Jay Wright

B etween 1967 and 1980, Jay Wright published five volumes of poetry so remarkably unified and consistent in subject, theme, tone, and technique that they might all constitute a single work.[1] Of the thematic reasons for that unity, two are most significant; one is general (but *essential*), the other specific (but "accidental").

First, religion—the religious experience, faith and belief—occupies its center. Wright is *essentially* a religious poet. "Essentially" meaning fundamental to his identity as a poet. His is not a poetry, like Milton's or Eliot's, in which comforting belief in a fixed, orthodox system predominates; rather, like the religious poetry of Yeats and Whitman, Wright's is questing, eclectic, dialectical ("how a poet will wrestle with a god,/ risking his mind"; "Arrogant like this,/ I have begun to design/ my own god." *Soothsayers and Omens*, 17, 74).

Second, the specific unifying element in Wright's poetry derives from African religion and myth. The reader is aware of its presence from the very beginning, in *Death as History* (1967), and throughout the succeeding volumes, but its specific source is not fully identified by Wright until *The Double Invention of Komo* (1980). In the 'Afterword' to that book he says he has been the beneficiary, "for some fifteen years" of his life, of expeditions to Africa by a group of French anthropologists. This enterprise resulted in published works that became the major texts

From *Callaloo* 19 vol. 6, no. 3 (Fall 1983). © 1983 by *Callaloo*.

for Wright's poem. He uses Dogon and Bambara cosmology (specifically, the Bambara initiation rite of Komo) as a ritualistic metaphor for spiritual redefinition and growth—a "double growth," in that the initiate grows both into his own ritual maturity and "in comprehension of himself in the world" (*Komo*, p. 115).

> This necessary chaos follows me.
> Something to put in place,
> new categories for the soul
> of those I want to keep.
> What I needed was to be thrown
> into this toneless school,
> an arrogant rhythm to release
> my buried style.
> > *This journey will end*
> > *with a double entry,*
> > bought by poems
> > to all my hidden loves.

> I have covered
> more than six miles
> to uncover
> my necessary gestures,
> > From city to city,
> > from tongue to tongue,
> > *I move in settled style,*
> > *a journey of the soul,*
> > accomplished once,
> > accomplished
> > with what is mine.   (Italics, my emphasis)

Those lines might have come from *The Double Invention of Komo*. In fact they were written (or published) thirteen years earlier; they are the concluding lines of "Destination: Accomplished," the poem that concludes *Death as History*, Wright's first collection.

With the first book, the destination and its outcome were already known. Indeed, the unity of Jay Wright's work makes surprise at the richness and difficulty of his later books a gratuitous response. In *Death as History* and *The Homecoming Singer* he arrives with his technique nearly mastered and the themes of his future books already identified. Even the images, motifs, and symbols of the later work are present from the beginning: masks, eggs, seeds, doubleness and twinning, birds, dance, song. In addition to religion, other prominent subjects and themes common to all of Wright's poems are death and resurrection, family relationships, the desolation and alienation of cities, travel, exile, and history. As the titles of his books indicate, if Wright had a classical muse it would be Clio, who presides over history. Even *The Double Invention of Komo* has as its "first subject" (Wright's phrase) not religion or myth, but history.

Wright's technique is another factor responsible for the effect that each book is part of a greater design—a section of one grand work. A Jay Wright poem has a characteristic form and look. The basic unit of his normally short line is the phrase, and because he tends to write long poems, often unbroken by stanzas, his long lean verses may snake their leisurely uninterrupted way through two, three, or more pages. The stacking up of end-stopped phrases has the disadvantage of often producing a tensionless, choppy poetry. But at their best, the lines modulate easily between speech and thought rhythms.

> Out on Seventh Avenue again
> I watch the legs challenge
> the blase evening.
> The streets bump and grind
> to the brass-endowed juke boxes,
> and I jut up in bars
> with winding mirrors,
> for a quick beer,
> a quick glance at some
> unapproachable liaison.
> The pimps are like priests,
> scratching their hips
> to the archaic dances,
> offering their eyes as tacit redemption.
> The cameo-faced go-go girls
> tussle their cages,
> envious of my eyes' leisure,
> horrible in the gregariousness of their thighs.

These lines from *Death as History* ("On the Block") illustrate the basic pattern of all his poetry, from which and to which his variations in line and stanza depart and return. Thus Wright's form, like his subject matter, is *established* at once, so permanently as to become a donnée, a fact—an organic, internal principle that allows the reader to note with efficient ease the changes in tone or emphasis produced by variations in lining (how long a line is, and where it stops). In contrast to the above passage, the following is "heavier," almost Shakespearian in tone and rhythm:

> Here I sit in the stolid temper of my study,
> fidgeting with the system of a myopic Frenchman,
> trying to find my politic self.
> But this perversion mocks the Florentine,
> would have stung the Philosopher to mockery.
> And you, now unphilosophical,
> have made up your mind to cousin ethics.

("Idiotic and Politic,"
The Homecoming Singer, p. 71)

Jay Wright is a difficult poet, a learned poet, a discursive poet, a brilliantly intellectual poet, even (he admits) a "bookish" poet (*Komo*, p. 109). That might explain why he is not more widely known by that amorphous, somnolent beast, The Reading Public.

Dimensions of History and *The Double Invention of Komo* (each conceived of as a single poem) are both heavily indebted to numerous texts, many of which, inevitably, will be unfamiliar to (another shaggy beast) The Average Reader. Each book, consequently, is glossed and annotated. In the notes to *Dimensions of History*, Wright declares that "almost every line in my poem is derivable from some historical event or its consequences" (p. 105). In his exploration of the rites and acts, the aesthetic and the physical dimensions of history, the poet makes use of social and religious ceremonies of the Dogon, Aztec, Ndembu, Dinka, Ashanti, Yoruba, and Egyptian peoples, integrating them into the Black experience and history of Africa, the Caribbean, and the Americas. He uses European, African, Caribbean, and South American musical, artistic, and craft forms. The Average Reading Public is obviously much dependent on the poet's notes in a work that mixes such unlikely sources as "Celtic and Yoruba mythology" (p. 110), or that contains a "Villancico," which Wright identifies as "a 15th and 16th century Spanish idyllic or amorous poetry" (p. 109). It *can* be heavy going. "Books are obviously important to this poem" is Wright's understatement on *The Double*

Invention of Komo. In addition to Marcel Griaule's *Masques Dogons* and *Dieu d'eau,* to Germaine Dieterlen's and Youssouf Tata Cissé's *Les fondements de la société d'initiation du Komo* (the poem's "well-spring and base"), other sources include Goethe, Augustine, Dante, Duns Scotus, the renaissances, and many many more. What is true of *Dimensions of History* is equally true of *The Double Invention of Komo* and poems in Wright's other books, that is, that "The landscape and some of the indigenous cosmologies of Mexico and South America" contributed to their shaping. For one who describes himself as "black and bilingual" ("Bosques De Chapultepec," *The Homecoming Singer,* p. 44) and who announces that "I elevate the trinity of races in my blood" (*Komo,* p. 105), the use of such diverse sources in his work is no surprise.

I suspect that Wright's poetry has been perceived as "hard" for reasons that may have little to do with its actual content. I can attest to the reaction of one tentative reader of *The Homecoming Singer* who, upon opening the book, exclaimed at the formidable *appearance* of Wright's long poems—line after line of unbroken text. However, it is harder to pinpoint the reasons for what has been the dearth of critical and scholarly attention to Wright's poetry. Surely, members of this community are accustomed to reading difficult, even obscure, poetry. Certainly it cannot be denied that Jay Wright has produced a substantial body of work. Nor can I imagine that its significance and merit as poetry could long be denied by discerning readers. In anticipation, therefore, of what admirers of his work hope will be his belated "discovery" by both readers and critics, an examination of Wright's early poetry in *Death as History* and *The Homecoming Singer* may serve as an introduction.

II

Death as History contains fifteen poems, seven of which were later included in *The Homecoming Singer.*[2] Common to the poems excluded from the latter volume is a romantic sensibility and imagery:

> The birds have flicked
> the torpor of this city
> from their wings,
> and still your hand
> lucidly sings within my own.

The season's quickness
frightened us.
Whole days were spent,
designing traps for memories.

Now,
I come home to a room laden
with rarities and work,
charge the light and charge
the darkness to be gentle.

The birds will beggar
other cities for the season,
perform with grace
wherever they appeal.

It isn't the too familiar
season that returns
the pain of our retreat,
but your hand sadly
singing our imitative art.

("Against Imitation")

Singing—whose dominance of Wright's early and middle work as motif, metaphor, and symbol is nearly absolute—makes its thin-voiced debut in this first poem. The combination of birds and city will also appear again, more forcefully, in later work:

The city sinks   and stinks.
And in the air the cry of an eagle.
A shackled Black wrist claps the clouds.
I sit over a dish of moros y cristianos,
bitter communion,
bitter memory of no communion,
bitter memory of the padre's death.

(*Dimensions of History*, p. 25)

In others of the rejected poems there is the same tepid romanticism in rather conventional language and images ("Time closes in like a box/

emptied of content,/ throwing its weight against any reentry—/ like your arms, like your forbidding heart./ Through those limpid days/ we made love tenaciously"). However, in "The Drums" there is the combination of Christian and African ritual:

> In this black ghetto,
> Sundays and festival days
> change their direction.
> It is Easter,
> and I'm enchanted by a girl ...
> She leads a shy goddess
> through the proud paradiddles
> of a Yoruba ritual.
> . . . .
> Easter, and the drums
> are singing an endless grace.
> The rhythms choke your separate sense,
> and some new god has learned to dance.

The synthesis culminates in *The Double Invention of Komo*:

> Komo's dance designs the spine,
> in sacred air, in the space around the body. (p. 102)

Further, in the course of the poem, the Komo initiation ceremony is explicitly associated with the Christian ritual ("This Easter Eve of double death/ and double resurrection," p. 52) and finally in the poem's climax at the initiate's rebirth:

> I rise, at the touch of the pool's water,
>   to my person.
>   I forget my name;
>   I forget my mother's and father's names.
>   I am about to be born.
>   . . . .
>   . . . .
> You take me to kneel, forehead to earth, before Komo.
> You present me to sacred things.
> I am reborn into a new life.
> My eyes open to Komo.

Frequent correspondences between such elemental details of Wright's first and last (i.e., most recently published) book suggest how early and how clearly the design had been determined.

"Wednesday Night Prayer Meeting" and "The Baptism" are given the important positions as the first two poems in *The Homecoming Singer*. The contrast between the joyous inevitability of rebirth in *The Double Invention of Komo* and the ambiguous attitude toward Christianity in *The Homecoming Singer* is striking.

"Wednesday Night Prayer Meeting" is 134 lines (three pages) of unbroken verse that unrolls scroll-like in a continuous narrative in which the poet relates the uncertain, inconclusive encounter between man and God in a Black church.

> On Wednesday night,
> the church still opens at seven
> and the boys and girls have to come in
> from their flirting games of tag,
> with the prayers they've memorized,
> the hymns they have to start.
> Some will even go down front,
> with funky bibles,
> to read verses from Luke,
> where Jesus triumphs, or Revelations,
> where we all come to no good end.

The mild, faintly amused ironic tone is the first indication of the narrator's ambiguous attitude.

Outside, while the "pagan kids" enjoy themselves playing and kissing in the darkness, the older people linger, in no hurry to enter,

> having been in the battle of voices
> far too long, knowing that the night
> will stretch and end only
> when some new voice rises
> in ecstasy, or deceit, only
> when some arrogant youth
> comes cringing down front,
> screaming about sin, begging
> the indifferent faced women
> for a hand, for a touch,

for a kiss, for help,
for forgiveness, for being young
and untouched by the grace
of pain, innocent of the insoluble
mysteries of being black
and sinned against, black
and sinning in the compliant cities.

The increasingly bitter irony is ambiguous in that it is difficult to pinpoint: is it the attitude of the narrator, or of the worshipers in the poem? Is it the religion and its efficacy that is being questioned, or the sincerity of those who profess it?

What do the young know
about some corpulent theologian,
sitting under his lamp,
his clammy face wet,
his stomach trying to give up
the taste of a moderate wine,
kissing God away with a labored
toss of his pen?

However, the poem's central ambiguity is whether the Christ whose presence the worshipers are expecting actually comes to them. On the one hand—in a long passage of vivid, concrete details—the narrator suggests that he does appear, and becomes one of them, becomes one with them:

But Christ will come,
feeling injured, having gone
where beds were busy without him,
having seen pimps cane their number running boys,
the televisions flicker over heaped up bodies,
having heard some disheveled man
shout down an empty street, where women
slither in plastic boots, toward light,
their eyes dilated and empty;
will come like a tired workman
and sit on a creaky bench,
in hope, in fear, wanting to be pleased again,
so anxious that his hands move,

> his head tilts for any lost accent.
> He seems to be at home,
> where he's always been.

A haunting, memorable passage.

Yet, he [Christ] seems not to know the "danger of being here,/ among these lonely singers," among those who resent giving up their Wednesday nights "while the work piles up for Thursday." But "caught in this unlovely music," he falls to the floor and "writhes as if he would be black" as the sisters circle him. However, as he stands up to sing (like a "homecoming singer"?), the narrator's apparent vision is broken by the wail of a young girl from the mourner's bench. Although the narrator (and the reader) has "seen" the waited-for Christ among them, they have not. They rise and prepare to leave the church. Now the narrator states flatly, "This is the end of the night,/ and he has not come there yet,/ has not made it into the stillness/ of himself, or the flagrant uncertainty/ of all these other singers." Has their *uncertainty* blinded them to his presence and made them incapable or unworthy of sharing the poet's vision? The poem gives no conclusive answer.

> They have closed their night
> with what certainty they could,
> unwilling to change their freedom for a god.

One of several aspects of Jay Wright's poetry awaiting critical examination is his varied (and sometimes puzzling) manipulation of point of view. In "Wednesday Night Prayer Meeting" the point of view is not only that of an omniscient narrator, but a narrator whose tone suggests cool detachment from the poem's events and persons. Because of this rigorously objective persona, the single exception in his use of the pronoun "we" generates the irony and sly humor in "where Jesus triumphs, or Revelations,/ where we all come to no good end."

In contrast, the second poem, "The Baptism," begins "We had gone down to the river again,/ without much hope of finding it/ unmuddied" (p. 8), and that perspective holds through the first four stanzas. The "we" are awaiting the arrival of the candidates for baptism, who come "naked under white robes,/ their hair pressed down in stocking caps,/ hesitating." In the fourth stanza the speaker says

> Now, we were singing,
> and the vowels seemed enough

> to threaten those confessed sinners,
> who would leave another world
> and be buffeted by our voices,
> who would take the terror in our eyes
> to enter ours.

That is the last explicit use of "we" in the poem; the narrator then seems to recede or withdraw from his identification with the others, and the point of view thereafter remains objective.

> Along another path,
> as if he would have nothing
> to do with these uncleansed ones,
> until the exact moment,
> the minister came, detached,
> seeming to be part of nothing
> except the disordered day.

Then this curiously detached man baptizes the "newly confessed." But there is no joy in the ceremony, one of them "now crying,/ now shaking/ as if he would turn/ and run, back,/ where he would reconsider/ his steps." "The Baptism" ends as uncertainly as "Wednesday Night Prayer Meeting," the imagery suggesting death without true spiritual rebirth. Furthermore, the subjunctive, doubtful "as if," denies us the unequivocal vision of new life with which *The Double Invention of Komo* concludes.

> one by one,
> he buried the stiffened bodies,
> bringing them up,
> swathed like mummies, screaming,
> *as if* they had found
> some new harmony,
> there at the pit of the river,
> *as if* they would take charge
> of the rhythm of those,
> waiting at the bank,
> still unsmiling, still
> disengaged from this rhythm,
> waiting for the hard
> and distant confirmation
> of their own *unsteady truths.* (pp. 9–10; Italics, my emphases)

Other poems in *The Homecoming Singer* also present Christians and their ceremonies in negative—or ambiguous—images, implying an unfavorable contrast with African myth and ritual.

In "Morning, Leaving Calle Gigantes," the poet is in Guadalajara. Conscious of his "own wet and beer-laden,/ stale and anxious smell," he passes a "clamorous church" and sees "black-veiled women *grovel*/ up the aisles on their knees, / their hands sweep as if they would *clutch*/ and *buffet* me into penitence" (p. 38, italics my emphases).[3] In his second "Variation on a Theme by LeRoi Jones," the poet would have the "stiff Jesus" come down from his cross, to break free and become "a living gesture, unearthed, / yet rooted in earth, in flesh" (p. 68), as did the Jesus in the narrator's vision in "Wednesday Night Prayer Meeting."

"The Regeneration" appears to be a dreadful allegory of the crucifixion:

> The wind, taut as piano wire,
> peels me apart.
> I go down, down through the evening,
> standing somewhere between light and dark.
> On this hill,
> I hear a child's voice
> grumble like a soldier's,
> and feel the weight of some dead man on my back,
> his fingers tightened around my throat ... (p. 78)

The poem's details—"wooden monuments," "shabby cathedral," "three candles," "twelve men," "wine," "the hill"—are images from a nightmare ("I run, under the dead man's stutter") rather than icons of faith.

"Collection Time" is particularly effective in suggesting the narrator's ambivalence toward Christianity. He seems to understand, admire, and share in the fervor, the sublimated sexual energy of the church service. Yet, the descriptive details add the taint of vulgarity to it all, and there is conveyed to the reader a hint of the speakers disapproval and, perhaps, revulsion.

> The bleeding Jesus hangs
> just where the preacher nailed him,
> and the wooden church rocks
> like a storm-caught fishing boat.
> A gap-toothed, fat and rouged soprano gurgles

as if she were going under a wave.
My preacher stops, gasping,
sweating, his hips still tossing,
his fingers stretched in the ecstatic air.
. . . .
Someone smacks the table.
and calls for every nickle in the house.
White-robed sister, still smelling
of Saturday's lavender-scented dives,
wrestle the aisles,
and shove the platters at you. (p. 88)

If the phrase "My preacher" caught your attention, then you've noticed one example of the way Wright creates complexities of tone through the manipulation of point of view. When the narrator says

You will mourn
you will come down front.
My preacher whirls to frighten you,
descends to lay his knotty hands
where the hurt is.
You will mourn for us

the reader is suddenly confronted, and unexpectedly pulled into the poem by the double-voiced speaker: as narrator and as a member of the congregation. And just as unexpected, and puzzling, is the tone. Is "You will mourn for us" prophetic, imperative, or ironic? And what a curious reversal of roles: why should we (the readers) mourn for them (the congregation)? And when? Before, or after, we join them?

In another poem, "First Principles," these questions are put into perspective. The jerking hips of the preacher and the gurgling voice of the soprano and the uncertain hearts of Christians are replaced by authentic worship and life-giving symbols.

when dancers
argue with the earth,
and black men speak in tribal tongues,
it is not a festival of the damned,
it is a feast of the living,
who move toward the past,

not in the fantastic,
but in the certainty of myth,
in the tongues of the exiled dead,
who live in the tongues of the living. (p. 84)

"It is that African myth/ we use to challenge death," Wright asserts in the
title poem to *Death as History*. "What we learn is that/ death is not
complete in itself,/ only the final going from self to self." Thirteen years
later (in the "real" time of book publication), the "certainty of myth"
transcends the "unsteady truths" of "Wednesday Night Prayer Meeting"
and "The Baptism." In *The Double Invention of Komo*

I have come,
past fear,
to be put to death,
and to be taken
by the new word,
to my resurrection.
. . . .
I am, reborn into a new life.
My eyes open to Komo. (pp. 97, 108)

III

What sets *The Homecoming Singer* apart from the books that follow is the
rich variety of its content. Both *Dimensions of History* and *The Double
Invention of Komo* are long poems and develop single themes (more or less).
Soothsayers and Omens in its first three sections is devoted primarily to
family relationships; the few remaining poems develop (either wholly or in
part) Wright's themes of travel, religion, and Black history. The material
of part IV of *Soothsayers and Omens* (The only titled section: "Second
Conversations with Ogotemmêli") is entirely that of the African myth on
which the later Komo is based. *The Homecoming Singer*, in addition to all
of the subjects and themes I have discussed and that appear in Wright's
other books, contains some not found in the others—or that do not
receive the emphasis that they do in this volume.

For example, there is a group of five poems whose subject matter
makes them unique to *The Homecoming Singer*. As their titles reveal (except
for the first two), they are about work experience—occupations: "The

Fisherman's Fiesta" (a summer job in a tuna cannery), "Jason's One Command" (work in a shipyard); "Two House Painters Take Stock of the Fog," "Track Cleaning," and "The Hunting Trip Cook." What these poems contribute to the volume is a rich texture of commonplace, everyday realism. No less important, they round out the poet's identity for the reader. If he becomes a "bookish poet" in succeeding volumes, in *The Homecoming Singer* he is eminently a man of solid flesh whom we see time and time again in dynamic relationships with the realities from which he makes his poems:

> and all summer long we rose at three
> to take the flaky ferry to the Island,
> standing three deep with buxom Slavic women,
> who smelled of dead fish, and never spoke English,
> going to the canneries, to stand
> in salty water up to the hip,
> without boots, hauling overpowering fish
> up onto the conveyor, where slight
> and chattering Filipinos slit them from stem
> to stern with one, sweet shaving stroke.

("The Fisherman's Fiesta," p. 14)

Another subject for study in Jay Wright's work is the family. Relationships between parents and children, husbands and wives, between siblings, are treated realistically, symbolically and mythically throughout his poems. (*Soothsayers and Omens* has the greatest concentration of his family poems-and the best.) The poet's father (and father–son relationships) is a frequent subject, as in "A Non-Birthday Poem for My Father" in *The Homecoming Singer*.

> Fathers never fit in poems
> and poems never please fathers.
> On my father's seventieth birthday,
> I tried to work him up a sonnet.
> I guess I did,
> and sent it off
> with some kind of prefessional pride. (p. 26)

This is a "typical" Wright poem, a continuous narrative, in about 150 phrasal lines, of his father's life and family history. "First Principles"—

written in exactly the same form in just over 100 lines—is a moving account of the father's fear that the son has been injured or killed in what the reader must assume was a so-called urban riot. It is one of Wright's finest works. "I see my father/ standing in the half-moon/ that the ancient lamp throws on the street," the poem begins; and the speaker walks toward his father, unable to believe that he is here—

> even if he's only come
> to pick up the pieces,
> to make sure that I'm alive.
> I can imagine his coming
> to identify me,
> lifting the sheet with emphatic hands,
> nodding briefly and turning out
> into the crowd, where he could
> bury himself and scream tears,
> as if he were one of them,
> giving in to his rage,
> and not to his loss. (p. 82)

Another theme that is unique to this collection—almost an oddity— is associated with Wright's several poems on travel and cities—cities inhospitable, bleak, and destructive. In his travels from city to city in the United States and Mexico, there emerges in a small number of poems a strange and unexpected Romantic strain: a Byronic, "Childe Harold" figure of loneliness and melancholy; the poet in exile, wandering to escape some nameless dread, but carrying some vague guilt with him. This is probably a continuation and deepening of the weak romanticism of *Death as History*; however, it is strange and unexpected because Wright is ordinarily a tough-minded poet who seems incapable of such sentimentality. One example will suffice:

> Ah, the pain I could tell,
> but that is not my choice.
> Before you, I'm not even virtuous.
> . . . .
> I think of how
> I walked this bridge,
> and would have leaped,
> leaving only my wallet

to identify me ...
. . . .
Ah, but I've come away
from that death desire.
("Beginning Again," 93, 94, 95)

If there is irony intended here, at least one reader has been taken in. However, the evidence for irony isn't strong enough to rescue the poem from an uncharacteristic failure of tone in Wright's work. Other poems in which this "Byronic" anomaly appears are "Jalapeña Gypsies," and "Pastel."

IV

The Homecoming Singer may be, for many readers, Jay Wright's most satisfying book, rewarding in its variety of experience. *Dimensions of History*, *Soothsayers and Omens*, and *The Double Invention of Komo* are also varied and complex works, likewise charged with the electricity of human hope, fear, love, ambition, etc. They transport the reader on intellectually stimulating and spiritually optimistic journeys through African, Caribbean, North–South American, and European history and culture. Moreover, these books have added to them the interest and fascination of unfamiliar myths and rituals. On the other hand, in one sense they are "narrow" in their focus and concentration on specific topics, notably God/religion and history, to the exclusion of a number of subjects and themes prominent in the earlier works. However, each book, and each stage of Wright's growth, has its specific rewards for the reader—whether one prefers the challenge offered by *Dimensions of History* and *The Double Invention of Komo*, or the greater familiarity and accessibility of *Death as History*, *The Homecoming Singer*, and the greater part of *Soothsayers and Omens*.

The chief attraction and charm of Wright's early poetry lies in witnessing the poet's discovering and making of himself through (to repeat a phrase I used earlier) his dynamic relationship with the materials of his world—and his art. The process is dramatic and unequivocal. From *Death as History*, the first book:

I've grown intellectual,
go on accumulating furniture and books,

damning literature, writing "for myself,"
calculating the possibilities that someone
will love me, or sleep with me.

> ("The End of An Ethnic Dream")

To *The Homecoming Singer*

Walking here,
I still feel I can sing
like a poet, a mad prophet,
caught in my own cadences ...

> ("First Principles," p. 84)

And, "Like a singing god,/ I stand and call the names of all my dead."

They fall and distract the living.
And in this forest of motives,
I pretend with the pretenders
to enter in here
in the night
with my urban chatter
transformed,
my mackin step weighted
with the grace of a ritual dance.

> ("A Nuer Sacrifice," p. 85)

Earlier, I invoked the ghost of that Good Gray Poet Whitman by saying that like him, Wright is a religious poet of eclecticism, synthesis, and myth. Grant me that gratuitous comparison between two poets who could not conceivable be more different otherwise, and I'll take it one step further. Read again the excerpts from the three poems by Wright, above. No, they are not "exactly" like anything from Whitman. Not exactly. It is not my intention to suggest that you will find anywhere in Wright's work any Whitman "influence." No one would be more surprised than I to discover more than accidental similarities between any two poets who happen to write about death, cities, religion, myth, occupations, travel, or history. But consider: In Whitman's early poetry, too (e.g., "Song of Myself") we find just such a process of self-discovery achieved through the poet's interaction with his world. The resulting self-knowledge then becomes the starting point for a spiritual journey. Although the whole of

Leaves of Grass records the process of Whitman's quest for personal and spiritual identity, and, true, his achievement of it occurs in crests and cycles, the single poem that shows best the process and the means whereby it is accomplished is "Passage to India." *The Double Invention of Komo* is Wright's current parallel to Whitman's great poem. I say "current" because I think we are witnessing, in process, the creation of an important body of work by Jay Wright. Perhaps one cycle has been completed. If so, the reader can discover its genesis in *Death as History* and *The Homecoming Singer*.

The poems speak for themselves.

NOTES

1. *Death as History*. A chapbook of 15 poems in 22 unnumbered pages. It is an edition of 200 copies by the Poets Press, New York, 1967.

> *The Homecoming Singer*. New York: Corinth Books, 1971.
> *Dimensions of History*. Santa Cruz, CA.: Kayak, 1976.
> *Soothsayers and Omens*. New York: Seven Woods Press, 1976.
> *The Double Invention of Komo*. The University of Texas Press, 1980.
> Hereafter cited as *Komo*.

Subsequent references to these works will appear in the text.

2. Included in *The Homecoming Singer*: "Crispus Attucks," "The End of an Ethnic Dream," "The Neighborhood House," "Chapultepec Castle," "Death as History," "Historical Days," and "Destination: Accomplished." Not included: "Against Imitation," "Exile," "The Musical Night," "The Voice of an Early Wind," "On the Block," "The Drums," "A Plea for the Politic Man," and "A Prelude."

3. In "Family Reunion," a poem in *Soothsayers and Omens*, the word "grovel" appears in a similar context.

> My saintly sister,
> you are more than a woman,
> more than the saintly body and soul
> you desire for yourself.
> You tell me,
> but I know you do not walk
> with Jesus or his saints,
> nor do you grovel up the paths
> you know he took. (p. 40)

ROBERT B. STEPTO

"The Aching Prodigal":
Jay Wright's Dutiful Poet

" ... this familiar music ... demanded action...."
—*Ralph Ellison*

I have been asked to provide a few words that might introduce Jay
Wright and his poetry to the general reader. This is an overwhelming
task—so much is there, so much is good—and it is a presumptuous one as
well since I, too, am the general reader. Perhaps I qualify for this work
because I own copies of the books and I have read them. Perhaps I should
therefore begin by saying something easy, such as, "Don't worry about
biography, or about the Anglo-American, Afro-American, and other
transatlantic traditions; don't worry about the history to be learned or the
myths to be dispelled or the language which is yours but which you do not
speak, just read the poems—let them introduce themselves." Jay Wright
would, I think, approve of this statement. But more must be said, all of it
having to do with how one may prepare one's self for reading a truly New
World poet.

Think of New Mexico. Consider it not so much as a place of birth
but as a "dimension of history," a physical dimension of fact, a bead of the
"map of beads." There are towns with Anglo names like Hobbs, Gallup,
and Farmington; other towns are called Las Cruces, Los Alamos, Las

From *Callaloo* 19 vol. 6, no. 3 (Fall 1983). © 1983 by *Callaloo*.

Vegas. Albuquerque is on the Rio Grande, and so is Truth or Consequences. "New Mexico assumed its present boundaries in 1863." (What else was going on in 1863?) Forty-nine years later, it was admitted as a State to the Union. It had been a Territory; while a "dimension" of Mexico, a Province and a Department.

The people of New Mexico are, and have been for some time, brown, white, red, and black. One could rehearse a history of people-in-place sometimes living a "feast of the living," at other times killing or at least distrusting each other; a history which begins, from one view, when Spanish explorers first ventured North from Mexico in the 1530's. But there is an easier route to seeing what is at hand: consider the Santa Fe Railroad.

Santa Fe. Named that by whom? "Settled" by whom and who else? There was a massacre there in 1680; four hundred "settlers" were killed and Santa Fe was "recaptured"—by whom, for whom, for how long? Santa Fe is almost 400 years old; it is the second oldest city in the United States. One can go there today and live a kind of "feast of the living"—the hills are gorgeous, the haciendas win decorating awards, a college or two blithely teach western civilization, anglos and Indians alike peddle craftwork of high quality, blue-corn tortillas are still available and still a manna from heaven. But one cannot get there easily by railroad.

Railroad. Built by whom? Stretched across whose land and when? And why? Who engineered, who conducted, who waited table and pointed out sights? Who observed from the observation car and saw what? Whose "noble image" graced the four-color posters and timetables that helped to fill the coffers? Who is the "we" in these lines?

> We'd learned that,
> when the snow was deep enough,
> we could show up by the tracks,
> looking ready and fit to work,
> and after the other men had been counted out,
> and sent trudging along the tracks,
> the foreman would sometimes turn to us.
> He always saved us for the last,
> even the giants, standing ready,
> with their uncommon eyes gripping him.[1]

What New World rituals are enacted here? What grip—as force, as disease—claims all?

State, Territory, Province, Department; Brown, White, Black, Red. These are not terms but tongues: "tongues of the exiled dead" but also, as we must intuit, "tongues of the living." They are the keys of our "own cadences," of our own literacies; they are for those of us gripped in this geography the keys to the kingdom of this world ("el reino de este mundo"). They are also beads upon a very particular "secular rosary" fashioned for those who, like Wright's poet, may " ... come, black and bilingual,/ to a passage of feeling" (*HS* 44) and sense that the journey must be undertaken again:

> Now I invoke my map of beads.
> I coil the spirit's veins about my wrists.
> I kneel at Ocumare to worry
> > the saint's bones,
> and rise on the walls of Cumaná.
> Poco a poco,
> I cut my six figures
> on another coast, in a western sunrise.
> In Carolina darkness, I push
> my jangada to the blessed water.
> I ask now:
> all the blessed means my journey needs,
> the moving past, the lingering shadow
> of my body's destination.[2]

This is a useful passage for anyone being introduced to Wright's art because it is at once complicated and straightforward. Complication comes, I suppose, with the references. Denizens of this world that we are, we nonetheless have to be told (in notes Wright probably did not want to write) that Ocumare and Cumaná are in Venezuela, and that *jangada* is a Brazilian balsam wood raft. While the notes clear up something, they in no way clarify everything, for it is precisely at this point that the predictable—and in some measure, insidious—culturally-prescribed questions set in. Is this poet black? Is this poet Catholic? (If he is a black Catholic, why?) Why does this poet go to South America? Are Ocumare and Cumaná in black South America? (Somebody better check.) Does this black poet consider South America home, if so, why? Why is there some Spanish in those lines? (How many black people "around here" know Spanish?) What kind of reading led to these lines? What kind of living let to these lines? Is this a religious poem? Is this poem black?

I should hope that in constructing these hypothetical questions, and in suggesting here and there motivations for them, I have also presented the worst possible hypothetical scenario. But something tells me that I am touching, in Wright's words, less upon the "fantastic" than upon the "certainty of myth." One wants to say that complication, as it is represented by these questions, is merely the result of ignorance or, to shift to another plane, illiteracy. (How much Spanish must a New World citizen know in order to translate "poco a poco"?) But that will not do. What we must see as well is how the myths and rituals of American living, including some of the most meaningful ones, tether us. We travel but do not journey; we read but cannot translate; we are wise but usually only in terms of a local wisdom. We are, in short, the father in these lines:

> But he, with good reason,
> never read my poem,
> and I think he must have sat
> in his small living room,
> with the dying dog lying at his feet,
> drowsing under the television's hum,
> thinking how little I knew. (*HS* 26)

Perhaps we are right to think such thoughts. They are, after all, a currency with which we have purchased a survival. But we must begin to come to terms with how all such thinking sends our children away, and only occasionally makes of them poets (the making having so pitifully much to do with childhoods becoming undone). And even then, not all of these poets are like Wright's "aching prodigal," who dares to sing "without metaphor" of

> What it means to spring from the circle,
> and come back again. (*HS* 28)

Complication thus appears with the return, which stands at once for what is contemporary in our lives and post-modern in our literature. The return is a radical, contemporary act because it forces a new dimension of history in place; it is aesthetically post-modern because it is the nether side of the journey, the cloth unwoven (nightwork, starwork), the city left, the lid (or mantle) as colon between two worlds instead of a figure of one world or another. The return is a complication full of decision and, on a fully evoked ritualistic level, incision: we know how to send our children away, or at least how to watch them go, but can we imagine and suffer the "cut" of their new, "trembling" presence?

But to speak of the return is in some sense to leap ahead. The end is in the beginning in Wright's poetry (as elsewhere), but it is with journeys not returns that we usually begin. Journeys are as essential to Wright's art as are the returns, and it is they which provide the points of entry, as it were, to many poems. This is what is straightforward, what should be familiar.

An early poem, "The Baptism," begins this way:

> We had gone down to the river again,
> without much hope of finding it
>   unmuddied. (*HS* 8)

"An Invitation to Madison County" has these first lines:

> I ride through Queens,
> out to International Airport,
> on my way to Jackson, Tougaloo, Mississippi.
> I take out a notebook,
> write 'my southern journal,' and the date. (*HS* 50)

The powerful final stanza of "The Death of an Unfamiliar Sister" declares:

> Sister, I have walked to here,
> over this compassionate dust,
> to wait in this moving light
> for your last movement,
> the one movement
> that these others will not
> and cannot understand.[3]

These lines from *Dimensions of History* seemingly rehearse those above:

> I strain to clasp my dust again,
> to make it mine,
> to understand the claims the living
> owe the dead. (*DH* 7)

Soon thereafter, we read,

> And so I start in search of that key,
> the ankh,
> that will unlock the act. (*DH* 8)

One image of what may then transpire is offered in the most recent book, *The Double Invention of Komo*:

> I forget my name;
> I forget my fathers and mothers names.
> I am about to be born.
> I forget where I come from
> and where I am going.
> I cannot distinguish
> right from left, front from rear.
> Show me the way of my race
> and of my fathers.[4]

In the first three passages, the referents appear to "bare" a North American stamp—quite possibly a North *Afro*-American one as well: baptism and burial, Mississippi and New Mexico, past and present—all these converge "down by the river side." In contrast, the final three passages provide no familiar referents. The geography is utterly nonspecific; the descent, insofar as the journey is of that nature, seems decidedly non-western; the image of the poet seeking and achieving the state of *tabula rasa* in order to gain the "way" of race and fathers alike unsettles and possibly offends more than one New World black culture. And yet, who presumes to declare that the final three passages depict foreign travel—or travail? Which "I" is the homeboy, which the alien, the *stranièro*? International Airport ("As I fly, I insist that nothing/ may now turn to itself, alone, again" (*DI* 87)) receives us all and disperses us upon our one-but-many journeys: Tougaloo and key; King and Komo; kin and cadence; river and dust. Albuquerque and Africa both require passports and preparation. In the North American South, the poet muses,

> I wonder how long I'll have to listen
> to make them feel I listen, wonder
> what I can say that will say,
> 'It's all right. I don't understand,

a thing. Let me meet you here, in your home.
Teach me what you know,
for I think I'm coming home.' (*HS* 51)

In the midst of "The third phase of the coming out of Komo ...", he continues,

I have been trying to create a language
to return what you have lost,
and what you have abandoned,
a language to return you to yourself,
to return to you. (*DI* 89)

There is difference here. In both passages, the poet is an apprentice or initiate; however, in the second, more recent passage he is more mature and, one suspects, better travelled. His statement of vocation clearly tells us that while he has not yet mastered his craft, he has passed through listenership to that level of authorship achieved only when responsiveness prompts responsibility. But there is similarity as well. "Home" is imaged in both passages, and in both images it is a shared language not merely to be found but performed. Here, then, is a key matter for the general reader to understand: Wright's art is one which forces us to make the all-important distinction between poems which describe or simulate performative acts—consider, among North Afro-American forms, the sermonic poem and the blues poem—and those which *prepare* us for performative acts. Wright's poems close, often arrestingly; but full closure exists within the imagined act that is just beyond the "circumference" of written art and possibly of language itself.

In poetry, and perhaps in other art forms as well, to speak of home is to suggest how that art seeks its tradition. And so we must ask of Wright's art, who travelled this road before? Who also travels now?

Vera Kutzinski, in her essay-review of *The Double Invention of Komo*, assists us here when she declares, "Du Bois' weary traveler has indeed come a long way," and adds, "Even though Jay Wright may not exactly be another 'cowboy' in Ishmael Reed's 'Boat of Ra,' he certainly is a fellow *traveler*, another one of those uncanny presences that people and traverse Afro-America's post-modern landscape."[5] To Du Bois and Reed, I would add, keeping in mind the landscape just cited, Jean Toomer: "I wonder how long

I'll have to listen/ to make them feel I listen, ..." is not from *Cane* but worthy of it. Consider as well Robert Hayden. Some of Wright's best early poems— "Crispus Attucks" and "W. E. B. Du Bois at Harvard" to mention two—are distinctly Haydenesque. In intensity, control, and angle of vision, and perhaps in their "angle of ascent" as well, they complement the work of Hayden, the American poet I first think of when I come upon a Wrightian phrase such as "the master of the spear" or "The star I see awakens me."

However, as I have already suggested, Wright's art is neither American nor Afro-American in any familiar, provincial sense. The boundaries of the United States, even in this post-modern era of expansion (military and cultural), cannot contain Wright's poet's "fact of history," any more than the rhythmic structures of ballads and blues can fully define that poet's ancient cadences. In *Dimensions of History*, the "brothers" include Crispus Attucks and Frederick Douglass. However, the "strict black brothers" are Du Bois and Saint Augustine. That pairing in itself charts a larger, transatlantic geography and historical ritual ground. Albert Ayler, Dante, Goethe, Wilson Harris, and Wole Soyinka are among the artists most often cited either in Wright's poems or in his notes. They figure deeply in the poems, partly because they provide models (of vocation as well as craft) and myths. But they are also central because they collectively signify an even larger landscape, one which perhaps is *the* map of the fact for Wright's poetry precisely because it delineates the triangulating routes of new world black culture and consciousness while exploring a still larger world, an "enhanced world" as Wright has put it.

The tradition Wright's poetry seeks is thus a puzzle for most of us, chiefly because it does not readily align itself with any one culture or cosmology—it is not a homing pigeon sure of its cage or sure that the cup of water and that of seed promiscuously placed therein is worth the price of incarceration. This troubles us, especially we who teach literature, since we are in a sense the pigeon-keepers, the custodians of the fragile cages which are variously courses and pedagogies on the one hand, and literary histories *cum* cultural fences on the other. Our problem in great part is that deep down something tells us that we should throw away the cages— including even those with the "comparative literature" tags and other travel stickers—and Begin Again. But how! And where does one start? An "enhanced world" is hard enough to fathom; an "enhanced world literature" complete with a tradition seems virtually incomprehensible.

I suggest that we begin, as Jay Wright often has, with the counsel of Wilson Harris. In "Some Aspects of Myth and the Intuitive Imagination," he writes:

With the fall of Pre-Columbian civilizations in America—and indeed with the sudden vulnerability of the ancient civilizations of China, India and Africa accompanying the circumnavigation and renewed penetration of the globe by European navigators and conquistadores—it would appear that a latent capacity, a latent restlessness, a sorrow, an anguish, an ecstasy as well, affected native craftsmen and a leap began to occur, the leap of the craftsman into the modern ambivalent artist. That leap was the beginnings of a community that brought Durer into dialogue with the arts of Pre-Columbian America as it was to bring centuries later Picasso into dialogue with the masks of Africa.[6]

This is useful; it offers both an idea of the modern and an image of the modern world community that is distinctly, as Frederick Turner would put it, "beyond geography."[7] But we need something more, if for no reason other than to avoid the mistake of packing Wright, Soyinka, Harris, Walcott, Schwarz-Bart, Carpentier, and all such writers into world literature courses that remain as conceptually thin as they may be bibliographically new. Hence, Harris continues:

That complex descent into the modern age is less than 500 years old. It scarcely yet possesses criteria of evaluation though I would suggest such criteria must accept the deep fact that all images (or institutions or rituals) are partial, are ceaselessly unfinished in their openness to other partial images from apparently strange cultures within an unfathomable, and a dynamic, spirit of wholeness that sustains all our hopes of the regeneration of far-flung community in an interdependent world.[8]

Statements of this kind effectively qualify the free-and-easy definitions of world literature that are soma of our flimsiest constructions. This particular assertion has further value in that it yields a language with which we can describe Jay Wright's art and the "enhanced world" it letters.

Wright's poet is, in one of his guises, the new world craftsman impaled upon the cusp of the modern, and in another, that same craftsman extracted (most likely, self-extracted) from that horn and healed. In one instance, there is assault from pain and rupture, in the other, there is that of memory and perhaps, too, that of the astonishing thought that the healing process will never end. In either case, the poet is a dutiful, aching prodigal, whose images of home and of a lasting inner health strain to prompt the act that will make all of us whole.

NOTES

1. Jay Wright, *The Homecoming Singer* (New York: Corinth Books, 1971), p. 19. All future page references to this volume are preceded by the letters, HS.

2. Jay Wright, *Dimensions of History* (Santa Cruz, CA.: Kayak Books, 1976), p. 93. All future page references to this volume are preceded by the letters, DH.

3. Jay Wright, *Soothsayers and Omens* (New York: Seven Woods Press, 1976), p. 56.

4. Jay Wright, *The Double Invention of Komo* (Austin, TX.: Univ. of Texas Press, 1980), p. 108. All future page references to this volume are preceded by the letters, DI.

5. Vera Kutzinski, "Something Strange and Miraculous and Transforming," *Hambone*, 2 (Fall, 1982), p. 129.

6. Wilson Harris, *Explorations: A Selection of Talks and Articles, 1966–1981* (Aarhus, Denmark: Dangaroo Press, 1981), pp. 98–99.

7. Frederick Turner, *Beyond Geography: The Western Spirit Against the Wilderness* (New York: Viking, 1980), *passim*.

8. Harris, p. 99.

VERA M. KUTZINSKI

The Descent of Nommo: Literacy As Method in Jay Wright's "Benjamin Banneker Helps to Build a City"

In the creative word,
there is the act of separation
and the act of falling.
—Jay Wright, *The Double Invention of Komo*

It has almost become a critical commonplace to note that Afro-American literature seems to be obsessed with history, as in fact it is. But this fact, in and by itself, is neither particularly meaningful nor very surprising given that American literature from all parts of the New World has always been preoccupied with history. For New World writing has constantly tried either to verify and lament, or else to overcome, what it felt as a profound lack of history: it simply could not call upon the kinds of historical origins to which Europe could—or in any case did—lay claim. Although it may be argued that Afro-American literature epitomizes this dilemma or crisis more than other American literatures because it suffered from a double denial of its cultural identity, the fact remains that the quest for history is not a unique phenomenon on the American literary scene. In a somewhat neglected essay entitled "History and the American Intellectual: Uses of a Usable Past," Warren Susman has pointed out that "the idea of history itself, special kinds of historical studies and various attitudes toward

From *Callaloo* 19 vol. 6, no. 3 (Fall 1983). © 1983 by *Callaloo*.

history always play ... a major role within a culture. The strange collection of assumptions, attitudes and ideas we have come to call 'world view' always contain a more or less specific view of the nature of history. Attitudes toward the past frequently become facts of profound consequence for the culture itself."[1] At a time when literary criticism seems to join other social institutions in adopting a dangerously indifferent attitude toward history, Susman's dictum should serve as a reminder of our need to return to history, not by way of substituting a naive neo-positivism for various types of formalism in the hope that they will simply go away, but by confronting history and/in literature as a series of conflictual interpenetrations of various forms and contexts.

There is obviously a need for clarifying literature's involvement with history, and in this particular context for asking more specific questions about the nature of Afro-American literature's obsession with history. The first, and perhaps most important, of these questions is, What does it mean for Afro-American literature to have a history, to be able, in other words, to entertain the idea of distinct historical origins? What does it mean to take notice of the traces that verify the historical existence of an Afro-American culture? And how does this act of taking notice manifest itself in those texts which comprise the Afro-American literary canon? In short, what are the literary *dimensions* of Afro-America's idea of and attitude toward its history?

What I am talking about is the evolvement of a particular kind of literacy out of Afro-America's perception of its own history. Robert Stepto has suggested that the Afro-American literary tradition is governed by what he calls a "pre-generic myth," which "is the quest for freedom and literacy."[2] But where does this myth come from? What happens to it once freedom and literacy have been achieved? Given the existence of a substantial body of texts written by Afro-Americans, it may be argued that these objectives have indeed been fulfilled. But the quest continues, and the question is, Why? It seems to me that what we are talking about is not freedom and literacy, but freedom *through* literacy. Literacy, taken literally as the ability to read and write, affords a very particular kind of freedom, namely the freedom to generate and disseminate knowledge about one's self in the form of written statements. Literacy, in this sense, is a kind of *method* for self-knowledge, which grants the Afro-American writer the freedom to interpret history and even to create his or her own myths about that history. In short, the quest for freedom through literacy is a quest for new methodologies. I am suggesting that the methods and methodologies Afro-American writers have devised since 1845 have changed significantly, and that these changes tell us a great deal about the nature of that self-knowledge that is being generated and thus about the nature of Afro-American culture as it exists today.

At the risk of stating the obvious, I want to go back in history, literary as well as social history, to recall some of the basic facts about Afro-America, facts which tend to get drowned in most current critical debates. One of those facts is that the vast majority of the African slaves imported into various parts of the New World, approximately since the beginning of the seventeenth century, did not have a written language of their own. In addition, blacks, especially in North America, were systematically denied access to the language of white society while at the same time being forced to substitute that very language for their various native tongues. In the North American slave states, more so than in other New World countries, literacy was used to create and reinforce both legitimate and illegitimate cultural differences between blacks and whites. Literacy thus quickly evolved into an ideological vehicle for the perpetuation of white supremacy. The historical link between freedom and literacy is clear: not only did the ability to read and write afford the black slave intellectual freedom by rendering accessible for interpretation and criticism the texts and documents used to legitimize his bondage. Literacy also granted actual physical freedom in those cases where slaves forged free-papers to facilitate their escape. Both instances have been well documented by the countless Afro-American slave narratives.

Since it was writing, not the spoken word, that was used as a means of social control and cultural imperialism, Afro-Americans resorted to their oral tradition to retain a sense of cultural authenticity and cohesion. They developed a form of literacy that questioned and actively circumvented the authority of "formal" writing as a vehicle for self-knowledge. The continued efforts on the part of Afro-American writers to unsettle this authority of "formal" writing manifest themselves both thematically and formally in their use of Afro-American folk materials as well as in their reliance on dialect, musical forms of expression, and oral modes of composition. This has led, especially but by no means exclusively, in poetry to the emergence and practice of a substantial number of distinct poetic forms, ranging from the blues poems of Langston Hughes and Sterling Brown and the poetic sermons of James Weldon Johnson to the jazz poetry of Michael Harper, the dozens of Don L. Lee, and the *sones* and *rumbas* of Jay Wright.

But things are not as easy and as clear-cut as they may seem, because no matter how strongly indebted to an oral tradition these new forms of poetry are, the fact remains that they are written forms. And because they are written forms, the initial idea of subverting the authority of "formal" writing becomes a highly ambiguous concept. The problem is this: How does the Afro-American writer maintain a dialogue with his or her culture at the moment of writing? How is it possible to perpetuate a culture, whose tradition is an oral one, without reifying that culture by turning it into something else, something other than itself? This issue is not resolved by defining literacy or freedom through literacy as concepts that go beyond or against writing simply because of their allegiance with Afro-America's oral tradition. What is implicit in such a definition is an identity between written and non-written systems, an analogy which has been widely questioned by recent literary theory, and justifiably so, because there are undeniable differences between an oral performance and a written text.[3] What is involved in literary writing is clearly more than a mere transcription of spoken words. Consequently, if the quest for freedom through literacy continues in Afro-American writing, as indeed it does, then we have to be very specific about what it is that Afro-American literature is trying to subvert and the ways in which that subversion takes place.

Modern Afro-American poetry's sustained quest for freedom through literacy is best described as a search for a reliable repository of meaning, on the basis of which the Afro-American writer can, in Amiri Baraka's words, "propose his own symbols, erect his own personal myths,"[4] in short, create his or her own language. This reliable repository of meaning is history, not a history that is self-contained and unchangeable in its pastness, but a history that consists of fragments to be assembled and woven together into "new categories for the soul/ of those I want to keep."[5] These last lines are taken from and best characterize the work of Jay Wright, one of the most important Afro-American poets to date. In neglecting his poetry, the criticism of Afro-American literature has deprived itself of one of the most fascinating and most fruitful resources for a true critical revisionism.

Wright's work is a remarkable contemporary example of an Afro-American poet maintaining a very active subversive dialogue with his culture while at the same time exhibiting an acute awareness of the problem of writing within the specific context of Afro-American culture. Wright is a most skillful weaver of poetic textures that well deserve to be called mythical, but which also embrace the kind of radical and inevitable historicity induced by the act of writing itself. There is no doubt that Wright is creating an Afro-American mythology, but he is also constantly reminding himself and his readers of the precariousness of such an endeavor. His best poetry emerges from an ongoing confrontation between history and myth, in which myth is rendered historical and history mythical. Although it is difficult, and at times almost impossible, to separate the two, we nevertheless have to distinguish these forms of discourse to be able to experience the effects of their interpenetration and to extract those categories which I have earlier described as the methodology of Afro-American writing. I shall explore Wright's poetic method(ology) by way of commenting in some detail on what I consider one of his best shorter long poems, "Benjamin Banneker Helps to Build a City." It is accompanied, in *Soothsayers and Omens* (1976), by its shorter "version," "Benjamin Banneker Sends His 'Almanac' to Thomas Jefferson," a poem which will not be considered separately here, but as a kind of double which revoices most of the important aspects of the former poem. "Benjamin Banneker Helps to Build a City" has the advantage of being more manageable than Wright's longer pieces, *Dimensions of History* (1976) and *The Double Invention of Komo* (1980), while at the same time sharing with them many prominent features. It is thus the perfect object for what I hope will be an inspiring introduction to the poetics of Jay Wright as it exemplifies Afro-American poetry's changing idea of literacy.

Both "Benjamin Banneker Helps to Build a City" and "Benjamin Banneker Sends His 'Almanac' to Thomas Jefferson" are as much about Banneker, the first self-trained Afro-American astronomer and doubtlessly one of the numerous grandfather figures which populate twentieth-century Afro-American letters, as they are about the founding of modern America. The point in American history to which Wright returns us in these two poems is the last decade of the eighteenth century, a period which marks North America's transition from colonialism to modern nationhood. This particular historical passage, which is symbolized by the founding of the national capital, the city which Banneker did indeed help to "build," is significant for a number of reasons, all of which have to do with language and with writing.

Like *Dimensions of History* and *The Double Invention of Komo*, "Benjamin Banneker Helps to Build a City" is preoccupied with origins, and more specifically with the controversial origins of the New World and with the role blacks played in the creation of an America that was more than just an "inspired invention of the European spirit," as Edmundo O'Gorman has called it.[6] This concern for historical origins pervades all of Wright's poetry and is frequently associated with the figure of the city, a connection which is not unusual in light of the historical significance of the founding of cities in the New World since the times of Columbus.[7]

But there is more to this figure; for Wright, the modern city as the center of all cultural activity emblematizes Europe's logocentric dream of totalization (and totalitarianism), a concept introduced to the New World by the Conquistadores. But its echoes are also present among the early Puritan settlers of North America, where this kind of logocentrism manifested itself in the notion of the "covenant of grace" and its secular extensions. The particular city alluded to at the beginning of "Benjamin Banneker Helps to Build a City" is the culmination of this logocentrism: the new capital of the United States is to be the seat of political power and thus the nation's new center, the very embodiment of its autonomy. A monument to modernity, it is a structure designed to commemorate the end of one era and the beginning of another, the era of American independence. In this sense, the national capital incarnates the American Revolution as a break with the old center, the England of George III. However, given the rest of the poem, especially the contents of the two quotations from Banneker's letter to Thomas Jefferson to which we shall have to return shortly, it would be quite erroneous to think that Wright is celebrating the spirit and the achievements of the American Revolution as the one historical event that could be a potential source of cultural authenticity. In fact, he is doing quite the opposite, which is rendered evident by the specific historical date implicit in both the quotations and the references to the founding of the national capital: The survey, in which Banneker participated, was launched in 1791 by President George Washington; Banneker's letter to Thomas Jefferson, then Secretary of State, was also written in 1791.[8] In other words, both events are separated from the signing of the Declaration of Independence by approximately fifteen years, but that alone is not the point here. What, then, is the significance of the year 1791 with respect to the origins of American (and Afro-American) history? What inevitably comes to mind—although it is nowhere directly mentioned in the text of the poem—is an event whose significance for Afro-America is vast and whose echoes in African-American literature are countless: this event is the Haitian Revolution. It is also worth mentioning that 1791 recalls two other "central" points in American history, both of which mark profound transitions: The first one happened three centuries earlier in 1492, when Columbus first landed in Santo Domingo; the second one occurred a century later in 1892, which is the date of the dedication ceremonies for the World's Columbian Exposition, the founding of "White City."[9] All of these fragments cluster around the date 1791 and the kinds of transitions it represents.

Although the poem does not invoke the names of Toussaint, Dessalines, or Henri Christophe, this underlying date itself is quite sufficient to shake the foundations of the future metropolis and to displace the center it aspires to represent. Even in its absence, the Haitian Revolution in particular provides both an analogy and a contrast to the American Revolution and its future emblem. The contrast is perhaps more obvious than the analogy: The Haitian Revolution, unlike its North American counterpart, was aimed at overthrowing the island's slave-holding society and replacing it with a black government; no such radical changes were ever envisioned for North America. This difference is important in that it substantiates the claim that the American War of Independence was the only revolution in modern times motivated by the desire to prevent drastic social change. But the similarity between the two upheavals is even more disturbing, because with regard to the black population of both Haiti and the United States, each was essentially, in Alejo Carpentier's words, a "rebirth of shackles," a prelude to reenslavement.[10]

In the same way that Haiti's mulatto elite, which replaced the government of the French slaveholders, continued to oppress blacks, slavery in the United States was far from having been abolished by the humanitarian principles inscribed in the Declaration of Independence and the Federal Constitution. I cannot, at this point, resist calling attention to another passage from Carpentier's *The Kingdom of This World* (1949), which is perhaps the best-known modern novel about the Haitian Revolution, and which is all the more relevant to our present discussion for narrating the story from the perspective of a black protagonist. Near the end of the novel in a chapter significantly entitled "The Surveyors" (!), Carpentier's Ti Noel, now an old man, is observing the work of the mulatto surveyors. At some point he raises his eyes to the old Citadel, sadly thinking that "[t]he word of Henri Christophe had become stone and no longer dwelt among us. All of his fabulous person that remained was in Rome, a finger floating in a rock-crystal bottle filled with brandy."[11] This vision of words turned to stone, of idealism quite literally turned to conservatism, is precisely what Jay Wright's poem associates with the future capital of the United States: the epitome of words devoid of any meaning, of empty gestures "with/ no sign, of what gave them strength."[12] This last citation is a passage from Baraka's "Poem for Willie Best," which Wright used as an epigraph to his "Variation on a Theme by LeRoi Jones. II." This earlier poem comments on the plan of transformation—the "alphabet of transformation" as it is called in *Dimensions of History*—elaborated in "Benjamin Banneker Helps to Build a City."

The image of the city is prefigured in "Variation" in the form of those "massive limestone crosses" which "measure the American continent."[13] They are the stony monuments left by previous "surveyors," whose measure(ment)s almost completely erased all traces of the continent's native civilizations. These crosses, in short, symbolize death,

> ... a stiff Jesus,
> with his impassive beard,
> driven staunchly on a mountain,
> impervious as well to the babble
> of tongues as to the absurd heights.

But Wright "would not have him there,/ marking some inaccessible point"; instead, "[h]e would have to come down,/ and bend his back on the line/ ... / feeling an insatiable desire/ to break free and become a sign,/ a living gesture, unearthed,/ yet rooted in earth, in flesh." Wright literalizes the Christian doctrine ("the word become flesh") in order to emphasize the absurdity of worshipping death as a form of salvation, as the measure of all living things. Passivity and imperviousness, the characteristics of sacred immobility, have to give way to the impact of historical experience. Once the "stiff Jesus" begins to take notice of the "babble of tongues" around him, once he is "listening/ to the groomed merchants of the soul/ bargaining guardedly for every part of him,/ letting the echo of exile change him," his poetic features change dramatically as the language of the poem itself breaks free and bursts into a rapid sequence of present participles and unfinished verb forms. The change we witness here is the creation of desire or "uneasiness."[14]

In "Benjamin Banneker Helps to Build a City," this "uneasiness" is a disturbance of the faith, not primarily in the rituals of Christian religion, but in the ritual of revolution and specifically the American Revolution. This ritual of revolution, represented by the lining out of the land according to precise mathematical laws ("the language of number" [p. 24]) is a self-contained process, a ceremony of imprisoning language by locking it into a definitive symbolic shape. This process is analogous to the legal rituals involved in the symbolic act of drawing up the Declaration of Independence, the new nation's *charter*, which is to be reproduced in the form of a *map* or *chart* of the site of the city. But,

> These perfect calculations fall apart.
> There are silences

that no perfect number can retrieve,
omissions no perfect line could catch. (p. 27)

What are those silences, those omissions, those imperfections in the
design? And what language can retrieve them? The most obvious instances
of such retrieved silences are the two passages from Banneker's letter to
Jefferson, which cause, within the text of the poem, a disturbance of no
small consequence. This letter, which was enclosed with the 1792 Almanac
Banneker sent to Jefferson, was written about six months after the black
astronomer had become involved with the survey project for the new
capital. It is the only known instance of Banneker's publicly expressing his
thoughts about slavery—he himself, it should be noted, was a free man.
Jefferson's reply was favorable; he informed Banneker that he had
forwarded the manuscript copy of the Almanac to the Secretary of the
Royal Academy of Sciences in Paris as evidence of the talents of the black
race. Ironically enough, it was never received. But Banneker's letter to
Jefferson and the latter's reply, first published in pamphlet form and later
included with Banneker's Almanacs, were widely circulated by abolitionist
societies in the United States and also in England. Several of Banneker's
"abolition almanacs" appeared between 1793 and 1797 in a number of
editions, and their great popularity made them some of the most
important publications of their time.[15]

All of this is to say that it is hardly an exaggeration to label
Banneker's letter to Jefferson one of the founding texts of modern
America—one, however, which unsettles the authority of the nation's
official charters. With the exception of a few minor changes, the
quotations from this letter as they appear in the poem are true to the
original.

> Here was a time, in which your tender feelings for yourselves
> had engaged you thus to declare, you were then impressed with
> proper ideas of the great violation of liberty, and the free
> possession of those blessings, to which you were entitled by
> nature; but, Sir, how pitiable it is to reflect, that although you
> were so fully convinced[16] of the Father of Mankind, and of his
> equal and impartial distribution of these rights and privileges,
> which he hath conferred upon them, that you should at the
> same time counteract his mercies, in detaining by fraud and
> violence so numerous a part of my brethren, under groaning
> captivity, and cruel oppression, that you should at the same

time be found guilty of that most criminal act, which you
professedly detested in others, with respect to yourselves.
(p. 24).

The contradictions exposed and expounded by this memorable passage are
significant beyond their well-known historical implications. Their
reverberations are felt throughout the poem as Wright himself is
"struggling for a city/ free of that criminal act,/ free of everything but the
small,/ imperceptible act, which itself becomes free" (p. 25), struggling for
"different resolutions" and different *measurements*.

Documents, as Joseph Riddel has pointed out, "decenter the lyrical
voice, the centering or narrative subject."[17] In the context of Wright's
poem, this particular kind of displacement corresponds to the
subversiveness of Banneker's letter when viewed as a specific historical
datum. We have already examined the traces of historical events which
cluster around that date and undermine the centrality of the American
Revolution by introducing the notion of multiple origins to the concept of
American culture. On the level of textuality, this idea of multiple origins
is corroborated by the poem's claim to multiple authorship, a
compositional principle which frees it from the singleness of vision
associated with a commanding origin or a central consciousness. The title
of the poem already anticipates this multiplicity. Not only does the use of
the name "Benjamin Banneker" displace the name of the author as it
appears on the cover of the book. In addition, "helps to build" instead of
"builds" indicates that the city, which is being built here, that is to say, the
text of the poem, is not the product of a single individual consciousness,
which authorizes its meaning. The poem, in short, is itself decentered. It
becomes a play of originating forces, or what Charles Olson has called a
"field" of intersecting lines, of crossing paths,[18] so that it is ultimately an
emblem of original and originary multiplicity. There is no question that
Wright's poetry on the whole partakes of the American tradition of the
long poem, whose achievement is "essentially a freedom from the
commanding origin."[19] What Wright is after is a "coherence," to borrow
another term from Olson,[20] and this coherence is precisely what I have
described as a method(ology), which would invest this play of originating
traces with culture-specific meanings. So we return again to Afro-
America's quest for freedom through literacy.

Free. Free. How will the lines fall
into that configuration?

How will you clear this uneasiness,
posting your calculations and forecasts
into a world you yourself cannot enter?
Uneasy, at night,
you follow the stars and lines to their limit,
sure of yourself, sure of the harmony
of everything, and yet you moan
for the lost harmony, the crack in the universe.
Your twin, I search it out,
and call you back;
your twin, I invoke
the descent of Nommo. (pp. 25–26)

The link between freedom and writing, and more specifically with writing as (con)figuration, is obvious enough in this citation. But what exactly is that freedom and how can it be realized in writing? To be sure, it is a freedom from that "most criminal act," from the "great violation of liberty" that is slavery. But if we want to be rigorous about such a referential reading, we also have to consider that Banneker, unlike Douglass for example, was never a slave. It could be argued that this difference is relatively insignificant given the actual treatment of free blacks in the antebellum South and also the continued oppression of Afro-Americans well after Emancipation. But the implications of Banneker's status as a black man, who was not only free, but also literate in a very special sense (he was a scientist), are nevertheless important to the rhetorical strategies of the poem. For it is this seemingly irrelevant difference which enables Wright to charge Banneker's definition of slavery as "criminal act" with a literary and cultural meaning which surpasses historical referentiality in the strict sense. He sees the "criminal act" as a slavish subscription to the fiction of a single commanding origin, which, in its turn, generates the fiction of the "harmony of everything." Wright's criticisms here are not simply directed at the injustices perpetrated in the name of slavery, but at those elements in Western thought used to sanction slavery, which are the same conceptual categories later employed to perpetuate slavery in the form of cultural imperialism. Those categories are rooted in the Christian doctrine and the religious fiction of a divine consciousness as a single figure of authority (the "Father of Mankind"). This figure had been invented in the image of those, who called themselves God's prophets, who were the interpreters (and authors) of the biblical myths which served to unify the story of the creation of the world by attributing it to a single source. However, this particular mythical version of history was sharply contradicted by the events which led to the "discovery" of America. This discovery produced a "crack in the universe" of Western thought by upsetting its previously harmonious, unified image of the world. It is this "lost harmony," this disruptive movement of displacement and transition, to which Wright appeals in order to unsettle the fiction of centrality and to recapture the turbulence generated by the existence and interpenetration of America's multiple origins.[21] Wright's poetry cuts through that image of America projected by its European inventors; it cuts through the New World's superficial newness down to the marrow of history. This deceptive quality of being new is what is represented by the founding of a city that would reinstate the very center from which it seeks to break free. What seems like an autonomous act, then, is really only an imitation of the European spirit and its desire for centralization. In this sense, "the sight of the lesser gods/ lining out the land" (p. 25) is a figure for historical mimetism. Rather than an act of liberation, it is an act of reproducing and repeating the paradigms of western culture in the form of its foremost imperial symbol: the modern city.

> How pitiable it is to reflect
> upon that god, without grace,
> without the sense of that small
> beginning movement,
> where even the god
> becomes another and not himself,
> himself and not another. (p. 25)

What is "pitiable" is the unmediated imitation, which is all the more "graceless" for being inauthentic, unaware of the doubleness at the origin of American history. That double origin is the point at which the "god," who, as we shall see, is a figure for the poem's design, becomes *both* himself and another. This simultaneity of self and other now generates figures which are true emblems of doubleness; they condense the essence of Afro-America's historical experience, exile and slavery, and relate that essence to the schism which was caused by the discovery of the New World. Those figures are "Amma's plan" and "the descent of Nommo." According to Dogon mythology as described by Marcel Griaule and Germaine Dieterlen,[22] Amma's plan is the design for the creation of the universe, the matrix which eventually becomes Nommo, the first being created by Amma. As Amma's twin, the Nommo embodies the very principles of its creation, that is to say, the process of twinning, of doubling. In this sense, the Nommo is a living design. Its descent, its creation, is a movement from abstraction to representation, from "the lines in your head" to "these lines," which are the lines we are actually reading.

A closer look at the poem's language will clarify this movement, which accounts for the difficulty of much of Wright's poetry. Part of that difficulty is that Wright's language offers very few representational images for the reader to hold on to. In fact, the main image that can be extracted from the text of "Benjamin Banneker Helps to Build a City" is that of Banneker contemplating the movement of the celestial bodies. But even that picture, which appears at the very beginning of the poem and recurs several times, is semantically highly unstable.

> In a morning coat,
> hands locked behind your back,
> you walk gravely along the lines in your head. (p. 22)

This is, if you will, the point where the "vibration" starts. This vibration is an unsettling of language's representational capacities, an effacement of sorts, which makes possible the projection of another, different, image: What we see, yet cannot *see*, as "morning" vibrates into "mo[u]rning" and "gravely" into "grave[-]ly," is an image of the poet himself, traversing a burial ground, which is clearly a figure for the act of memory Wright has to perform in order to produce an image that appears to be representational. The following remarks by Paul de Man are helpful here. "All representational poetry," de Man writes, "is always also allegorical, whether it be aware of it or not, and the allegorical power of the language undermines and obscures the specific literal meaning of a representation open to understanding. But all allegorical poetry must contain a representational element that invites and allows for understanding, only to discover that the understanding it reaches is necessarily in error."[23]

All the reader is offered in the case of "Benjamin Banneker Helps to Build a City" are remnants of that representational element, traces of an image as it is prefigured in the poet's consciousness. The point is that these traces never evolve into a fully graspable representation; instead, they undergo a series of transformations, which culminate in the act of naming at the end of the poem. "And so you, Benjamin Banneker, / walk gravely along these lines" (p. 26). With the exception of the title of the poem, this is the only other instance where Wright uses this name; and this final baptism is directly preceded by the invocation of "the descent of

Nommo," which announces the completion, that is, the final articulation, of the poetic design.

But much happens prior to this final articulation, and it is necessary to trace the evolvement of the poem's initial vibrations into their literate configurations. The second "stanza" already introduces some important transformations: The gravesite is now more fully figured as a field of ruins, and what had previously appeared to be an act of remembrance is now revealed to be an act of reading.

> Now, I have searched the texts
> and forms of cities that burned,
> that decayed, or gave their children away. (p.22)

The poet now poses as an archeologist attempting to decipher the ruins of ancient cities (Rome, perhaps, but more likely cities such as Cuzco or Tenochtitlán[24]) in order to recover the cultural origins of the New World. All the while, he is "watching [his] hands move"; they are no longer locked behind his (or Banneker's) back. Their movement, as it produces the very lines we are reading, picks up on the kinetic trope of "walking," which significantly reappears as "the weight and shuttle of my body," thus inviting us to apprehend this movement as a kind of weaving, one of Wright's main figures for the act of writing.[25]

In the third "stanza," the journey back into time, so far figured as a survey of a variety of ancestral sites, leads us to "the time/ of another ceremony" and to the creation of "another myth." Now, a "familiar tone" enters the poet's voice as the opening of the site, the breaking of the ground, suddenly begins to assume the qualities of a *rite de passage*, which is, more specifically, a purification ritual.

> A city, like a life,
> must be made in purity.
>
> So they call you,
> knowing you are intimate with stars,
> to create this city, this body.
> So they call you,
> knowing you must purge the ground. (p. 23)

It is at this point that we first encounter a quotation from Banneker's letter to Jefferson. The extent to which this document itself constitutes an invocation by continuing the rhythmic movement of the preceding lines, is quite striking. This becomes more evident if we extract certain phrases, which may be identified as "calls," and line them up differently:

> Sir, suffer me to recall to your mind that time ...
> look back, I entreat you ...
> reflect on that time ....

What these lines urge us to recall is Afro-America's history of exile and slavery, which now begins to reveal its mythical dimensions. In the realm of myth, the cut of the umbilical cord connecting Afro-America with Africa ("These people, changed,/ but still ours") can be seen as the beginning of an initiation into self-knowledge. What makes this transformation possible is Wright's vision of the cut into exile as a sacrificial act, an excision which purifies the initiate while at the same time *marking* him as member of the Afro-American community. The fact that the two passages from Banneker's letter should be called upon to serve as purifying agents, which prepare, "exorcise," the ground for the inscriptions of the signs of self-knowledge, is quite telling, not only because of this document's connections with the beginnings of abolitionism. This is yet another instance of Wright's creating a myth, of turning an historical context into allegory, only to render that allegory literal again. Put differently, once the predicament of exile and slavery ceases to be viewed simply as a period in Afro-American history that is best forgotten and becomes part of a larger historico-mythical pattern, which may be described as a ritualistic worldview, then it assumes the qualities of a communal sacrifice which opens old wounds as new paths toward self-knowledge. History, in this sense, does yield a myth, which is Afro-America's myth of exile. This myth is "the seed vibrating within itself,/ moving as though it knew its end, against death" (p. 22). This myth is an "open space," a place where the fiction of being, and of culture, can be entertained, but it is also a "shelter" from history in that it is a timeless space. So in order for myth to reenter history, the seed has to "break into the open." It has to become articulate, literate, and this process of becoming articulate and literate is the transformation of myth to text. It becomes evident, then, that the seed, although a figure for culture, for cultivation, and thus for the "city, "is not a figure for the origin of culture in nature, but a figure for the origins of culture in language.

Myth may be able to shelter language from history; it may preserve it, like the finger of Henri Christophe, in a rock-crystal bottle filled with brandy. But that is not its "end." Rather than being a mechanism for preservation, a container of sorts, it is a functional design for the invention of language, a language which has metaphorical powers effective enough to participate in history, a language which does not just follow paths, but cuts them itself. Writing, then, is a taking literal of the cut into exile; it is a method that renders this particular myth both literate and literary. For Wright, the double cut into exile and kinship is the ultimate configuration of freedom through literacy. It shows that, in fact, the only way in which the Afro-American writer can maintain an authentic dialogue with his or her culture is precisely, and quite paradoxically perhaps, through the act of writing, which reenacts, instead of reifies, the small movement at the double origin of Afro-America. In doing so, writing generates knowledge about that mythical origin by constantly decomposing it into historical fragments, by transforming it into something other than itself. According to Wright, Afro-American poetry has to be an ongoing invocation of the descent of Nommo, the god who is both himself and another, who is twinned at the moment of self-knowledge, which is also the moment of sacrifice, or, in Wright's own words, of "death as history." [26]

NOTES

1. *American Quarterly* (Summer, 1964), p. 243.

2. *From Behind the Veil. A Study of Afro-American Narrative* (Urbana: University of Illinois Press, 1979).

3. Writing does not have access to the qualities of voice, nor to the repertoire of gestures, which a storyteller utilizes to mediate between story and audience. All of the above are part of a performance, but not part of a transcription of the text of the story told. In writing, the mediation between story and audience, text and reader, is always an integral part of the text itself. What mediates between the two in a written context are the postures adopted by the author vis-à-vis both his story and his readers. These postures manifest themselves *in* language, not outside of it, and they consequently affect the story in ways that may resemble, yet differ substantially, from the performative effects of intonation and gesture. For more detailed information on oral performance, see Harold Scheub, "Oral Narrative Process and the Use of Models," *New Literary History*, 6 (1975), 353–377.

4. Baraka quoted in Kimberly Benston, *The Renegade and the Mask* (New Haven, CT: Yale University Press, 1976), p. 110.

5. *The Homecoming Singer* (New York: Corinth Books, 1971), p. 75.

6. *The Invention of America. An Inquiry into the Historical Nature of the New World and the Meaning of its History* (1958; Westport, CT: Greenwood Press, 1972), p. 4.

7. See, for example, *Christopher Columbus. Four Voyages to the New World. Letters and Selected Documents*. Bilingual Edition. Translated and edited by R.H. Major (Gloucester, MA.: Peter Smith, 1978), pp. 49–50; also *Hernando Cortés. Five Letters*. 1519–1526. Translated by J. Bayard Morris (New York: W.W. Norton, 1928), pp. 17–18.

8. Silvio Bedini, *The Life of Benjamin Banneker* (New York: Charles Scribner's Sons, 1972), pp. 104–105 and 152.

9. Alan Trachtenberg, *The Incorporation of America. Culture and Society in the Gilded Age* (New York: Hill and Wang, 1982), see especially Chapter Seven, "White City," pp. 208–234.

10. *The Kingdom of This World*. Translated from the Spanish by Harriet de Onís (New York: Collier Books, 1970), p. 178.

11. *Op. cit.*, p. 177.

12. *Selected Poetry of Amiri Baraka/LeRoi Jones* (New York: William Morrow and Co., 1979), p. 23.

13. *The Homecoming Singer*, pp. 67–68.

14. *Soothsayers and Omens* (New York: Seven Woods Press, 1976), pp. 25 and 27. All further references to this volume will appear in the text by page number only.

15. Bedini, *The Life of Benjamin Banneker*, pp. 158–201.

16. What is missing here is "of the benevolence"; see the reprint of Banneker's original letter in Bedini, p. 155.

17 "Decentering the Image: The 'Project' of 'American' Poetics?" in Josué Harari, ed., *Textual Strategies. Perspectives in Post-Structuralist Criticism* (Ithaca, NY: Cornell University Press, 1979), p. 357.

18. "Projective Verse," in *Selected Writings of Charles Olson*. Edited, with an Introduction by Robert Creeley (New York: New Directions, 1966), pp. 15–26.

19. Riddel, "Decentering the Image," pp. 344–345.

20. See Olson, *Human Universe and Other Essays*. Edited by Donald Allen (New York: New Directions, 1967), p.19. It would be very fruitful to compare Wright's poetics to Olson's, but such a comparison goes beyond the limits of this essay.

21. See the last two stanzas of Wright's "Homecoming" in *Soothsayers and Omens*, p. 58:

> From line to line,
> from point to point,
> is an architect's end of cities.
>
> But I lie down
> to a different turbulence
> and a plan of transformation.

22. The work of Griaule and Dieterlen is of crucial importance to all of Wright's poetry. See especially *Le renard pâle. Tome 1–Le mythe cosmogonique* (Paris: Institut d'Ethnologie, 1965).

23. *Blindness and Insight. Essays in the Rhetoric of Contemporary Criticism.* Second, revised Edition (Minneapolis: The University of Minnesota Press, 1983), p. 185.

24. See, for example, the end of *Dimensions of History.*

25. See especially "Second Conversations with Ogotemmêli," *Soothsayers and Omens*, pp. 61–78.

26. See *The Homecoming Singer*, pp. 62–63.

CHARLES H. ROWELL

"The Unraveling of the Egg": An Interview with Jay Wright

ROWELL: Most of your poems published after 1971 force me to rethink and re-evaluate my own concept of *the poem* or of *poetry*. What is a poem— or, what do you, a working poet, conceive poetry to be? And what are its functions? My questions seem strange, I'm certain, in 1984, but your poetry evokes them from me. The main of your poetry after *The Homecoming Singer* (1971; the poems in section two of *Soothsayers and Omens*, 1976, are, however, similar to those in *The Homecoming Singer*) is quite different as constructs, for example, from the contemporary poetry I have read.

WRIGHT: Theory is the angel in twentieth century intellectual life, but I'll risk a hip. I sometimes enjoy setting forth my paradigmatic relationship to the words *poetry* and *poem*. I almost said derivational, but that leads us into the tricky area of fixed laws, and any conception of fixed law introduces the troubling necessity of finding the origin of such a law. I suppose I shouldn't worry about that. So much of Anglo-American, and, unfortunately, black African-American, talk about poetry simply ignores that problem, and sets out a comfortable notion of poetry that accepts unspecified (and, when specified, contradictory) compositional rules. In developing my theory, I've begun by asking whether it is not true that poetry is what a particular literary community at a particular time says it

From *Callaloo* 19 vol. 6, no. 3 (Fall 1983). © 1983 by *Callaloo*.

is. The literary histories available to us suggest that this is so, up to a point. I haven't gone far, but you can see that I've already begun by acknowledging that no poet can be without the civilizing impress of history and tradition. Clapping that mathematical word, derivational, on the table wasn't as ingenuous as it may have seemed to you. Poetry, if I may rearrange some bones for a moment, does deduce one function from another. In recent years, I've been energized by Samuel Akpabot's statement that "the African lives in music and in number." My reading of history impels me to think that music, speech and calculation (the measuring of time and event) have been the complex relationships in which human spirit, action, social and political relationships have been most gloriously exemplified. I realize that asserting this makes literary phenomena seem primary. You would expect a poet to insist upon literature's central position in human affairs. We hardly apologize for this insistence any longer. But I should stop here to say that I include in the speech community all those practitioners of verbal art who are not normally included: the griot, the old Testament prophet, the ritual chanter, the fabulist, the legist, the chronicler, the preacher, even the mathematician, among others. Quite a list, you say. What's left out? Why, nothing. Not even poetry. Among the various speech communities, poetry finds its voice, and its unique functions, which, nevertheless, are like those of other disciplines—the discovery, explication, interpretation, exploration and transformation of experience. I've now come to the point where I can set down the basic elements of my theory, the one by which I'm guided in writing poetry. Poetry is a concentrated, polysemous, literary act which undertakes the discovery, explication, interpretation, exploration and transformation of experience. It differs from some other forms of speech (such as that used by the legist, the chronicler, the mathematician) in that it handles its "facts" with more disdain, if I might put it that way, insisting upon spiritual resonance. It differs from some other forms of speech (such as that used by the preacher, the ritual chanter, the fabulist) in that it handles its spiritual domain with slightly more critical detachment than they do. The paradox of the extreme manipulative consciousness of the two domains—spiritual and material— indeed, their association to produce what is at least a third and unique domain—is what distinguishes poetry from the other forms of speech. I was almost going to say that I assume that we can recognize the formal differences between a poem and a statute, or a mathematical formula, or a sermon, but I would have left the field too soon. A poem distinguishes itself by rhythmic balance, accent and imaginative dissolution and reconstruction of its materials. It has a rhetoric we recognize as something peculiar to what we call a poem, irrespective of its line count, its imagery or lack of it, its rhyme or lack of it, its metaphor or absence of it, its adherence to any accepted paradigm. What the new poem tries to do is to establish itself as a member of that class of things we call poems and thereby establish a paradigm, one that still serves to create the third domain. This ought to be an unremarkable statement. There are, though, more complex matters involved in what I've said. Who is the *we* I mean? I'll answer that in a minute. What should be remarkable is that I consider poetry to have a functional value equivalent to all other forms of speech in a social and historical community. Putting things this way means that I consider poetry to have social and historical responsibilities. The poet cannot escape these. These responsibilities manifest themselves in the act of writing poetry and in the act of the poem. The *we* is the corporation of human beings who require and accept poetry's charter within it. I have now to elaborate upon certain terms in my definition. By concentrated I mean the kind of intensity and density that give great weight to suggestiveness, to resonance. Polysemous here means capable of translation from one meaning to another. Can we say a poem discovers anything? Yes, we can. It first finds the experience, in all its complexity, to be revealed and talked about. I talk this way to avoid begging the question of the given. There are no givens in poetry, not even your feelings. One does not recreate an emblematic state of anything; one works to create the act of becoming aware, attentive, active and transformed. I take the term, explication, from Willard Van Orman Quine's work in logic. Explication, he says, is elimination, beginning with an expression, or form of expression, that is somehow troublesome and resolving it by some new channel. Explication is analysis. In fastening on the terms, elimination and analysis, I have enough cloth for my sail and, therefore, do not have to be rigorous about the logical term, explication; I've changed it to a term usable for poetry. Interpretation is another logical term I've appropriated. You can find it most conveniently defined in Susanne Langer's introduction to symbolic logic, where she tells us that finding applications for concepts is called interpretation of an abstract form. Interpretation is the opposite of abstraction. Abstraction begins with a real thing and derives a concept; interpretation begins with an empty concept and tries to find some real thing to embody it. You must notice the importance of an operation here, an act of fitting. These last two terms, explication and interpretation, should call attention to one of my basic assumptions: that naked perception (just seeing something), directly expressed, is misprision in the highest degree. Every perception requires explication and interpretation. Exploration means just that. A simple report of experience, if you could make such a thing, isn't good enough. Finally, the whole process of making leads to transformation, the radical creation, of experience, the making of a new body and new heart, the breathing of a new spirit, what Soyinka urges upon you when he exhorts you to follow Ogun through the fourth stage. This last term's appearance in my definition should give you some idea of which sources have been most important to me in this formulation. My sources, apart from the obvious Judaeo-Christian ones, are in Africa and the Americas. The impulse behind my application of this theory of poetry arises from my attention to Wilson Harris's discourse on vision as historical dimension. To be guided by vision and spirit in poetry is a reputable task. The African and American sources provoke attention to vision and spirit, and call for different terms to describe the poetic act. The words I used before—line counts, imagery, rhyme, metaphor—are inadequate to describe the creative processes of the particular speech community to which I belong. I am not, as one might guess from the gossip, alone. I must say here, before I end with this question, that I believe all true poets do have theories and that they are very conscious makers. I give no credit to the taster who says, oh, I don't know, or, you work so hard and hope that what you're doing is right, or, I don't know where I'm going with this. As the Dogon say, speech is knowledge. An unconscious artist is a contradiction in terms. Now, I must finish by insisting that my theory accommodates poetry that is not written like mine. That is why I've said very little about form. Black African-American poetry can, should and will encompass any number of various paradigms. What remains common to all of them is the urge to express within them the claims of history, vision and spirit. I realize that I have time here to be no more than provocative. But that's all right; it's time for a little provocation. And I can, after all, refer the reader to my poetry where the thing is done by one member of the class who takes these matters seriously.

ROWELL: The poems in *The Homecoming Singer* and section two of *Soothsayers and Omens* remind me of the "autobiographical" or "confessional" voices in contemporary poetry. That is, your early poetry seems grounded in "personal" experience, but your later poetry seems to grow out of scholarship and events not immediate to our individual experiences. You even say in the Afterword to *The Double Invention of Komo* (1980) that books "are obviously important to this poem." *Dimensions of*

History (1976) and *The Double Invention of Komo* are different as aesthetic constructs from the poems in *The Homecoming Singer*. For example, they are different from *The Homecoming Singer* in language as a textured medium, experience as vision, and event as metaphor. Moreover, the later poems require us to use personal resources we are seldom asked to apply to "understand" contemporary—or even "modernist"—poetry. I immediately think of the aesthetic differences between "The Fisherman's Fiesta," "A Non-Birthday Poem for My Father," and "An Invitation to Madison County" as opposed to *The Double Invention of Komo* and "Twenty-Two Tremblings of the Postulant" (in *Explications/Interpretations*, Callaloo Poetry Series, Vol. 3, 1984).

WRIGHT: I did *The Homecoming Singer* in a way different from that of all the other books. I discovered the pattern of that book almost a posteriori. I had, as I looked at it, the record of my developing black African-American life in the United States, but I also saw that I had the beginning of forms to express lives that transcended that particular life. I have to say that, when looked at properly, all my poems are autobiographical and grounded in personal experience. The poems simply present this individual, the poet, within the cultural, historical, social, artistic, intellectual and feeling context in which he is asked to act, contribute and realize himself. Given the complex relationships and interactions with which the poet finds himself involved, and given the claims of that particular speech community upon him, scholarship and books, as well as spiritual and intuitive awareness, are important. The change you notice in language results from my decision to go further in uncovering the black African and American sources available to me and to use the linguistic processes, which appeared, to do this. Though I'm hesitant about the word metaphor, you put it nicely, experience as vision, event as metaphor. These are at least two of the linguistic resources of the communities I've indicated. Proceeding in this new way, I necessarily ask your active participation in the poetic act because I'm also asking your participation in the social and historical processes called forth. You haven't used the word, difficult, but so are the cultural and historical processes they intend to present. These processes and my poetry have an understanding: they will not cheat on nor devalue each other, they will respect complexity and difficulty, and urge aspiration and profound discovery in each other. From my second book, *Soothsayers and Omens*, onward, I have plotted and carried out books as books, not as collections of poems which just happen to make a book. I had the end of a series in mind. *The Double Invention of Komo* closes that phase. *Explications/Interpretations* stands third in the series. I thought, at first, I would have an octave progression. I see now that I have only a dominant one, and I'm working toward the tonic in a new progression.

ROWELL: Are we to read *Explications/Interpretations*, *Dimensions of History* and *The Double Invention of Komo* as three single poems or as some other kinds of poetic constructs? Haven't you referred to *Explications/Interpretations* as "a poem in movements?" What does that mean?

WRIGHT: My books should be read in the following order: *The Homecoming Singer*, *Soothsayers and Omens*, *Explications/Interpretations*, *Dimensions of History*, *The Double Invention of Komo*. Each is itself, but they are all related. *Explications/Interpretations*, like the whole series, is a dramatic process, with all its tensions and resolutions.

ROWELL: Am I justified in saying that we are asked to do more than merely read and "understand" these three book-length poems? Aren't we asked to surrender ourselves to their magical power and "to become" with the voices in them? Isn't the poet as voice a kind of priest in these poems?

WRIGHT: The poems do ask you to enter a process that requires thought, intuition, memory, factual and imaginative comprehension. I wouldn't use the word surrender; it's better to say that you are asked to accept the poem's challenge and to listen to, walk along, sing along and be with the poem. You are right in saying that you're asked "to become" with the voices. You are also asked to understand, and one thing you will understand is the process of entering in (I keep the redundancy to emphasize the double embrace of poem and percipient; in fact, here you can say that the poem sees you and is itself a percipient, and that makes you, in a sense, a poem, doesn't its). Perhaps, I should have said you will understand one process of entering, and that understanding should make you aware of the many ways and complexity of entering. I should also like to impress upon you that becoming with the poem is like becoming with your social context. Both require the same things. They support you and offer you a freedom, one that entails responsibility in your own becoming. They release you to realize your moral, imaginative and creative powers. I've come to the point where I must say that poetry is a distinct and very valuable mode of knowledge. It is not the only nor is it a pure mode of knowledge. I've talked to you about understanding, and that has almost led me to get into my African-Hellenic-Judaic discourse on understanding and wisdom. Understanding is a first step. J. B. Danquah, the Ghanaian politician-philosopher, in his book, *The Akan Doctrine of God*, defines three aspects of one God: Onyame, Onyankopon and Odomankoma. Kwesi Dickson quarrels with Danquah over the idea that the Akan know only one God. I continue with the formulation, anyhow, because it has a justifiable aesthetic relevance. Danquah calls these postulates, anyway. Onyame, he tells us, reveals an apprehension of Him as Understanding, Extension (Space) and Order. Onyame's antithesis, Onyankopon, is Experience, Time and Knowledge. Odomankoma corresponds to Reason, Reality and the Absolute. You can't fail to note the Hegelian ring of the formulation, but you can't fail to notice Danquah's imaginative way of filling the concepts with a complexity of motives and exemplifying them as active principles. I have substantiated Danquah's Absolute as wisdom. That gives me the opportunity to say that wisdom itself is an act, a process, a growth, in need of constant nourishment, cultivation and attention. So the poet here asks you to reach for wisdom, and you ask is the poet a priest. No, he's a poet, with the unique functions and claims upon him I brought forth earlier.

ROWELL: In fact, there is a concern for religion in all of your poems. In your poems after 1971, isn't religion more ritual than belief or faith? That is to say, ritual as order. I don't mean that your work is "religious poetry"; rather, religion seems to be, in one way or another, a central concern in your poetry. Will you talk about the function of religion—and myths and cosmologies—in your poetry; e.g., "Wednesday Night Prayer Meeting," "Collection Time," "Sources," section four ("Second Conversations with Ogotemmêli") of *Soothsayers and Omens*, and *Dimensions of History*.

WRIGHT: This would take me a few feast days. I can say something, though I'll also have to call attention to the essay I have coming in an MLA anthology that John O'Reilly and Robert Stepto are editing. I've also treated some of these matters in my inaugural lecture as Joseph Compton Creative Writing Fellow at the University of Dundee. Now, from the start, I make some distinctions. A poem is not ritual. I say that to obviate any misconceptions your readers may have on the point. Secondly, we are too ready to dismiss self-consciousness and a critical spirit from the realm of mythical thought; myth, being a human process, cannot escape being historical. Ignoring these facts makes it easy to see ritual, in which sometimes myths appear, as simply emotional outlets, things to which you completely surrender yourself. Now, to come back to me. I don't mind being called religious. That makes me very African. My reading in history, anthropology, cosmology, religion, social thought, the various things that engage me in Africa, shows me that African societies, at least the traditional ones, are moral and spiritual, one might say as well, metaphysical. If these are some of the attributes of religion, then I accept my religious calling. I'd prefer to say that, in my poetry and plays, spirit and social and historical responsibilities concern me, claim me, really. I claim, in my MLA essay and here now that these are black poetry's central concerns, and I even assert that the ritualistic pattern that Sunday Anozie has seen in Christopher Okigbo's poetry—a process of separation, transition and incorporation—motivates most, and the best, black African-American poetry. I take a cue from Wole Soyinka, "To dare transition is the ultimate test of the human spirit," and insist that that test is a paradigm of black African-American experience: a consciousness of risk, separation, self-alienation and, ultimately, reconciliation. I have said that the ritualistic pattern can define an epistemology of poetry. When the poet reaches for fulfillment in this way, it leads to what Soyinka says is not a difference between "I" and "we" but a deeper subsumption of the self into vision and experience, and keeps us from splitting the physical from the psychic, from separating action from poetry. The religious resources—and myths and cosmologies—available to me in the earlier poems are in quality and quantity different from those in the later ones. I must emphasize, however, that the poetry's goal, early and late, has always been to bring a critical and creative vision to bear on an enlarged realm of experience, and, as I have put it at the end of my essay, to offer itself in the service of a new and capable personality at home in the transformative and transformed world.

ROWELL: History is also important in your poetry. Is it also used as an organizing, as well as a thematic, principle in your work? Obviously, it is important to *Dimensions of History*. In that poem, we are in many times and places at an instant. Will you discuss history as concept, theme, etc., in *Dimensions of History* and the Benjamin Banneker poems in *Soothsayers and Omens*. History in your poems is global; it is something broader, and much more exciting and humanistic than the narrow Eurocentric notion perpetuated by departments of history in universities in this country.

WRIGHT: Again, it's a large topic. I've discussed history and its relationship to black poetry in other places—an essay I did for a Francis

Fergusson festschrift, my inaugural lecture at Dundee, my MLA essay, the afterword to my fifth book—where I've been a little more formal than here and where I've been more elaborate and detailed than I'm going to be here. My interest in history goes back to my teenage years. My friend's mother, Mrs. Daisy Mae Fine Cline, who was family by marriage and a friend of W.E.B. DuBois, pushed DuBois, Garvey, John Hope Franklin, Rayford Logan, Benjamin Quarles, Saunders Bedding, Sterling Brown, Alain Locke and J. A. Rogers on us. She said we ought to be learning some proper history. I can't say I understood any of these people. Franklin, Logan, Quarles, Redding, Brown and Locke receded until recently, even though Mrs. Cline had special relationships with their work. I remember, though, her overwhelming enthusiasm for DuBois, Garvey and Rogers. I didn't learn historiography from her. What I learned was that history mattered. At the same time, she was running us through the writers of the so-called Harlem Renaissance; so it became rather natural for me to associate history and literature, or to think, at least, that they treated the same matters. Of course, now I'm an old horse on this course, and have busied myself with documenting and exploring what was urged upon my youth. For my theoretical self, I have the examples and help of people like Soyinka, Wilson Harris, and Robert Hayden. Soyinka claims that people live in a comprehensive world of myth, history and mores. Harris's insistence on essential unity within forms of latent and active historical diversity, his "vision of consciousness," his phrase "vision as historical dimension," seem to me other and most fertile American paradigms. There is nothing academic about these claims and assertions, and a trained historian might find them rather unappetizing. But one can't dismiss these things so easily, and there is great argument among historians and philosophers of history about their own ways with methodology, sources and origins. I have a new issue of *History and Theory*, in which Hayden White, writing about narrative in historical theory, discusses the relationship between historiography and literature, a relationship he finds as tenuous and difficult to define as that between historiography and science. The difficulty, he says, may be the result of historiography's rise, in the West, against the background of literary, or fictional, discourse, which itself had arisen from an even more archaic discourse, myth. He goes on to say that, in its origins, history differentiates itself from literature by virtue of its subject matter—real rather than imaginary events—rather than by form. Form, he tells us, refers not only to the appearance of historical discourses but to the systems of meaning-production (modes of emplotment, he calls them) which historiography shared with literature and myth. Then he says (and like B.B. King, this is the part I like) that we shouldn't be embarrassed about this affiliation because the systems of meaning-production shared by all three are distillates of the historical experience of a people, a group, a culture. I claim that historians have always understood these matters, even those in the "Eurocentric departments of history in universities in this country." At least the best historians, those not bound by career considerations and those aware of and ready to acknowledge the political trappings of their calling. Ernst Kantorowicz taught Robert Duncan that history and poetry have the same creative ground. Thinking about Hellenic and Judaeo-Christian thought and practice ought to assure us of the truth of that insight. The word, history, derives from the Ionian Greek, ἡ ἱστορία: learning by inquiry, inquiry, the knowledge so obtained. That word stems from ἱστορέω: to inquire into a thing, to examine. Now, for me, myth is a mode of knowledge. Traditional societies revere knowledge. Those who know the most, who think most acutely and accurately, who have developed a crucial ability to incorporate the many available forms of historical experience are the honored ones, the leaders. I don't want to rehearse everything I've said in other places. But I should say that, when we turn to ritual (the place where myth is often found), what we discover it teaches is what poetry embodies: reverence and compassion, visual and auditory rigor, emotional and intellectual rigor (what I call the discipline of imagination, the freedom of rule), respect for history and memory, respect for vision and desire and the ability to face up to the seriousness of life and the inevitability of death. Wilson Harris tells us that on society "literature has a profound and imaginative bearing wherein the life of tradition in all its complexity gives a unique value to the life of vocation in society." You can see that I keep coming back to the Americanness and Africanity of this vision of history in literature. The reason for that is that I find the vision most dramatically and profoundly expressed in the Americas and Africa, particularly in traditional societies. That is also why I composed a poem called *Dimensions of History*, based on Wilson Harris's phrase. The two Benjamin Banneker poems intend to get this comprehensive vision into another American context and to put forth the idea that black African-Americans have always strived to participate in all historical processes. You mention the global nature of my history. That is more than faith. Let me stop a moment for another kind of illustration. In a recent issue of *Isis*, Jonathan Spence, writing on Joseph Needham, tells a story about Matteo Ricci, a Jesuit missionary who lived in China from 1583 to 1610. The story concerns the making of a clock in Chao-ch'ing for the prefect, Wang Van. Ricci's associate, Ruggieri, went to Macao to raise money and to buy a clock. When Ruggieri couldn't turn up the money for the clock, he decided to send the best clockmaker in Macao to Ricci in Chao-Ch'ing. The man who agreed to go was, according to Ricci, "a black from the Canary Islands who had lived in India." Now, Spence later refers to the man as an Indian, but Ricci's formulation suggests that the man was what he would understand to be a black. What about that black man? A craftsman. Listen to Ellison on black African-Americans' intellectual and technical capabilities, and on their desires to work, to live and to be in the world that surrounds them. A young man, hearing me read some of my poems, said that I seemed to be trying to weave together a lot of different things. My answer was that they are already woven, I'm just trying to uncover the weave. People have never been that removed from each other and wherever you find black people in history, you're going to find black people acting in history. One of our tasks is to recall the forgetful to this fundamental truth. That is why my poetry looks for the basic human connections in experience and why it is one which includes many voices.

ROWELL: What do you mean when you write in the notes to *Dimensions of History* that the "poem is creation of a first order, not that of a second order, nor the kind of creation involved in more strict historical writing"?

WRIGHT: These are, again, logical terms. A first-order function is one "that involves reference to no totality other than that of individuals." Second-order functions sometimes have non-logical constituents. You can see that my poem is not strictly first-order. All I wanted to do was to keep the reader geared to the logic of the poem before reasoning away from it, to treat the poem as poem first. The poem and my own theory, of course, make that difficult, a salutary contradiction. Strict historical writing, at least that practiced by the "Eurocentric departments of history in universities in this country" would be content to treat every event as singular and undocumented and non-authoritative evidence with great caution.

ROWELL: Why did you append notes and commentaries to your last three published books?

WRIGHT: The individual publishers asked me to make them.

ROWELL: I have heard you give two readings—one at the University of Kentucky and the other at the University of Pennsylvania. At each reading you seem to have been very much concerned about the arrangement of your poems in the reading—that is, you shaped and maintained each reading as a tightly fixed pattern, a very tight structure, which transformed us from listeners to participants, however passive, in your reading as ritual. You have also expressed to me your concern that your readers know the order of the composition of your books. *Explications/Interpretations* (1984) was written before *Dimensions of History* (1976) and *The Double Invention of Komo* (1980). Why is it important for us to know the order of the composition of your work?

WRIGHT: I shape the readings for just the reason you have given, as well as to suggest that there is a comprehensive pattern in my books. I have been following a dramatic movement, which the end of my first book suggested and the subsequent books have challenged me to accomplish.

ROWELL: Will you talk about *Death as History* (1967), your first book of poems. It was not made available to many readers. Apparently, the title poem was republished in *The Homecoming Singer*. Have you republished any of the other poems that appeared in *Death as History*?

WRIGHT: *Death as History* is not really a book I set out to publish, but a group of poems selected from those I had on hand. I had been working with Carolyn Kizer for the Central Atlantic Regional Educational Laboratory in Virginia. She had confidence in my ability to do the job needed on a tour of black southern schools for the Woodrow Wilson-National Endowment of the Arts program. I had no book, and she thought I should have one. She helped me to publish, with Diane DiPrima at Poets Press, the pamphlet you have. The two women won't mind my saying that I don't consider it part of my canon. Some of its poems were in *The Homecoming Singer*.

ROWELL: The fate of *Soothsayers and Omens*, a beautiful book, is not overly unlike that of *Death as History*. *Soothsayers and Omens* has not been readily available. Why?

WRIGHT: You'd have to ask its publisher, George Koppelman, that.

ROWELL: I mentioned your use of African sources. Actually, your poems absorb multi-cultural sources of various periods of human history. And, ironically, it is for this very characteristic of your poetry that some of your readers have attacked it (though not in print). Some of them describe it as "inaccessible." You have offered notes, afterwords and other commentaries as assistance for reading your work, but will you give your readers other aids, guides, or directions/scores on how they might make *The Double Invention of Komo* and *Dimensions of History*, for example, "accessible."

WRIGHT: This gives me an opportunity to add to what I was saying earlier. I am convinced that human history will continue to reveal more and more of the fundamental interrelations of people, things and the other creatures of the universe. For me, multi-cultural is the fundamental process of human history. I must say here that we black African-Americans have been much too ready to allow other people to divest us of our other selves. No black African American can have escaped grounding in other cultures. You can have escaped critical confrontation with and assimilation of them, though I think that impossible. What is necessary is to think carefully about what you possess, and I contend that we all possess more than we know and are willing to acknowledge. Every individual is as complex as my poetry; I will continue to honor that gift. It's a shame that your computer won't register my laugh. Inaccessible. Perhaps, I should introduce some of my readers to the two old black African-American elders, who came to hear me read in a Baptist church in Salt Lake City, and who chewed every word and sometimes grunted with the pleasure of full recognition. Or, perhaps, to my white neighbor down the road here in New Hampshire, your basic struggling countryman, who characterized one of my books to my wife with such humanity and insight that her heart filled. No, I have no sympathy for the kind of cowardice that would prefer to dabble in whispers and psychic injury. A black woman at Wellesley asked me if my poetry weren't too intellectual for black people. Her response demonstrates a complete ignorance of the intellectual and spiritual resources of the people in the cultural tradition to which she belongs. The attitude this woman and my lazy readers manifest brings us close to that discourse where we'd use such words as plantations, house niggers, slaves and your proper place. I think I've said enough to nudge these readers toward more rigorous application. I regret having to introduce such harsh terms into the discussion. But those engaged to the failing will know who and what I mean; those not so engaged will suffer no injury. The books—their forms—remain my contribution to a continuing cultural and historical tradition. They refer the reader, over and over again, to the many forms of his or her own multi-cultural possessions.

ROWELL: Your readers often compare your poetry to that of Melvin Tolson, Robert Hayden, Ezra Pound, and Louis Zukofsky. What is your response to such a comparison?

WRIGHT: Pleasure. Though I no longer find Tolson deserving of such a high place, he was at one time an able guide. The other three men are excellent poets whose artistic and intellectual integrity, aspiration and achievement temper my pride and encourage my steps. You haven't asked me, but I'd like to add, if I may, that, for me, the poet is the man Samuel Beckett calls The Poet, Dante. To have conceived such a poem is a miracle, to have carried it out displays a divinity that is rare among us.

ROWELL: Why did you dedicate *Explications/Interpretations* to Robert Hayden and Harold Bloom?

WRIGHT: They are men of superior humanity, intelligence, learning and spirit who have shown me every kindness and given me every encouragement.

ROWELL: Your concept of the poem—and this takes us back to my first question—seems different from that of the four poets I mentioned. Their poems are static art objects to be examined; your poems are living aesthetic creations that pull us to their centers. Of course, your poetry admits a knowledge of "modernism," but then, your poetry also admits a knowledge of traditions "modernists" never explored.

WRIGHT: I don't want to treat your question in a cavalier fashion. I think, though, that a careful look at their poems would show that they aren't so static. It is true that my poems try to provoke a more overt engagement with their forms and the process of creating them and it is true that using the particular traditions I do allows me to exploit these strategies as freely and fully as I can, but my creative behavior is possible, in part, because I do know Melvin Tolson, Robert Hayden, Ezra Pound and Louis Zukofsky, among others. This is just another way of saying that I'm not alone and that I have accepted the charge this knowledge makes imperative and possible.

I hope that you will permit me now to say thank you for the honor of this special section in your magazine. I hope that my answers to your questions, along with my other contributions to this issue, will be found worthy of your readers' concern.

VERA M. KUTZINSKI

Jay Wright's Mythology of Writing: The Black Limbo

All great poetry is concerned with the true stature of things.
—ERICH HELLER, *The Disinherited Mind*

In an essay entitled "The Place of the Poet in Modern Society" (1966), Wilson Harris declares that "the crucial problem for the modern poet ... is to visualize a structure which is, at one and the same time, a structure of freedom and a structure of authority."[1] My task in the following pages is to describe such structures of simultaneous freedom and authority as they emerge in the work of the Afro-American poet and playwright Jay Wright, one of the most remarkable contemporary authors in the New World. According to John Hollander, "Jay Wright's poetry is some of the most original and powerful that is being written in America."[2] To date, Wright's poetic canon consists of five books of poetry: *The Homecoming Singer* (1971), *Soothsayers and Omens* (1976), *Explications/Interpretations* (1984), *Dimensions of History* (1976), and *The Double Invention of Komo* (1980), this being the order in which Wright suggests his poetry be read.[3] Of this series, *The Homecoming Singer* is the only book that is properly described as a collection of poems, while the other four texts constitute what Wright calls his first poetic cycle.

From *Against the American Grain: Myth and History in William Carlos Williams, Jay Wright, and Nicolás Guillén*, © 1987 by The Johns Hopkins University Press.

101

At the risk of violating the integrity of that cycle, I have decided to focus on *Dimensions of History*, which, in my view, best exemplifies the literary processes defined above as structures of freedom and authority. Wright frequently envisions those structures as a city, a compound trope that translates specific cultural and historical relationships into spatial configurations, that is, into writing. The trope of the city, quite reminiscent of Williams's *Paterson*, first appears in "Benjamin Banneker Helps to Build a City" (in *Soothsayers and Omens*), a poem I treat as a kind of introduction to *Dimensions of History*, where the city as a locus of transformation plays a dominant role. Frequent excursions, particularly to *The Double Invention of Komo* as well as to some of Wright's other poems, form a necessary and, to my mind, inevitable part of any reading of *Dimensions of History*. A poem best characterized as "contact-high,"[4] *Dimensions* brings into literary contact cultural "geographies" (that is, traditions identified with more or less specific geographical locations) generally conceived as separate entities: Europe, Africa, and the Americas.

Wright's territory is the New World, and I am employing this term very self-consciously to de-emphasize as much as possible the nationalistic connotations the term "America" has acquired as a result of being used as a shorthand expression for the United States. If "America" in any way suggests a potentially unified area of study, it does so, as we have already seen, only by subordinating all cultural elements of a non-European origin to the claims of the so-called Anglo-North American cultural establishment.[5] In contrast, the "New World" is what Auerbach has called a *Sinnganzes*,[6] and this is exactly how Wright perceives it: not as a political entity, but as a "geography" that derives its coherence from a long history of cultural exchange. This coherence liberates it from the need for the kind of false unity imposed by forms of nationalism which are ultimately nothing but feeble disguises for cultural imperialism. Wright would no doubt concur with Auerbach that "our philological homeland is the earth; it cannot be the nation any longer."[7] Consequently Wright's well-charted poetic journeys lead into territories almost completely unfamiliar to most North American readers. Under the careful guidance of his poet (or poetic persona), this "dark and dutiful dyeli," we travel to the most remote corners of European and New World history and mythology and to the even less familiar realms of African religion. This intense unfamiliarity is, at least in part, due to contexts such as Dogon, Bambara, and Akan cosmologies and Ifa divination, but even more so to Wright's poetic method. The language of his poems appears familiar at first, but on closer look we become increasingly doubtful that what we are reading is adequately described as "English." These doubts are justified: Not only does Wright avail himself of a variety of languages, ranging from Spanish and Arabic to the ritual signatures of the Dogon *sigui*. He also interweaves different grammars to enlarge the semantic capacities of the English language.

Yet there is one thing we can be certain about: Wright's poetry is obsessed with history and with the history of the New World in particular. To be more precise, it is motivated by the desire, and in fact the need, to comprehend the complex relations between history, myth, and literature as different forms of self-knowledge. Wright's poet's journeys are set in motion by the search for a language that accommodates both myth and history, that plays off one against the other without submitting to the constraints of either. This interplay of myth and history also offers a key to Wright's use of ritual. *The Double Invention of Komo*, for instance, is explicitly described as a poem that "risks ritual's arrogance."[8] At the same time, it is important for us to understand that poetry, as Wright insists elsewhere, is not ritual.[9] Yet ritual, as we shall see, can be used in poetry, Wright and Harris would agree, "not as something in which we situate ourselves absolutely, but an unravelling of self-deception within self-revelation as we see through the various dogmatic proprietors of the globe within a play of contrasting structures and anti-structures."[10] It is this play of contrasting structures and antistructures (that is, of myth and history) that Wright's poetry seeks to articulate through linguistic and formal rigor. The results are spectacular: Wright is one of the poets in recent literary history who, to use Williams's words, is "making the mass in which some later Eliot will dig."[11] In neglecting his poetry, the criticism of Afro-American (and American) literature(s) has deprived itself of one of the most fascinating and fertile resources for a true critical revisionism.

What form would such a critical revisionism take, and what alternatives can it offer to the established rituals of modern American literary and cultural criticism? Out of a certain protective attitude developed largely in response to those established rituals, Afro-American literary criticism has cultivated its own biases and clichés, which have gradually hardened into an impenetrable crust. But this safe crust of bias is no viable substitute for a critical methodology, one that would duly recognize Afro-American literature's comparative nature instead of attempting to maintain illusions of canonistic purity. Along those lines, a critical revisionism would have to accomplish, to return to Harris's phrase, a rigorous "unravelling of self-deception within self-revelation." The self-deception in this case is the belief in the efficacy of cultural nationalism, manifest in the attempt at defining an Afro-American literary canon in the classical sense. This belief tends to disregard the fact that the Afro-American writer is heir to far more than just the African cultural and literary traditions. Afro-American literature is not simply a matter of certain so-called African retentions. Rather, it is a matter of conscious choices on the part of the writer, choices that enable him or her to compare the different values, aesthetic and moral, embodied by each of the cultural traditions to which he or she has access in the New World. Wright exercises this freedom of choice and comparison rigorously and challenges his readers to do the same.

We witness in Wright's poetry the emergence of a particular kind of literacy out of his perception of the place of Afro-American history within the larger patterns of New World history. Robert Stepto has suggested that the Afro-American literary tradition is governed by a "pregeneric myth," which he defines as the "quest for freedom and literacy."[12] But where does this myth come from? How did it evolve? And, what happens to it once freedom and literacy have been, in some sense, achieved? Although the existence of a substantial body of texts written by Afro-Americans seems to suggest that these objectives have been fulfilled, the quest continues and the question is not only why but also how. It continues mainly because of several vital questions concerning the involvement of Afro-American texts with history, and it is these questions that Wright's poems address: What does it mean for Afro-American literature to have a history, to be able, in other words, to entertain the idea of distinct historical origins?[13] What are those historical origins, and what do they suggest about the nature of Afro-American culture(s) in relation to other New (or Old) World cultures? What does it mean for a writer to take notice of the traces that verify the historical existence of Afro-American culture(s)? And, finally, how does this act of self-realization affect the processes of writing and reading?

The issue at hand is not so much freedom *and* literacy, but freedom *through* literacy, as well as freedom *with* literacy.[14] Literacy, understood at the most elemental level as the ability to read and write, affords a very special kind of freedom, namely the freedom to generate and disseminate knowledge about one's self in the form of written statements, texts. Literacy, in this sense, is a method of gaining self-knowledge, which grants the Afro-American writer the freedom to interpret and to create his or her own myths about history. In short, the quest for freedom-through-literacy is a search for new methodologies. This further implies that the methods and methodologies, that is, the formal strategies Afro-American writers have devised since 1845, have changed substantially. These changes, as manifest in Wright's poems, tell us much about the nature of the self-knowledge that is being generated and thus about the current features of Afro-American writing.

At the risk of stating the obvious, let me briefly recall some of the basic facts about Afro-America, facts that tend to get drowned in most current critical debates. One of those facts is that the vast majority of African slaves imported into various parts of the New World approximately since the beginning of the seventeenth century did not have a written language of their own. A few knew Arabic, as is evident in the case of colonial Brazil, but their number was negligible. In addition, blacks, especially in North America, were systematically denied access to the written language of their white masters, while at the same time being forced to substitute that very language for their own various native tongues. In the North American slave states, more so than in other New World countries, literacy was used to create and reinforce both legitimate and illegitimate cultural differences between blacks and whites.[15] Literacy thus quickly evolved into an ideological vehicle for the perpetuation of white supremacy. The historical link between freedom and literacy is clear: Not only did the ability to read and write afford the black slave intellectual freedom by rendering accessible for interpretation and criticism the texts and documents used to legitimize his or her bondage. Literacy also granted actual physical freedom in those cases where slaves forged free-papers and other legal documents to facilitate their escape. Both instances have been extensively documented by numerous Afro-American slave narratives.[16]

Since it was writing, not the spoken word, that was used as a means of social control and cultural imperialism, Afro-Americans readily resorted to their oral traditions to retain a sense of cultural authenticity and cohesion. They developed forms of expression that actively circumvented writing as a vehicle for self-knowledge. The continued efforts on the part of Afro-American writers to unsettle the authority of writing manifest themselves both thematically and formally in their use of Afro-American folk materials as well as their reliance on dialect, musical forms, and oral modes of composition. As a result, Afro-American writers, in addition to appropriating classic European forms such as the sonnet and the ballad, also developed a substantial number of distinct poetic forms, ranging from the blues poems of Langston Hughes and Sterling Brown and the poetic sermons of James Weldon Johnson to the jazz poetry of Amiri Baraka and Michael Harper, the dozens of Don L. Lee, and the *sones* and *rumbas* of Jay Wright, to name only a few examples.[17]

But things are not as easy and as clear-cut as they may seem, because no matter how strongly indebted to an oral tradition these new forms of poetry are, the fact remains that they are *written* forms. And because they are written forms, the initial idea of subverting the authority of writing becomes a highly contradictory endeavor that raises a number of questions: If Afro-American culture is predominantly oral, how can a writer maintain a dialogue with that culture at the moment of writing? How is it possible to sustain an oral culture in writing? This problem is not resolved by defining literacy or freedom-through-literacy as concepts that somehow go beyond or against writing. Nor does such a definition take into account that the mere existence of an oral tradition is not a unique circumstance. No matter how we turn this argument, the fact remains that literacy is a concept inherently linked with the written, not the spoken, word. Moreover, any attempt to connect literacy with orality implicitly sustains an attitude that Derrida has labeled phonocentrism.[18] To stress Afro-American poetry's indebtedness to an oral tradition is not to emphasize its difference from Western literary discourse and its metaphysics but to situate it squarely within that framework and the metaphors that define it. The frequent claim that Afro-American texts subvert established literary conventions by introducing "oral" elements to written discourse is based upon an argument that unwittingly maintains one of the dearest assumptions of Western thought: the primacy of speech over writing. Afro-American literature's "oral" qualities are regarded as a kind of corrective capable of turning written language into an "authentic" expression of those mental experiences that go by the name of culture.[19] In other words, language that is invested with oral qualities is deemed capable of performing truthfully, or of performing the truth, whereas writing (being secondary and derivative) is the epitome of distortion, inauthenticity, and untruth. This association of speech with truth and authenticity is no doubt a familiar one that has been traced back all the way to Plato and Aristotle. As Derrida has shown quite candidly, Western culture has its own history of problems with, and suspicions of, writing's ability to articulate truth (or reality), and those suspicions seem oddly to coincide with those we attribute to Afro-American literature.

Most Afro-American poets are well aware of this contradiction, as well as of the subversive potential and the inherent unreliability of writing, qualities which, according to Derrida, the West has been at pains either to overlook or to conceal with an anxious and highly ambiguous reverence of the written word. This kind of reverence effectively serves to protect writing from the rigorous questioning that would expose its unreliability.

Reverence, like faith, implies distance, and in the case of literature an aesthetic distance that will make us believe in mysterious truths instead of encouraging us to look closely at the language that is supposed to convey them. Reverence and faith render language transparent, invisible.

What this is leading up to is my contention that Afro-American poets have undertaken their own systematic critiques of the sign, not by returning to some notion about re-creating "primary language" through a renewed emphasis on metaphors of voice or speech relating back to an oral tradition, but by exploring the possibilities for subversion that writing itself offers. Consequently, if we argue that the quest for freedom-through-literacy continues in Afro-American writing, as indeed it does, then we have to be very specific about what it is that is being subverted and about the ways in which that subversion takes place. Clearly, what is being subverted is not writing itself but the authority with which Western culture has invested certain forms of writing and certain kinds of texts. For that reason, it is of crucial importance that Afro-American writers frequently claim as part of their tradition texts that are either regarded as "nonliterary" or as the property of other literary canons. To show precisely what those texts are as well as how and why they become part of an Afro-American tradition of writing is one of my main objectives.

Contemporary Afro-American poetry's sustained quest for freedom-through-literacy is best described as a search for a reliable repository of meaning, on the basis of which the Afro-American writer can, in Amiri Baraka's words, "propose his own symbols, erect his own personal myths"[20]—in short, create his or her own language. This repository of meaning is history, not History as something self-contained and unchangeable in its pastness, but a history that consists of fragments to be assembled and woven together into "new categories for the soul / of those I want to keep."[21]

Wright's work offers one of the most remarkable examples of an Afro-American poet maintaining a very active dialogue with a variety of traditions while at the same time confronting the problems posed by the idea of writing within the specific context of Afro-American culture. Wright is a most skillful weaver of poetic textures that well deserve to be called mythological in that they embrace both the timelessness of mythical discourse and the radical and inevitable historicity induced by the act of writing itself. There is no doubt that Wright is creating a mythology of Afro-American writing, but he is also constantly reminding himself and his readers of the precariousness of such an endeavor. His best poetry emerges from a confrontation—or what Ralph Ellison would call an "antagonistic cooperation"[22]—between history and myth, in which myth is rendered historical and history mythical. Although it is difficult, and at times almost impossible, to separate the two, we nevertheless have to distinguish them as different forms of discourse to be able to experience the effects of their interpenetration and to extract those categories that constitute the methodology (and mythology) of Afro-American writing. I shall begin with what I consider one of Wright's best shorter long poems, "Benjamin Banneker Helps to Build a City." This poem is accompanied, in *Soothsayers and Omens*, by its shorter version, "Benjamin Banneker Sends His 'Almanac' to Thomas Jefferson," a poem that will not be considered separately here but as a kind of double which revoices most of the important aspects of the former poem.

Both "Benjamin Banneker Helps to Build a City" and "Benjamin Banneker Sends His 'Almanac' to Thomas Jefferson" are less concerned with the historical personality of Benjamin Banneker, the first self-trained Afro-American astronomer and doubtlessly one of the numerous grandfather figures which populate twentieth-century Afro-American letters, than with the founding of modern America. The point in American history to which Wright returns in these two poems is the last decade of the eighteenth century, a period that marks North America's transition from colonialism to modern nationhood. This particular historical rite of passage, which is symbolized by the founding of the national capital, the city that Banneker did indeed help to "build," is significant for a number of reasons, all of which have to do with language and with writing.

"Benjamin Banneker Helps to Build a City" is preoccupied with origins, and more specifically with the controversial origins of the New World and with the role blacks played in the creation of a cultural (and textual) space that was more than just an inspired invention of European thought. This concern for historical origins pervades all of Wright's poetry and is frequently associated with the figure of the city, not an unusual connection given the historical significance of the founding of cities in the New World since the times of Columbus.[23] These early colonial cities, founded by the conquistadors in the name of the Spanish crown, were the administrative outposts of the Hapsburg monarchy and can be viewed as emblems of Spain's desire for political and cultural totalization (and totalitarianism). But if the colonial cities in the New World were stony symbols of imperial power, they were also, at the same time, the first places of intensive cultural interaction of the kind that eluded official control and surreptitiously undermined the administrative foundations of the empire.[24] Both of these different historical functions of the city are relevant to my discussion of the representational dimensions of the particular city Wright evokes at the beginning of "Benjamin Banneker Helps to Build a City": The future capital of the United States is to be the seat of political power and thus the nation's new center, the very embodiment of its autonomy. Although conceived as a monument to liberty, the national capital is a structure motivated by the same kind of logocentrism that had produced the cities in the Spanish colonies. The desire for totalization was equally pervasive in North America, where it manifested itself in the Puritan concept of the "covenant of grace" and its secular extensions.[25] Once freed from the British empire, the former colonies were at liberty to pursue their own imperialistic aspirations. The construction of the United States capital was a symbolic act of replacing the old forms of British colonialism with the new forms of North American imperialism.

This view is substantiated especially by Wright's including in the text of his poem two quotations from Banneker's letter to Thomas Jefferson to which I shall return shortly. But it would be quite erroneous to presume that Wright is celebrating the spirit and the achievements of the American Revolution as a potential source of cultural authenticity. In fact, he is doing quite the opposite, which is rendered evident by the specific historical date implicit in both the quotations and the references to the founding of the national capital: The survey in which Banneker participated was launched in 1791 by President George Washington; Banneker's letter to Thomas Jefferson, then secretary of state, was also written in 1791.[26] What, then, is the significance of the year 1791 with respect to the origins of Afro-American cultural (and literary) history? What readily comes to mind, although it is nowhere directly mentioned in the text of this poem, is an event whose significance for Afro-America was vast and whose echoes in Afro-American literature are countless: that event is the Haitian Revolution.[27] By extension, 1791 recalls two other "central" points in New World history, both of which also mark profound historical transitions: The first one happened three centuries earlier in 1492, when Columbus landed in Santo Domingo. The second one occurred a century later in 1892, the official date of the dedication ceremonies for the World's Columbian Exposition in Chicago, the founding of "White City."[28] All of these fragments cluster around the date 1791, which is now no longer simply an isolated point in history, but a historical field.

Although the poem does not invoke the names of Toussaint, Dessalines, or Henri Christophe,[29] the implied date itself is sufficient to shake the foundations of the North American future metropolis and displace the center it aspires to imitate. Even in its absence, the Haitian Revolution provides both an analogy and a contrast to the American Revolution and its future emblem. The contrast is perhaps more obvious than the analogy: Unlike its North American counterpart, the Haitian Revolution was aimed at overthrowing the island's slaveholding society and replacing it with a black government; no such radical changes were ever envisioned for North America. This difference is important in that it substantiates the claim that the American War of Independence was the only revolution in modern times motivated by the desire to prevent drastic social changes, meaning, in this case, the prohibition of the African slave trade and the possible abolition of slavery on "recommendation" of the British crown. But the similarities between the two wars are perhaps even more disturbing: With regard to the black population of both Haiti and the United States, each revolution was, in Alejo Carpentier's words, a veritable "rebirth of shackles," a prelude to reenslavement.[30] In the same way that Haiti's mulatto elite, which replaced the government of the French slaveholders, continued to oppress blacks, slavery in the United States was far from having been abolished by the humanitarian principles of the Declaration of Independence and the federal Constitution.

I cannot resist at this point calling attention to a passage from Carpentier's *The Kingdom of This World*, perhaps the best-known modern novel about the Haitian Revolution, which is all the more relevant to my present discussion for narrating the story from the perspective of a black protagonist. Near the end of the novel in a chapter significantly entitled "The Surveyors," Carpentier's Ti Noel, now an old man, is observing the work of the mulatto surveyors in the Northern Province. At some point he raises his eyes to the old Fortress, sadly musing that "the word of Henri Christophe had become stone and no longer dwelt among us. All of his fabulous person that remained was in Rome, a finger floating in a rock-crystal bottle filled with brandy" (*Kingdom*, 177). Ti Noel's vision of words turned to stone, of idealism stiffened into conservatism, is precisely what Wright associates with the future capital of the United States: He sees it as the epitome of words devoid of any meaning, of empty gestures "with/no sign, of what gave them strength."[31] This last citation is from Baraka's "Poem for Willie Best." Incidentally, Wright uses these lines as an epigraph to his "Variation on a Theme by LeRoi Jones. II," an earlier poem that comments on the plan of transformation, "the alphabet of transformations" as it is called in *Dimensions of History*, now elaborated in "Benjamin Banneker Helps to Build a City."

The image of the city is prefigured in "Variation" in the form of those "massive limestone crosses" that "measure the American continent" (*HS*, 67). They are the stony monuments left by previous "surveyors," whose measure(ment)s almost completely erased all traces of the continent's native civilizations. Their former cities have turned into graveyards. The crosses are emblems of death, of

> a stiff Jesus,
> with his impassive beard,
> driven staunchly on a mountain,
> impervious as well to the babble
> of tongues as to the absurd heights. (HS, 67)

But Wright, "would not have him there,/marking some inaccessible point"; instead, "He would have to come down,/and bend his back on the line/ ... /feeling an insatiable desire/to break free and become a sign,/living gesture, unearthed,/yet rooted in earth, in flesh." Wright literalizes the Christian myth ("the word become flesh") to emphasize the absurdity of worshipping death as an abstract ("stiff") form of salvation, as the measure of all living things. Passivity and imperviousness, the characteristics of sacred immobility, have to yield under the impact of historical experience. Once the "stiff Jesus" begins to take notice of the "babble [or Babel] of tongues" around him, once he is "listening/to the groomed merchants of the soul/bargaining guardedly for every part of him,/letting the echo of exile change him" (*HS*, 68), his poetic features change dramatically as the language of the poem itself breaks free and bursts into a rapid sequence of present participles and unfinished verb forms. The change we witness here is the creation of desire or "uneasiness."

In "Benjamin Banneker Helps to Build a City," this "uneasiness" is a disturbance of the faith, this time not primarily in the myths of Christianity but in the ritual of revolution and specifically the American Revolution. This ritual of revolution, represented by the lining out of the land according to precise mathematical laws, "the language of number," is a self-contained process, a ceremony of imprisoning language by locking it into a definite symbolic shape. This process, in turn, is analogous to the legal rituals involved in the symbolic act of drawing up the Declaration of Independence, the new nation's *charter*, which is reproduced in the form of a *map* or *chart* of the site of the city. But,

> These perfect calculations fall apart.
> There are silences
> that no perfect number can retrieve,
> omissions no perfect line could catch.[32]

What are those silences, those omissions, those glaring imperfections in the design? And what language can retrieve them? The most obvious instances of such retrieved silences, examples of which we have previously encountered in Paz's *The Labyrinth of Solitude*, Williams's *In the American Grain*, and Carpentier's *El arpa y la sombra*, are the two passages from Banneker's letter to Jefferson, which cause, within the text of the poem, a disturbance of no small measure. This letter, which was enclosed with the 1792 *Almanac* Banneker sent to Jefferson, was written about six months after the black astronomer had become involved with the survey project for the new capital. It is the only known instance of Banneker's publicly voicing his thoughts about slavery—he himself, it should be noted, was a free man. Jefferson's reply was favorable; he informed Banneker that he had forwarded the manuscript copy of the *Almanac* to the secretary of the Royal Academy of Sciences in Paris as evidence of the talents of the black race. Ironically enough, it was never received there. But Banneker's letter to Jefferson and the latter's reply, first published in pamphlet form and later included with Banneker's other almanacs, were widely circulated by abolitionist societies in the United States and England. Several of Banneker's "abolition almanacs" appeared between 1793 and 1797 in a number of editions, and their great popularity made them some of the most important publications of their times.[33]

All of this is to say that it is hardly an exaggeration to label Banneker's letter to Jefferson one of the founding texts of modern America, one, however, that unsettles the authority of the nation's official charters:

> Here was a time, in which your tender feelings for yourselves had engaged you thus to declare, you were then impressed with proper ideas of the great violation of liberty, and the free possession of those blessings, to which you were entitled by nature; but, Sir, how pitiable it is to reflect, that although you were so fully convinced [of the benevolence] of the Father of Mankind, and of his equal and impartial distribution of these rights and privileges, which he hath conferred upon them, that you should at the same time counteract his mercies, in

detaining by fraud and violence so numerous a part of my brethren, under groaning captivity, and cruel oppression, that you should at the same time be found guilty of that most criminal act, which you professedly detested in others, with respect to yourselves. (*SO*, 24)

The contradictions exposed and expounded in this memorable passage are significant beyond their well-known historical implications. Their reverberations are felt throughout the poem as Wright himself is "struggling for a city/free of that criminal act,/free of everything but the small,/imperceptible act, which itself becomes free" (*SO*, 25), struggling for "different resolutions" and, like Williams, for different *measure(ment)s*.

Documents, Joseph Riddel has pointed out, "decenter the lyrical voice, the centering or narrative subject."[34] In the context of Wright's poem, this decentering or displacement corresponds to the subversiveness of Banneker's letter when viewed not just as an isolated historical datum but as a historical field. I have already examined traces of the historical events which cluster around that date and undermine the centrality of the American Revolution by introducing the notion of multiple origins of New World culture. At the level of textuality, this idea of multiple origins is corroborated by the poem's claim to multiple authorship, a compositional principle that frees it from the singleness of vision associated with a commanding origin or a central consciousness. The title of the poem already anticipates this multiplicity. Not only does the use of the name "Benjamin Banneker" serve to displace the name of the author as it appears on the cover of the book. In addition to that, "helps to build" (instead of "builds") indicates that the city, which is being built here, that is to say, the text of the poem, is not the product of an individual consciousness that alone authorizes its meaning. The poem, in short, is itself off center. As a result, it becomes a play of originating forces, or what Charles Olson has called a "field" of intersecting lines,[35] of crossing paths, so that it is ultimately an emblem of original and originary multiplicity. Most of Wright's poetry unquestionably partakes of the American tradition of the long poem, whose achievement is, Riddel argues, "essentially a freedom from the commanding origin."[36] Wright is after a "coherence," to borrow another term from Olson,[37] and this coherence is precisely what I have described as a method(ology) that would invest his play of originating traces with culture-specific meanings, although without arresting its motion. So we return again to Afro-America's quest for freedom-through-literacy.

Free. Free. How will the lines fall
into that configuration?
How will you clear this uneasiness,
posting your calculations and forecasts
into a world you yourself cannot enter?
Uneasy, at night,
you follow the stars and lines to their limit,
sure of yourself, sure of the harmony
of everything, and yet you moan
for the lost harmony, the crack in the universe.
Your twin, I search it out,
and call you back;
your twin, I invoke
the descent of Nommo. (*SO*, 25–26)

The link between freedom and writing, and more specifically with writing as (con)figuration, is obvious enough in this citation. But what exactly is that freedom, and how can it be realized in writing? To be sure, it is a freedom from that "most criminal act," from that "great violation of liberty," which is slavery in its numerous guises. But if we want to be rigorous about such a referential reading, we also have to consider that Banneker, unlike Douglass, for instance, was never a slave. Although it could be argued that this difference is merely nominal, given the actual treatment of free blacks in the antebellum South, the implications of Banneker's status as a black man who was not only legally free but also literate in a very special sense (he was a scientist) are nevertheless important to the rhetorical strategies of the poem. It is this seemingly irrelevant difference that enables Wright to charge Banneker's definition of slavery as "criminal act" with a literary and cultural meaning that surpasses historical referentiality in the strict sense. Wright sees the "criminal act" as a slavish submission to the fiction of a single commanding origin, which, in its turn, generates the fiction of "the harmony of everything." Wright's criticisms here are not simply directed at the monstrous injustices perpetrated in the name of slavery but at those elements in Western thought used to sanction them, incidentally the same conceptual categories later employed to perpetuate slavery in the form of cultural imperialism. Those categories are rooted in the Christian doctrine and the theogonous postulate of a divine consciousness as a single figure of authority (the "Father of Mankind"). This figure had been invented in the image of those who, calling themselves God's prophets, were the interpreters and authors of the biblical myths that served to unify the story of the creation of the world by attributing it to a single source.

However, this particular mythical version of history was, as suggested above, sharply contradicted by the events that led to the "discovery" of the New World. This discovery produced a "crack in the universe" of Western thought by upsetting its previously harmonious, unified image of the world. It is this "lost harmony," this disruptive movement of displacement and transition, to which Wright appeals in order to recapture the fertile turbulence generated by the existence and interweaving of the New World's multiple origins. His text, like Williams's *In the American Grain*, cuts through that image of America projected by its European inventors; it cuts through the New World's superficial newness down to the marrow of history. This deceptive quality of being new is what is represented by the founding of a city that would reinstate the very center from which it seeks to break free. What seems like an autonomous act is really only an imitation of European thought and its desire for centralization. In this sense, "the sight of these lesser gods/lining out the land" (*SO*, 25) is a figure for historical mimetism. Rather than an act of Liberation, it is an act of reproducing and repeating the paradigms of Western culture in the form of its foremost imperial symbol, the city.

> How pitiable it is to reflect
> upon that god, without grace,
> without the sense of that small
> beginning movement,
> where even the god
> becomes another and not himself,
> himself and not another. (*SO*, 25)

What is "pitiable" is the act of imitating, which is all the more "grace"-less for being inauthentic, unaware of the doubleness at the origin of New World history. That double origin is the point at which the "god," who, as we shall see, is a figure for the poem's design, becomes both himself and another. This simultaneity of self and other now generates emblems of doubleness; they condense the essence of Afro-America's historical experience—exile and slavery—and relate that essence to the schism caused by the discovery of the New World. Those figures are "Amma's plan" and the "descent of Nommo." According to Dogon mythology as recorded by Marcel Griaule and Germaine Dieterlen, "Amma's plan" is the design for the creation of the universe, the matrix that eventually becomes Nommo, the first being created by Amma. As Amma's twin, the Nommo embodies the principles of its own creation, that is to say, the process of twinning, of doubling. In this sense, the Nommo is a living design.[38] Its descent, that is, its creation and sacrifice, is a movement from abstraction to representation, from "the lines in your head" to "these lines," which are the lines we are actually reading.

A closer look at the poem's language will clarify this movement from abstraction to representation, which accounts, at least partly, for the difficulty of Wright's poetry. Part of that difficulty is that Wright's language offers very few representational images in the traditional sense for the reader to hold on to. In fact, the only image that can be culled from the text of "Benjamin Banneker Helps to Build a City" is that of Banneker silently contemplating the movement of the stars. But even that picture, which appears at the very beginning of the poem and recurs several times, is semantically highly unstable.

> In a morning coat,
> hands locked behind your back,
> you walk gravely along the lines in your head. (SO, 22)

This is the point where the "vibration" starts. The vibration is an unsettling of language's representational capacities, an effacement of sorts that makes possible the simultaneous projection of another, different image: What we see, yet cannot *see*, as "morning" vibrates into "mo[u]rning" and "gravely" into "*gravely*," is the poet himself traversing a burial ground, which is clearly a figure for the act of memory Wright has to perform to produce an image that appears to be representational. Paul de Man's remarks are helpful here: "All representational poetry," de Man writes, "is always also allegorical whether it be aware of it or not, and the allegorical power of the language undermines and obscures the specific literal meaning of a representation open to understanding. But all allegorical poetry must contain a representational element that invites and allows for understanding, only to discover that the understanding it reaches is necessarily in error."[39]

All that the reader is offered in "Benjamin Banneker Helps to Build a City" are fragments of that representational element, traces of an image as it is prefigured in the poet's mind. The point is that these traces never evolve into a fully graspable representation; instead, they undergo a series of transformations, which culminates in the act of naming at the end of the poem. "And so you, Benjamin Banneker,/walk gravely along these lines"

(*SO*, 26). With the exception of the title of the poem, this is the only other instance where Wright uses Banneker's name. This final baptism is suggestively preceded by the invocation of "the descent of Nommo," which announces the tentative completion of the poetic design. But much happens prior to this apparent closure, so that it is necessary to trace in more detail the development of the poem's initial vibrations into their literate (and literary) configurations.

The second stanza already introduces some important transformations: The grave site is now more fully figured as a field of ruins, and what had previously appeared to be an act of remembrance is revealed to be an act of reading.

> Now, I have searched the texts
> and forms of cities that burned,
> that decayed, or gave their children away. (*SO*, 22)

The poet now poses as another kind of surveyor, as an archaeologist attempting to decipher the ruins of ancient cities (Rome, perhaps, but more likely cities such as Cuzco, Labná, and Tenochtitlán) in order to recover the cultural origins of the New World. All the while, he is "watching [his] hands move"; they are no longer locked behind his (or Banneker's) back. Their movement, as it produces the very lines we are reading, extends the kinetic trope of *walking* that reappears as "the weight and *shuttle* of my body" (my italics), thus inviting us to apprehend this movement as a kind of *weaving*, one of Wright's main figures of writing.[40]

In the third stanza, the journey back into time, so far figured as a survey of a variety of ancestral sites, leads to "the time/of another ceremony" and to the creation of "another myth." A "familiar tone" enters the poet's voice as the opening of the site, the breaking of the ground, begins to assume the qualities of a *rite de passage*, which is, more specifically, a purification ritual.

> A city, like a life,
> must be made in purity.
> So they call you,
> knowing you are intimate with stars,
> to create this city, this body.
> So they call you,
> knowing you must purge the ground. (*SO*, 23)

It is at this point that we encounter the first quotation from Banneker's letter to Jefferson. What this document urges us to recall is Afro-America's history of exile and slavery, which now begins to reveal its mythical dimensions. In the realm of myth, the cut of the umbilical cord connecting Afro-America with Africa ("These people, changed,/but still ours") becomes an initiation into self-knowledge. However, the connection itself has not been completely severed, only it is no longer a genealogical imperative that links Afro-America with Africa. This transformation is possible because Wright envisions the cut into exile as a sacrificial gesture, an excision that purifies the initiate while at the same time *marking* him as a member of his community. That the two passages from Banneker's letter should be called upon to serve as purifying agents that prepare, "exorcise," the ground for the inscriptions of the signs of self-knowledge is quite telling, and not merely because of this document's connections with the beginnings of abolitionism in the United States. We have here another instance of Wright's creating a myth, of turning a historical context into allegory, only immediately to render that allegory literal again. Once exile and slavery cease to be viewed as an episode in Afro-American history that is best forgotten and become part of a larger historico-mythical pattern that may be described as a ritualistic world view, then they assume the qualities of communal sacrifices opening old wounds as new paths toward self-knowledge. History, then, does yield a myth, which is Afro-America's myth of exile or displacement. This myth is "the seed vibrating within itself,/moving *as though it knew its end*, against death" (*SO*, 22; my italics). It is a secure enclosure, a place where the fiction of being, that is, of culture, can be entertained. Like any other myth, it provides a protective shelter from history. But what is it that is being sheltered here, at least temporarily, from the "harsh winds" of history? An answer to this question requires a further look at the rhetorical nature of myth and its uses in the emplotment of history.

As suggested in Part 1, myth is a culture's storehouse of historical knowledge. This knowledge is stored by rendering it timeless to protect it from change. To be even more precise, a myth is a fixed interpretation of a particular historical event, which is subsequently removed from its initial historical context so that it may serve as an interpretive model for other, future events. Myth is thus a conceptual device that, in the context of a given culture, promotes a sense of order and continuity. Its function is to bring about cultural unification by not admitting any dissenting interpretations of the past events that generated it in the first place. Myth monopolizes historical interpretation for the sake of establishing ideological consensus. For this reason, the historical knowledge stored in the form of myth is generally apprehended as *truth*, a truth, however, whose origins are not directly accessible to all members of the community.

The epic of Sundiata (or Sun Dyata), King of Mali, alluded to in *Dimensions of History* (27), provides a concrete example of the limited accessibility of the knowledge preserved by myth. A written version of this epic was first published in a French transcription by D. T. Niane in 1960. Most relevant to us are not the intricacies of the story of Sundiata itself but the remarks of the *griot* from which Niane received his version of the epic. These remarks, which frame the actual story, clarify the nature and the function of mythical discourse as a strategic device for sheltering historical knowledge. Here, then, are the introductory words of the Mali storyteller:

> I am a griot. It is I, Djeli Mamoudou Kouyate, son of Bintou Kouyate and Djeli Kedian Kouyate, master in the art of eloquence. Since time immemorial the Kouyates have been in the service of the Keita princes of Mali; we are *vessels of speech, we are the repositories which harbour secrets many centuries old*. The art of eloquence has no secrets for us; without us the names of Kings would vanish into oblivion, *we are the memory of mankind*; by the spoken word we bring to life the deeds and exploits of kings for younger generations.
>
> I derive my knowledge from my father Djeli Kedian, who also vulgar it from his father; *history holds no mystery for us*; we teach to the vulgar just as much as we want to teach them for it is we who keep the keys to the twelve doors of Mali [the twelve provinces of which Mali was originally composed].
>
> I teach kings the history of their ancestors so that the lives of the ancients might serve them as an example, for the world is old, but the future springs from the past.
>
> *My word is pure and free of all untruth; it is the word of my father*; it is the word of my father's father. I will give you my father's words just as I received them; royal riots do not know what lying is. When a quarrel breaks out between tries it is we who settle the differences, for *we are the depositaries of oaths which the ancestors swore*.
>
> Listen to my word, you who want to know; by my mouth you will learn the history of Mali.[41]

Djeli Mamoudou's prologue is clearly intended to establish his authority as a storyteller by identifying him as a member of an old family of royal *griots*, the traditional teachers of the princes of Mali, as someone, in brief, who has been properly initiated into the secrets of his country's history. He portrays himself as someone who simply passes on the truths he has received from his ancestors without embellishing or distorting them in any way. But at the same time as assuming the role of a mouthpiece of tradition, he also leaves no doubt about the fact that there is a significant difference between the knowledge he has received and that which he is willing to pass on to the "vulgar" in the form of his story. In short, he knows more than he tells. This is most evident at the end of the tale, where he flatly refuses to supply any details of Sundiata's death. In fact, the death is not mentioned at all. Instead, we are told that "Mali is eternal" and that it "keeps its secrets jealously. There are things which the uninitiated will never know, for the griots, their depositaries, will never betray them" (*Sundiata*, 83). Actually, he goes even further by warning his readers or listeners in no uncertain terms: "Never try, wretch, to pierce the mystery which Mali hides from you. Do not go and disturb the spirits in their eternal rest. Do not ever go into the dead cities to question the past, for the spirits never forgive. Do not seek to know what is not to be known" (*Sundiata*, 84).

What, then, is the "truth" we receive from the mouth of the *griot*? The knowledge he transmits as truth has been, as he freely admits, carefully preselected, and it is precisely that ability to select and edit that must arouse our suspicions about those things that are to be known as well as our curiosity about those that are not to be known. It is worth noting here that the *griots*, or *djelis* (*dyelis* in the spelling Wright adopts in *Dimensions of History*), are the official historians of traditional African societies, and that they, like all official historians, are bound by a set of rules prescribing the treatment of their materials. The decision about what to tell and what to omit is not their own, for it is part of their office to take "an oath to teach only what is to be taught and to conceal what is to be kept concealed" (*Sundiata*, 84). The truth-value of their stories depends on their societies' specific conventions, which determine how history is to be narrated.

The emplotment of history has therefore nothing to do with telling the truth in any absolute sense, because that truth is clearly defined as historical knowledge presented in conformity with social convention. It functions to uphold a society's belief in its conventions and thus guarantees cultural unification and stability. The traditional *griot*, or *djeli*, is a guardian of culture in the strictest sense of the term; he is neither a historian nor an artist in the modern sense, because his office renders him incapable of questioning received truths. He is not free to invent new modes of presentation for the myths he disseminates.

The value of myths as timeless truths can thus be seen to depend entirely and exclusively on an act of faith and obedience. The discourse of myth is not open to internal criticisms; it is not self-reflexive in the sense of being self-critical but rests comfortably in its self-definition as an idealized, sacred (and thus transparent) language, meaningful only to those who are willing to make a leap of faith and regard interpretation as a form of worship. But modern literature does not require faith; it demands methodological rigor.

In the context of Jay Wright's poetry, this rigor of method is best described as an act of disturbing the spirits in their eternal rest, of going into the dead cities to question the past. Wright does not consider myth an end in and of itself. Instead of a permanent shelter from history, it is a transition "from our knowledge to our knowing" (*DH*, 90). Myth as a form of human discourse is transitory or transitional in that it mediates between the objects of knowledge (that is, history as a body of factual events) and the actual experience of that knowledge. To be more precise, myth as a mediation is a formal language that determines the conditions that make knowledge possible, and these conditions, in turn, can themselves become objects of knowledge, which also means that they can be questioned.

This proposition is nothing extravagant or even unusual when placed in its proper context, that of the philosophy of history. It is equivalent to Schelling's (and Hegel's) contention that "as the process of self-knowledge advances, new stages in self-knowledge enrich the knowing mind and thus create new things for it to know. History is a temporal process in which both knowledge and the knowable are progressively coming into existence, and this is expressed by calling history the self-realization of the Absolute."[42] That "Absolute" is apprehended not as a presupposition of the historical process, that is, as a systematic plan or law existing prior to and thus outside of history, but as a dynamic element always in the process of becoming. (The former notion had governed the idea of history from Herder through Kant to Fichte.) Historical knowledge, in this sense, is always self-knowledge, that is, not the knowledge of empirical facts evidencing the workings of some preformulated law (be it natural or scientific), but an understanding of how those facts are (re)created in the mind of the historian. I am not talking about a radically subjective view of historical knowledge—Hegel, as is known, despised subjectivity—but about historical perspectivism and the awareness that historical facts are always conditioned or mediated by language. In de Man's words, "The bases for historical knowledge are not empirical facts, but written texts, even if those texts masquerade in the guise of wars or revolutions."[43]

In keeping with the goals of modern historicism, the emphasis of Wright's poetry is not so much on what we know or can know but on *how* we know, and on how a scrutiny of the conditions that make historical knowledge possible (i.e., forms of language) can lead to a heightened level of self-awareness—Wright calls it "understanding." Wright's poems, in this sense, are studies of what Barthes has termed "ideas-in-form."[44] To the extent that Wright is concerned not simply with the formal presentation of ideas but with questions about how certain ideas are formed and formulated, his poetry must be understood as a mythology in Barthes's sense: as a formal as well as a historical inquiry into the nature and function of myth. Wright's poetry is mythological (as opposed to mythical) in that it generates knowledge *about* myth: it is not the discourse of myth, but a discourse *on* myth. Consequently, it is not sustained by (in the sense of receiving meaning and authority from) the idea of Literature as a mythical system.

Afro-American literature in its perpetual quest for the freedom of literacy has always been at odds with that traditional idea of Literature, and for good reasons. Since the idea of Literature as a mythical system heavily depends on the postulates of Western metaphysics, which invest a literary text with meaning by assuming that these postulates constitute a system of beliefs and values shared by writer and reader alike, it is fairly self-explanatory why writers such as Wright who, for historical, cultural, and ideological reasons, refuse to accept those precepts as an absolute frame of reference would search for other, for them more reliable, repositories of meaning. The result is a systematic breakdown of literary form, the beginnings of which have already been witnessed in "Benjamin Banneker Helps to Build a City." This subversion of established principles of order, such as the aesthetic charters that determine our idea of what constitutes a poem, continues on a much broader scale in *Dimensions of History* and *The Double Invention of Komo*. Perhaps the most obvious indication of the breakdown of literary form in each of these two poems is their conspicuous resistance to poetic closure, which allows for the kind of "freeplay of substitutions" that Derrida has termed "the movement of supplementarity."[45] Conspicuous examples of such supplements evidencing the deferral of poetic closure are the notes in *Dimensions of History* and the afterword in *The Double Invention of Komo*. Both have to be considered not as substitutes for the poems but as parts of the poetic texts themselves. Even if we do not read any farther than the last line of what we regard as the text of each poem, and even if we respect that Wright was explicitly asked by his publishers to supply those annotations,[46] we cannot therefore pretend that those "appendices" do not exist or that they serve no purpose whatsoever with regard to the texts they supplement. It is not acceptable to discard them as useless simply because they do not facilitate the task of reading. But even assuming that the list of sources Wright offers in each instance were complete, which it is not, or that it were at all possible to give an exhaustive account of everything that inspired those two poems, it still would be erroneous to think that the sum total of such references would somehow add up to the poetic text. What, then, do these notes accomplish?

First it ought to be stressed that this practice of annotating one's text is far more common among novelists than among poets.[47] It suggests a dissolution of generic boundaries, or what Mikhail Bakhtin has called the "novelization" of genres,[48] whose most conspicuous manifestations in postmodern New World poetry are Williams's *Paterson*, Charles Olson's *Maximus Poems*, Allen Ginsberg's *The Fall of America*, and Nicolás Guillén's *El diario*. An earlier example that comes to mind even more readily are the notes on "The Waste Land," which Eliot nonchalantly brushed off as a kind of literary joke. Yet, it is not advisable to follow Eliot's lead, because, as we shall see, neither his nor Wright's notes can altogether be passed off as practical jokes at the expense of some perhaps overzealous critics. In short, since such annotations do not appear to help us understand the poetry, their function must lie elsewhere, as in fact it does.

If the notes and the afterword do indeed accentuate the poems' resistance to closure and thus assert the possibility of an infinite number of supplements, of which they themselves are already the first instance, then we have to ask how the absence of closure affects our reading of the poems, which is yet another supplement. *Absence of closure*, of course, does not mean that the poems do not, in the most literal sense of the term, end. What it means is that the tensions upon which the poem is built are not, in the final analysis, resolved or transcended. There is no point that arrests the movement of figuration and conveniently allows us to assign to each individual figure or trope a fixed representational value in the form of a more or less definitive meaning. Consequently, it becomes very difficult to view Wright's poems as anything else but fragments, not fragments of poems, but poems-as-fragments. Yet, how is it possible to read such poetry without submitting to the idea of radical indeterminacy? Does not every reading as an act of communication require a communicator, no matter how ineffable? Regardless of how one defines communication, one cannot answer this last question in the negative; and since that is the case, I must either postulate the existence of such a communicator or else terminate my discussion here and now.

Recall that the point that would arrest the movement of figuration and thus create the possibility of fixed meanings is what I have earlier labeled a "center." In short, the deferral of or resistance to closure as accomplished, albeit involuntarily, by Wright's notes and afterword identifies the movement of supplementarity as a process of decentering. The first thing that is decentered by Wright's annotations is the figure of the author. In the case of "Benjamin Banneker Helps to Build a City," the title of the poem itself already dislocates or effaces the figure of the author. In *Dimensions of History* and *The Double Invention of Komo* the same kind of effacement is achieved by the notes and the afterword: The name of the author seems to be just another bibliographical item. It becomes more and more elusive as other names arc added to and superimposed upon it, until it becomes one name and all names.[49] But what are those names that turn Wright's own name into "an interminable name,/made from interminable names" (*HS*, 37)?

In his afterword to *The Double Invention of Komo* Wright mentions as his major sources a series of studies of Dogon and Bambara cosmologies, conducted by a group of French anthropologists associated with Marcel Griaule and Institut d'Ethnologie of the Musée de l'Homme in Paris (*DI*, 109–10). The most important of these anthropological treatises are Marcel Griaule's doctoral dissertation, published in 1938 under the title of *Masques Dogons*, and his *Dieu d'eau: Entretiens avec Ogotemmêli* (1948); Germaine Dieterlen and Marcel Griaule's *Le renard pâle*, vol. 1: *Le mythe cosmogonique* (1965); as well as Germaine Dieterlen's *Essai sur la religion bambara*; and *Les fondements de la société d'initiation du Komô* (1972), a collaboration of Dieterlen and Youssouf Tata Cissé. Wright further acknowledges his debts to Wande Abimbola's translations of Ifa Divination poetry; Victor Turner's work on the Ndembu; L. O. Sanneh's historical study of the Jakhanke; and, above all, J. B. Danquah's *The Akan Doctrine of God*.[50] No further details are needed here to evidence the major role of anthropology and ethnology in Wright's work.

There is much more to Wright's interest in anthropology than meets the eye. I have earlier described his poetry as discourse on myth, and it does not require any elaborate explanations for us to discern that that is what constitutes the link between cultural anthropology and poems such as *Dimensions of History* and *The Double Invention of Komo*. The anthropological studies listed above are a major part of Jay Wright's *Archive*; they do not simply supply him with information about various African cultures, raw data of sorts to be transformed into poetry. They suggest, much more importantly, a comparative approach to cultural history that is particularly suitable for Wright's interest in the history of the New World. To a writer, whose cultural heritage does not *per se* constitute a unified whole that could be effectively sustained and mediated by any one mythical system alone, modern anthropology offers an attractive methodological starting point for charting relationships between different cultures and for creating a sense of coherence, in which those vital differences need not be negated or leveled. As proposed above, this kind of coherence is a structure without a center in that it is not founded on, and is thus not reducible to, a single, absolute frame of reference. In Part 1 I presented several decentered or acentric structures in my comparison of Williams, Carpentier, and Paz, whose respective texts dismantle the myth of America by subjecting it to the rigors of (re)interpretation. Anthropology is precisely such a (re)interpretation of myth, and it is therefore appropriate for it to mediate Wright's poetry.

To substantiate this linkage between poetic and social-scientific discourse, it ought to be stressed that the debut of anthropology as a human science tellingly coincided, around the turn of the century, with a rapidly declining faith in Western metaphysics. "One can assume," Derrida contends in one of his early essays, "that ethnology could have been born as a science only at the moment when a decentering had come about: at the moment when European culture—and, in consequence, the history of metaphysics and of its concepts—has been dislocated, driven from its locus, and forced to stop considering itself as the culture of reference."[51] The philosophical crisis ensuing from that dislocation of Europe as the central cultural reference point is, in many ways, analogous to the crisis brought about, several centuries earlier, by the "discovery" of the New World. This loss of the center, which affected both Europe and the New World in similar ways but with very different results, initiated a "rediscovery" of America, now led by chroniclers of a different kind in search not of gold but of new myths to replace those that had ceased to play the role of secure foundations. For Wright, however, national myths are no longer enough, and in his own search he comes to embrace the "different resolutions" modern anthropology suggests.

What, then, are the "different resolutions" anthropology offers the modern writer? Roberto Gonzalez Echevarría, with Lévi-Strauss's *Tristes tropiques* in mind, regards "anthropology [as] a way through which

Western culture indirectly affixes its own cultural identity. This identity, which the anthropologist struggles to shed, is one that masters non-historical cultures through knowledge, by making them the object of its study. Anthropology translates into the language of the West the cultures of the others, and in the process establishes its own form of self-knowledge through a kind of annihilation of the self."[52] We have already witnessed several instances of such a self-effacement (it is not really an annihilation) in Wright's work, and it now becomes clear that the identity he is trying to shed or efface in the process of gaining self-knowledge is the one that has been conceived and formulated on the premise of Europe's central position in world history. The goal of Wright's poetry is to show what, as Octavio Paz has asked, "happens to America as an autonomous historical entity when it confronts the realities of Europe." The traditional concept of the American self, invented by the European spirit at that moment when it "free[d] itself of its historical particulars and conceiv[ed] of itself as a universal idea," becomes an empty shell, a voided presence. The loss of the center renders its mythical identity transparent. It effaces its contours by divesting it of its truth-value, while at the same time preserving it as an instrument.

Wright's poetry is characterized by the attempt to separate truth from method, and this attempt further emphasizes the link between anthropology and literature as parts of the humanities. In much the same way that the separation of truth from method enables the anthropologist tentatively to employ concepts without maintaining their truth-value, it enables the poet to use language—that is, the language(s) of the West—without burdening it with a predetermined set of metaphysical significances. This double intention is essential to Wright's poetics. It characterizes his notion of exile, that principal trope which makes possible the *double invention*. of myth and history that links his poetry with the texts of Williams, Carpentier, Paz, and Guillén.

II

> take the earth beneath me
> as parchment and intention,
> memory and project of all
> movement it contains.
>
> —JAY WRIGHT, *Explications/Interpretations*

Wright's poems, as we have seen in the case of "Benjamin Banneker Helps to Build a City," are very much concerned with the problems and possibilities of writing. This concern serves as a point of departure for revising Afro-American literary history by situating it within a tradition of New World writing. Wright's preoccupation with writing leads him to challenge a number of compositional (and critical) clichés that, wittingly or unwittingly, regard the distinctiveness of Afro-American texts as a function of their oral heritage. Perhaps the most pervasive of these clichés is the idea of poetic voice, which, in an Afro-American context, is quite heavily invested with certain cultural significances: more often than not, the gaining of voice is seen as a form of liberation. I need not reiterate here my previous argument concerning the connection between freedom and literacy and the problems resulting from the fallacious association of literacy with orality. Still, it seems necessary to reemphasize that in Wright's poetry voice, as well as freedom, is gained only through writing.

It is well worth noting in this regard that Wright's poet is never cast in the traditional role of the singer of tales; he is a "bookman of the blood," a keeper of records and a chronicler, who becomes a kind of semiotician or grammatologist in his own right. Although Wright obviously uses the phonetic-alphabetic script of the English language, he tempers the metaphysical tradition with which that language is burdened by introducing into his poetry other, formalized languages: In both *Dimensions of History* and *The Double Invention of Komo*, as well as in *Soothsayers and Omens*, he uses a series of nonphonetic ideograms drawn from both Dogon mythology and the Komo initiation ritual of the Bambara. What the presence of those ideograms, some of which will be discussed in detail later on, indicates is that Wright does not treat writing as a more or less faithful transcription of speech. Instead, his poems seek to "translate" one formalized language into another, without assigning priority to either. For Wright, poetic voice is always mediated by writing. Like the ideograms themselves, it has no literal meaning if only because that literal meaning is always already figurative. In this way, Wright's use of ideogrammatic writing becomes an elaborate critique of the authenticity and truth-value associated with literalness and thus of the kind of writing that conceives of itself as secondary to, and derivative of, speech.[53] What happens in Wright's poetry is that figures of voice are systematically decomposed into figures of writing, and these poetic transformations have much to do with his use of ritual.

I have stressed before that Wright is not attempting to turn poetry into ritual. Rather, he is interested in the conceptual structures that underlie specific cultural rituals and in the problem of how to translate those conceptual patterns into linguistic ones. This process is analogous to using one language according to the grammatical rules of another: the outward appearance of the individual words remains unchanged, whereas the ways in which those words combine into meaningful messages are substantially altered. To see more specifically how this applies to poetic practice, we first need to know more about the workings of ritual. As both *Dimensions of History* and *The Double Invention of Komo* are based on initiation rituals, it is helpful to consider Lévi-Strauss's observations:

> No anthropologist can fail to be struck by the common manner of conceptualizing initiation rites employed by the most diverse societies throughout the world. Whether in Africa, America, Australia or Melanesia, the rites follow the same pattern: first, the novices, taken from their parents, are symbolically "killed" and hidden away in the forest or bush, where they are put to the test by the Beyond; after this, they are "reborn" as members of the society. When they are returned to their natural parents, the latter therefore simulate all the phases of a new delivery.[54]

An important addition must be made to this rather general account. As the anthropologist Michael Houseman points out, initiation rituals are characterized, above all, by a double process: They create at once continuity and discontinuity, sameness and difference.[55] On the one hand, the initiate remains the same individual as before; on the other hand, he undergoes a radical metamorphosis that changes his social identity and thus distinguishes him from the noninitiates. This paradoxical logic—in fact, a "double invention" of the initiate's identity—is one of the keys to Wright's poetics: It is his "alphabet of transformations." This "alphabet" consists of clusters of tropes that translate the language of ritual into the language of poetry. We may say that in this process the English language itself takes the place of the initiate: Its linguistic surface does not change in any noticeable way, but the ways in which its words produce meaning do.

This peculiar logic of the initiation ritual accounts for much of the semantic doubleness (and duplicity) of Wright's language, which seems to be invested with a kind of "double consciousness." The Du Boisian echo here is hardly coincidental.[56] It is particularly obvious in a poem entitled "The Albuquerque Graveyard," which recalls the Benjamin Banneker poems as well as anticipates *Dimensions of History*:

After so many years
of coming here,
passing the sealed mausoleums,
the pretentious brooks and springs,
the white, sturdy limestone crosses,
the pattern of the place is clear to me.
I am going back
to the Black limbo,
an unwritten history
of our own tensions. (*SO*, 38)

The tropological cluster that "double consciousness" generates in these lines immediately invokes the opening of "Benjamin Banneker Helps to Build a City." As in the previous poem, Wright's vision of traversing a burial ground studded with sturdy white limestone crosses is readily identified with the twin activities of reading and writing. The poet's journey is an articulation of the "pattern" inscribed on this place by the marks of time, a pattern quite different from the one represented by a landscape of "sealed mausoleums" and "pretentious brooks and springs." Wright appropriately calls it "an *unwritten* history." It would be erroneous to read that phrase as a reference to the fact that many aspects of Afro-American history have not yet been recorded in written form and are only transmitted orally. While this is doubtlessly true, the idea of walking across graveyards in search of oral histories would be absurd. "Unwritten" does not conveniently translate into "oral"; it is not, as we may initially think, a figure of voice, at least not in this poetic context. The possibility of such an easy equation is already precluded by the figure that directly precedes this line: "the Black limbo." The meaning of "unwritten history" is quite evidently held *in* (Black) *limbo*, suspended but not rendered completely indeterminate. The very act of using one trope to dislocate another is precisely what brings forth another, supplementary meaning of "unwritten": Wright does not perceive Afro-American history (and New World history) as something that has not yet been written, but something that has always yet to be *un-written*, undone through writing in the same way that the meaning of "unwritten" itself is undone by the *limbo*.

The disruptive effect of the trope of the *limbo* on the language in this poem evidences the workings of a different grammar which dislocates conventional meanings. It is in this sense that the *limbo*, which itself inscribes that unwritten history of cultural and linguistic tensions, becomes what Harris has called an "inner corrective": It allows Wright to work within a Western language while at the same time dismantling the underlying conceptual structures—that is, the metaphysics—that govern the way in which meaning is produced in that language.

If we further pursue the *limbo* as a cultural phenomenon, we find that it refers to the Middle Passage and thus implies a journey from an old space (Africa) to a new one (the New World). It is, in other words, closely connected with exile, both as a historical event and as a mental process of dislocation and transformation. Harris's comments on this are most suggestive:

> The *limbo* dance is a well-known feature in the Carnival life of the West Indies today though it is still subject to intellectual censorship .... The *limbo* dancer moves under a bar which is gradually lowered until a mere slit of space, it seems, remains through which with spread-eagled limbs he passes like a spider. *Limbo* was born, it is said, on the slave ships of the Middle Passage. There was so little space that the slaves contorted themselves into human spiders. *Limbo*, therefore, ... is related to *anancy* or spider fables .... But there is something else in the *limbo-anancy* syndrome, ... and that is the curious dislocation of a chain of miles reflected in the dance .... the *limbo* dance becomes the human gateway which dislocates (and therefore begins to free itself from) a uniform chain of miles across the Atlantic. This dislocation of interior space serves therefore as a corrective to a uniform cloak or documentary stasis of imperialism. The journey across the Atlantic for the forebears of West Indian man involved a new kind of space—inarticulate as this new "spatial" character was at the time—and not simply an unbroken schedule of miles in a log book. Once we perceive this inner corrective to historical documentary and protest literature, which sees the West Indies as utterly deprived ..., we begin to participate in the genuine possibilities of original change in a people severely disadvantaged (it is true) at a certain point in time. The *limbo* therefore implies ... a profound art of compensation which seeks to replay a dismemberment of tribes ... and to invoke at the same time a curious psychic reassembly of the parts of the dead muse or god.[57]

One recognizes in these remarks the ritualistic pattern of death/separation/dismemberment and rebirth/reintegration/reassembly.

One further notices an emphasis on the simultaneity of those two movements or processes, which is also precisely what occurs in writing. In Wright's poems, writing is always a simultaneous dismemberment and reassembly of meaning. Writing becomes unwriting in that it undoes its own underlying conceptual structures to clear a space for new meanings.

Since both *Dimensions of History* and *The Double Invention of Komo* are preoccupied with ritualistic structures of dismemberment and reassembly, or to use Wright's language, excision and circumcision, it is not very surprising that the *limbo* as a "gateway" should occupy a central place in each poem: "My instruments," Wright declares. "toll you into limbo" (*DI*, 39). In the following quotation the *limbo* is again used to signal the transformation of voice into writing, of sound into space:

> I know my double exile in song,
> and the way the heel comes down,
>   remembering a dance,
> on unfamiliar ground.
> I have been made serious
> by composing
>   in the bright afternoons
> of reticence and hay,
> what I want to say
>   without song. (*DI*, 22)

Immediately noticeable in this passage is the movement from knowing exile "in song" to articulating that knowledge "without song," that is, in writing. The difference between these two modes of knowledge is mediated by the figure of the dance, which, given the context established by the word "exile," can easily be read as an allusion to the *limbo*. The knowledge "in song" which, at least initially, appears to be a figure of voice, is significantly predicated on the memory of the dance, a spatial metaphor that evokes the journey implicit in the *limbo*. Voice or song, in other words, depends on a spatial movement (the dance as journey), and spatial movements for Wright are always figures of writing, of speaking, as it were, "without song." As in my previous example, dance or *limbo* dismantles a figure of voice—it "dislocates interior space"—only to reassemble it immediately into a figure of writing.

Wright's poetry emerges from an unwriting of a language that would otherwise not be able to articulate the tensions that characterize the New World as a cultural and historical space. As this formulation may falsely suggest that such an "un-written" language is, in the end, a mere reflection of a particular socio-cultural reality, it is necessary to stress that unwriting is a process that dislocates and supplements that reality as it is presented in historical documentary and protest ("realistic") literature. Wright seeks to demonstrate the process of various levels of conceptual dismemberment and simultaneous reassembly involved in transforming a borrowed language, in this case English, perhaps not into a different language altogether but at least into a different kind of language. His persistent decomposition of figures of voice into figures of writing, which is mediated by the trope of the *limbo*, exemplifies such a transformation. There may not be an Afro-American language in the same way that there is an English or a French language, but that in no way precludes the existence of distinct forms of Afro-American written discourse. Wright would no doubt agree with Octavio Paz that "the language that Spanish Americans [and Afro-Americans, for that matter] speak is one thing, and the literature they write another."[58] Wright explores in his poetry the tensions between different kinds of language, tensions that arise because each of these languages has its own distinct forms of discourse and its own grammar. These variegated patterns are superimposed upon one another and constitute a sort of master plan, a design that we may call the Afro-American concept of New World writing. In my comments on *Dimensions of History* we shall see in detail how Wright enhances the features of his "Black limbo" (that is, the "sea-change" to which he subjects certain aspects of Dogon, Bambara, and Akan-Ashanti cosmologies) with numerous Amerindian and Latin American/Hispanic elements.

Designs play a crucial role in *Dimensions of History*. Each of the three parts of the poem, as well as each of the four subsections in part 2 and, finally, the poem as a whole, has its own distinct ideogrammatic signatures, derived from the ritual languages of the Dogon and the Bambara. These signatures are very much part of the poetic text and have to be treated as such. Let us disregard, for the moment, the figure of the Nommo of the Pool which adorns the cover and turn to the ideogram that is reproduced below the title of the first part, entitled "The Second Eye of the World: The Dimension of Rites and Act." This Dogon signature, or *tónú* (schema), represents what Griaule and Dieterlen have translated as "The Separation of the Twins" at the moment of circumcision (see fig. 1), the symbolic cut that marks the transition from childhood to adulthood.[59] This transition is a movement from innocence to knowledge, an initiation into what Wright calls "the clan's knowledge," which is accomplished through the "ennobling" cut of the ritual knife. We need not probe the fine details of this circumcision ritual and its complex historical origins to understand why this particular signature appears as a frontispiece in *Dimensions of History*: The entire poem may be described as an initiation into the secrets of an extended Afro-American mythology of writing.

Similarly, the language of the poem must properly be regarded as ritualistic. Not unlike the *sigui* of the Dogon, *Dimensions of History* is presented in a special language, designed specifically as a medium for communicating with one's immortal ancestors.[60] Reading this poem is comparable, in many ways, to learning a new language, one that has relatively little in common with the "borrowed" language in which it is situated. I repeat this analogy to stress that Wright does indeed erode the metaphysical foundations of the English language, while still preserving its surface appearance. Simply to equate this process of erosion or subversion with the cliché "literary usage" would be to diminish the actual effects, as well as the scope, of the dismantling he undertakes. *Dimensions of History* does not offer the kinds of assurances that have always tempted critics into reducing literary texts to a set of supposedly unchanging meanings that serve as stable communicators. I am not suggesting that this cannot be done in the case of Wright's poem(s), but it ought to be done, if at all, with the understanding that such communicators are nothing but tools, grammars of sorts that help us translate this poetry into a language and a form of discourse that are organized very differently.

The problem of translation (and of interpretation-as-translation) indeed looms large in *Dimensions of History*. For instance, the above translation of the Dogon signature as "The Separation of the Twins," a translation already mediated by Griaule and Dieterlen's descriptions, is completely incapable of conveying what the actual shape of this ideogram communicates. The signature itself, consisting of three different circles laid out in the form of an open triangle, prefigures both the triadic structure of the poem as a whole and that of "The Dimensions of Rites and Acts," which is also composed of three parts. In addition, this schema represents, as the title "The Second Eye of the World" and its association with the Southern Cross already suggests, a constellation of stars which includes Sirius, also called "the second eye of Amma" (the other "eye" is the North Star).[61] Since the sign of "The Separation of the Twins" is a ritual figure representing a specific constellation of stars, there evidently exists a connection between initiation rituals and astronomy. This connection informs, either directly or indirectly, all of the poem's fundamental tropes. For example, the general notion that an initiation ritual is a movement from one state of consciousness (innocence) to another (knowledge) gives rise to the kinetic trope of the *journey*, which is not a linear progression but a series of internal transformations. It is further evident that such a journey, lest it be the kind of idle roaming of Whitman's poet, requires a "compass" (*DH*, 7), which also explains the relevance of astronomy and astrology to this initiation ritual: both are navigation aids.[62] All these metaphoric threads come together in the following three lines, which echo not only the Benjamin Banneker poems but also Aimé Césaire's *Cahier d'un retour au pays natal* [Notebook of a Return to My Native Land] (1939).

> I travel by the turning of a star
> through all the gates that lead me home,
> that lead me to my other self. (*DH*, 103)

Wright's poetic travels, like Césaire's, take the form of a *journey home*, a journey toward that "other self," which would represent the final achievement of the freedom accorded by self-knowledge (literacy). But, curiously enough, that journey "home" is also a journey into *exile*, which is already implicit in the association of "home" with the "other self." To explain the nature of and the reasons for this seeming paradox, it is necessary to call attention to the fact that the first line of the above quotation ("I travel by the turning of a star") contains an allusion to how runaway slaves, at least on the North American continent, found their way into freedom. In Wright's own language, running away from slavery may be described as *traveling by the turning of the North Star*, his equivalent of the Césairian neologism *marronner* [to run away like a slave].[63] It is hardly a coincidence that the North Star should have evolved as the foremost emblem of freedom in nineteenth-century Afro-North American writing or that Frederick Douglass should have named his first abolitionist newspaper *The North Star*. Although the direction of Wright's poetic travels is not exclusively determined by the light of the North Star, there is nevertheless an important connection to be found in his invocation of this emblem. Literacy, understood not as the ability to read and write in general but more specifically as the ability to read the stars and thus to navigate, made it possible for the runaway slaves to find their way into freedom and safety, no matter how tenuous that vision of the antebellum North as an abode of freedom and security may have been. In the same way, poetic writing as another, new form of literacy, one that would free literary language from Western metaphysics, now makes it possible for Wright to find his way out of a different kind of bondage. His writing

enables him to break out of the "prison house" of the English language
and its ideological underpinnings. He thus avoids the trappings of an
identity which, because it is cast in and defined by the same language
formerly employed to justify and perpetuate slavery, would prevent true
self-knowledge.

Wright's journey in *Dimensions of History* is a dynamic resistance to
the pull of a language so deeply entrenched in the history of the West that
it would inevitably confine and reduce any meaning to that cultural
framework and thus to a set system of references unable to account for the
broad metaphoric spectrum of Wright's ideogrammatic tropes. There
simply are no standard reference points in Western mythology for figures
such as "The Separation of the Twins" or "The Second Eye of the World."
This becomes quite evident when we consider that these two phrases,
themselves only relatively inadequate translations when compared to the
actual ideograms, already considerably reduce the semantic range and
repertoire these figures are capable of mobilizing. Translation is a tricky
business fraught with all kinds of ambiguities. As John Deredita has
pointed out, "All translation, considered as the rendering of an original,
involves traduction [that is, distortion caused by a reduction of language's
disseminating powers]. The parallel text that brings over the original
necessarily alters it; difference inscribes itself everywhere as the original is
led away from its mother language and its *écriture* points to the difference
inherent in that repetition and unsettles the representational myth that
traditionally has motivated translation."[64] At the same time as inevitably
impoverishing the original, translation also adds something to it,
supplements it. As a supplement, a translation is both *a part of* as well as
apart from the original in the sense that it makes up for a deficiency that it
itself has created in the first place. This process best characterizes
Wright's poetic method. The paradox of being both a part of something
and at the same time being apart, separated from it, corresponds to and
illuminates the perplexing relationship between "home" and "exile."

This requires still further clarification, since it would be evasive to
designate the relationship between "home" and "exile" an irreducible
paradox. Both figures are in fact different configurations of "self," as can
be seen in the following citation from "Meta-A and the A of Absolutes."

> I am good when I am in motion,
> when I think of myself at rest
> in the knowledge of my moving,
> when I have the vision of my mother at rest,

in moonlight, her lap the cradle of my father's head.
I am good when I grade my shells,
and walk from boundary to boundary,
unarmed and unafraid of another's speech.
I am good when I learn the world
through the touch of my present body.
I am good when I take the cove of a cub,
                    into my care.
I am good when I hear the changes in my body
echo all my changes down the years,
when what I know indeed is what I would
                    know in deed.
I am good when I know the darkness of all light,
and accept the darkness, not as sign, but as my body.
This is the A of absolutes,
the logbook of judgments,
the good sign. (*DH*, 90)

For Wright, to be "in motion" is to think of oneself (one's self) at rest in the knowledge of one's moving, or in other words, to be at home in the knowledge of one's exile. But since "there is no sign to *arrest* us/from the possible" (*DH*, 90; my italics), "home" is a mere fiction of being created by the mind as a temporary resting place for itself. That resting place is a myth produced by the knowledge of exile. As an idealized locus of self-knowledge, it is a projection of the poet's desire for closure, for the completion of a process of transformation that will not end. That process is history, and its knowledge is the knowledge of exile: It is the process itself of knowing history, of "walk[ing] from boundary to boundary," which promotes exile. The knowledge of being exiled, of being a part of history, is thus a knowledge of the impossibility of returning to one's origins, of becoming one with the source at the moment of perfect (unmediated) self-knowledge. This kind of "homecoming" is possible only in death, a death quite tellingly associated with speech!

And death enters with the word,
the conception of speech. (*DH*, 34)

The crucial question Wright implicitly poses is, How can we know death? It has to be taken into account when pondering that question in the context of his poetry that there are two levels on which to consider death:

First, the level of the individual, where death is an event that brings about radical discontinuity; second, the level of the community (and ritual), where death establishes the kind of continuity we call tradition. In the latter case, the one that concerns us here, death is not a closure but the point at which life (and experience) are transformed into the knowledge that constitutes tradition. This is the way in which the above citation has to be understood. It is only in this form and at this level that death can be apprehended as a meaningful and knowable event, one that marks not the end of history but a turning point in history. Wright's perhaps most explicit comments on the relationship between death and history can be found in one of his early poems significantly entitled "Death as History." For reasons of economy as well as emphasis, I will quote only the last two parts of that poem.

iv

It is always like the beginning.
It is always having the egg
and seven circles,
always casting about in the wind
on that particular spot;
it is that African myth
we use to challenge death.
What we learn is that
death is not complete in itself,
only the final going from self to self.

v

And death is the reason
to begin again, without letting go.
And who can lament
such historical necessity?
If they are all dying,
the living ones,
they charge us with the improbable. (*HS*, 63)

"Death as History" offers a first, fleeting glimpse of "that African myth" Wright uses in later poems to develop his poetic "categories for the soul/of those I want to keep." The singular form is somewhat misleading here because what Wright presents as a challenge to death is more than one particular myth. It is a dense admixture of a variety of different African mythologies drawn from Dogon, Bambara, Akan-Ashanti, and Yoruba sources, to mention only the most prominent ones. One of the most important aspects of Wright's own mixed mythology is the element of ritual sacrifice, whose vital link with exile has already been emphasized. Viewed as a sacrifice (a ritual "killing") required to ensure historical continuity, death is not an isolated event, "not complete in itself," but part of an elaborate ritual consisting of the three categories identified above: separation (excision), transition (hibernation), reintegration (circumcision).[65] Translated into my previous terminology, this schema, which recalls the Dogon signature used as a frontispiece in *Dimensions of History*, yields the following: exile—journey—home. We can now clearly see that "home," signifying incorporation or reintegration through circumcision, is not an origin or a center, that is, an ideal point that exists outside of and generates this structure. Instead, it is an integral part of it. "Home" signals the transformation of one self into another, "the *final going* from self to self (my italics)," but can only project that "other self" (or other selves) for a brief moment without being able to arrest the process of transformation as such. The (individual) self is thus never fully figured; it can only know itself *as other* because (self)-knowledge is always mediated by language. The self can only know itself as its own *text*.

Wright's concept of being "at rest/in the knowledge of [one's] moving" articulates the moment when self turns to text, that is, the moment of writing. In the context of the Afro-American literary tradition, this formulation is a variation on, and a tribute to, Robert Hayden's "For a Young Artist" and more specifically the last four lines of that poem:

> ... Then—
> silken rustling in the air,
> the angle of ascent
> achieved.[66]

The prominent display of the past participle ("achieved") at the end of the poem seems to suggest that what has indeed been *achieved* here is closure. On closer look, however, we realize that Hayden's "angle of ascent" is precisely a figure for thinking of oneself at rest in the knowledge of one's moving: of being airborne. It is a figure with which Hayden attempts, much like Wright himself, to capture—the very moment when self becomes text, or better even, trope. The result of this transformation is not closure but an instance of almost complete self-effacement at the moment of flight, which corresponds to the moment of separation (the "cut") in Jay Wright's poetry. (What Hayden effaces here is the figure of the old man with enormous wings, one of García Márquez's fabulous creations.)[67] We see in Hayden's poem, not the old man trying to lift himself up into the air, but only a line and a space ("Then—") to be immediately supplemented by "the angle of ascent/achieved." This substitution achieves knowledge of the self as other by rendering visible the way in which language, writing, effaces the self in order to make it knowable.

According to the Dogon, each being, as well as what we would consider inanimate objects, has its own "language," which is regarded as a kind of *double* of that being or object.[68] Since knowledge is acquired by decoding the symbolic language of each being or object, it is evident that the world can be known only through its double and, in fact, as its double. For the Dogon, the world is like a book to be read and interpreted. Most importantly, everything is apprehended in terms of the process it embodies, that is, in terms of the process that brought it into being: its history. Since the self participates in the flow of history through language, (self)-knowledge is always historical knowledge; nothing can be known outside of or apart from its history: therefore, "being will speak/with the tight voice of becoming" (*DI*, 36). And that "tight voice of becoming" is of course a figure of writing. The following passage from *Dimensions of History* readily turns that pronouncement into poetic practice.

> Speech is the fact, and the fact is true.
> What is moves, and what is moving is.
> We cling to these contradictions.
> We know we will become our contradictions,
> our complex body's own desire. (*DH*, 89)

This poetic manifesto, which is the "Meta-A and the A of Absolutes" of Wright's poetics, exposes as a necessary failure any attempt to divorce the concept of "being" from that of "becoming" (as well as, by the same token, speech from writing) and thus to define self as a static category outside of history. Modernism's often desperate preoccupation with questions such as "How can we know the dancer from the dance?"[69] is indicative of the attempt to achieve a knowledge of the self by stepping outside of time into a conceptual dimension where the self could presumably be contemplated as an unchanging entity, complete in and by itself. Wright, in contrast, is not interested in devising ontological distinctions between "dancer" and "dance." For him, as for Williams, the dance is the language that articulates the dancer, who exists only in the form of his or her dance and has no identity outside of it. The concept of being or self as something that is present, and in fact exists, only in the process of being articulated, finds its equivalent again in the Dogon view of language: For the Dogon, a thought or an idea that does not seek expression simply does not exist.[70] In this sense, speech is the (f)act, or, put differently, language is being.

Wright regards self (or what the Dogon call "personality") as a series of movements in time (history) that can be translated into spatial configurations (poetry), which render visible "our complex body's own desire." The dance (recall the *limbo*) is a trope for history, a structure visualizing the ritualistic pattern of separation, transition, and reintegration. It has to be stressed that these three categories, each of which represents a different aspect or dimension of the self in its steady fluctuation away from and toward its identity, do not constitute an actual sequence in time. Although they can be represented episodically, they nevertheless remain imaginary movements between fictional or fictionalized points. They are not stages in a development, in an evolutionary process that progresses toward an ideal point, but synchronic juxtapositions of different levels of meaning that constitute the complex historical dimensions of Wright's poetic self. These movements are best conceptualized with the help of a visual metaphor: They are like different exposures of the same object, which are superimposed upon one another to form dense clusters of tropes.

In *Dimensions of History* this ritual design or "alphabet of transformations" functions both diachronically and synchronically. While the poem as a whole moves from "The Dimension of Rites and Acts" to "The Aesthetic Dimension" and finally to "The Physical Dimension," or, as it does in the first part, from "The Eye of God" to "The Key That Unlocks Performance" and "The Second Eye of the World," similar triads can be detected in the individual metaphors that simultaneously pull the text in the opposite direction and thus disrupt episodic representation, the poetic narrative, if you will. As a result, the text becomes a vast *field* of signs and references, indeed a "landscape" that is already compressed into the frontispiece. In this poetic landscape, as in the Dogon signature, each of the three dimensions of the initiation ritual forms tropological clusters. Each of these clusters, in turn, emphasizes a different aspect of the whole by temporarily effacing all other aspects that are also latent in it. Consequently, the Dogon signature is a contraction, not a reduction, of the field of the poem.

A look at the poetic posture Wright assumes at various points in the poetic narrative of *Dimensions of History* best conveys the idea of tropological clusters and the relationships between them. One of the first things to notice when reading *Dimensions of History* (as well as Wright's other poetry) is that the narrative voice of Wright's poet is constantly engaged in alternative impersonations of both speaker or listener, or better, writer or reader. At no point is the poetic or narrative "I" ever confined to the space of an individual subject that could neatly be associated with the figure of the author. Instead, it is an intersubject, a figure capable of assuming multiple identities: "I"—"you"—"we." Let us consider the following examples.

> Under the tightly bound arms
> and the spirit of masks,
> I return to you,
>   to name,
>   to own,
> to be possessed and named myself,
> following the movement of the eye of God
> whose lids will close upon your greater claims. (*DH*, 8)
> . . . .
> But here alone I sit
>   with the tassel and the bell,
> holding the celebration of my people's love.
> I can hear these bells in the distance,
> and hear them shake the child's voice,
> singing his ox's name in your womb.
> We cut them into peacefulness,
> and breed them to witness
> our slow coming together,
> to bear the burden of the years
> in which you will meet me
>   again and again,
> each death a growth,
> a life rising into its clarity of being. (*DH*, 12)
>
> . . . .
>
> Who you are
>   and where you are

> we teach you to teach us.
> So I would wear myself
>   the feather of the lourie bird,
> and be the hand to cut you
> into this special kinship. (*DH*, 13)

Each of these three postures ("I"—"you"—"we") emphasizes a different dimension of the poetic self, which is associated with a different location in time. Their "slow coming together" is represented as a dialogue of the "I" with its "other self" (you), a figure that is alternately situated in the past ("I return to you") and in the future ("in which you will meet me"). It is not an umbilical cord that links these various manifestations of the poetic self and weaves them together in the figure "we." The "special kinship" Wright proposes is not a birthright but a matter of choosing to accept "the claims the living/owe the dead" (*DH*, 7). Wright, following Ellison here, chooses his ancestors, and this choice is a poetic gesture that cuts across as well as cuts genealogical lines. This double cut into exile and kinship is the ultimate configuration of freedom-through-(and with)-literacy. The cut itself is a figure of writing, which does not simply represent experience but deepens and purifies it as the pen cuts the paper. For Wright does not so much seek to create new experience or new molds for experience; his intention is to create a more profound understanding of the old ones. After all, the trope of exile is by no means a novel or even a recent invention in Afro-American literature. We have only to recall a famous passage from Frederick Douglass's 1845 *Narrative*: "My feet have been so cracked with the frost," Douglass writes, "that the pen with which I am writing might be laid in the gashes."[71] These gashes are marks of exile, wounds inflicted by slavery, and the Afro-American writer uses these wounds as molds for his or her historical experience. Writing, like Douglass's pen, fills these gashes. It attempts to heal these wounds by deepening our understanding of what they signify: "you must learn / the lesson of this sweet dispossession" (*DH*, 13). In this way, the wounds inflicted by centuries of bondage are transformed into the insignia of freedom.

> The solution is never to yoke,
> but to split.
> This is the gesture. This is the act.
> From every twoness cut from itself,
> the scar gives rise to one. (*DH*, 24)

A conjoining of Dogon mythology (again, the sign of "The Separation of the Twins") and Du Boisian "double consciousness," this brief citation invites us to apprehend and appreciate the poet's quest for literacy, not as a journey toward unified and integrated selfhood, but toward an understanding of the creative potential of his self-divided personality. For Wright, as for Du Bois, to be self-divided and to be conscious of one's doubleness is a "gift," a legacy to be fulfilled, and not a cultural handicap.[72] Wright clarifies this in "The Abstract of Knowledge / the First Test" that appears in *The Double Invention of Komo*.

> I now traverse love's dispersal
> through your body,
> here,
> in an exile's scriptorium.
> Love itself allows your opposition.
> Say that love permits me
> to publish my own decline,
> to here, where I am pitched up,
> waterless, a water spirit compelled
> toward a denser wood.
> Now, may your necessary injury
> guide me to what is true.
> What is true is the incision.
> What is true is the desire for the incision,
> and the signs' flaming in the wound.
>
> I am now your delegate.
> I give you order and determination,
> and your soul's syntax,
> extracted from God's speech. (*DI*, 48–49)

To "traverse love's dispersal / through your body" is to trace an inner geography and thus to translate an external passage into an internal one. The historical event of the Middle Passage, the physical journey into exile, is internalized as a *rite* of passage, something that is infinitely repeated and repeatable in the act of writing. Exile is a form of dispersal and dismemberment, of being cut off from one's community and one's origins. The separation is equivalent to the first stage of the initiation ritual: the ritual "killing," or excision. But this "necessary injury" is also, at the same time, a cut into kinship, a circumcision, in that it transforms the novice into a "delegate," a special member of his community, who is identified as such by the writing on his body: his scars. Writing, once linked with the grammar of the initiation ritual, assumes an explicit double significance: It wounds as well as heals. The scars, which are the signs that flame in the wound, now become the "soul's syntax"; they provide order and determination, but only when read according to that grammar. This syntax, in turn, is "extracted from God's speech," and this process of extraction creates yet another wound, or deepens the old one. Clearly, writing "wounds" speech: It creates a deficiency, an absence, which is represented here as a blank space on the page. This textual incision, the turning point at which the initiate becomes a "delegate," where excision becomes circumcision, and where cultural ritual becomes a linguistic process, again brings to mind the passage from Robert Hayden's "For a Young Artist" discussed above. The blank space equals Hayden's dash: "Then—."

A series of other transformations is occasioned by Wright's ritualistic grammar. The signs "flaming" in the incisive space between the lines consume the "denser wood," turn it into ashes. From these ashes the figure of the delegate arises like a phoenix ("a. bennu bird" [*DH*, 31]),[73] "manuring" the burned place, which Wright elsewhere images as a desert, with his "ashy soul" (*DH*, 25). This resurrection signals the emergence of a language "to publish" the initiate's "*decline*/to here, where [he is] *pitched up*." My italics here underline two different metaphorical movements— descent and ascent, return and flight—whose simultaneous occurrence follows the logic of the initiation ritual. But this opposition operates only on the surface of the poem. At the level of Wright's poetic grammar, descent or decline is equivalent to being "pitched up," to reaching a higher, but at the same time more profound, pitch. This transformation is also figured as the entering of a state of greater *density* (to be "compelled toward a denser wood"). The notion of density or complexity is, in turn, intensified by the figure of the flaming signs, suggesting the burning of this wood and its transformation into another, even more condensed shape—ashes, or to recall Williams, white ink.[74]

I have suggested earlier that Wright's intention is not to create new experience but rather to purify and deepen the "old" experience of exile, and that this is accomplished through sacrifice, another wounding. This becomes clearer if we engage in yet another reading of the above citation, one that identifies it as a rewriting of the Dogon creation myth mentioned in connection with the Benjamin Banneker poems. At the same time that the poet descends, his other self ascends in the form of Nommo, the "water spirit," who is transformed ("waterless") into a wooden ritual mask and then sacrificed. The sacrificial "burning" of the dense, waterless wood represented by the flaming signs is a figure for the ritual death of Nommo, who, after his necessary injury and because of it, returns to earth to establish a new order out of the chaos of experience.[75] Another important influence on Wright's poetics, J. B. Danquah's *The Akan Doctrine of God*, provides further understanding of the complexities of this new order that Wright labels the "soul's syntax." Danquah explains,

> There is the triad—Order, Knowledge, Death. There is also the divine triad, Onyame, the naturally given, Onyankopon, the experience of the given, and Odomankoma, reconciliation of the given and experience of the given, of being and the effort towards non-being, i.e., knowledge. If Odomankoma contains both in himself, then there is no real contradiction, but simply an appearance, what seemed merely to be contradiction ....
>
> These ideas are not easy of comprehension unless one has made a study of the elementary basis of the Akan conception of life. But, at least, on this level we can feel certain that the first of the given is Order. That is the thesis. The antithesis is knowledge and experience of that order. Knowledge analyzes, separates, complicates, and, by its own effort, seeks for new adjustments for a new and completed harmony, a striving for development of a whole within which the basis of knowledge, mind, seeks expression.
>
> What then is the *conclusion*, the reconciliation? It is found even in the most simple fact of physical growth. Life is a harmony in which individual experience, the seed that is planted, must first perish, in order to find itself in a new ripened order.... The individual dies to himself in order to find himself in a whole that is completely ordered.[76]

This triad, Order–Knowledge–Death, which we have already encountered in the form of exile–journey–home and separation–transition–reintegration, is Jay Wright's "nexus of exchange" (*DI*, 9). It informs both the narrative (episodic or diachronic) and the metaphoric (synchronic) structure of *Dimensions of History*, two movements whose interweaving is most strikingly exemplified in the following lines.

We are born to trade upon and build
the head's intent

in the river's seed,
the seed's irruption,
the milk of the lamb,
the star's sudden fall,
the rock's mountain breaking shape,
the saint bickering with birds,
the sceptre, flail, and crook,
the coffin at the neck of things,
the joker at the soul's bequest,
the eye,
the key,
the second eye.

This, before you,
    is the life
of a dark and dutiful dyeli,
searching for the understanding of his deeds.

Let my words wound you
into the love of the emblems
    of the soul's intent. (*DH*, 35–36)

When reading this passage, notice that Wright's "emblems of the soul's intent" further qualify the "soul's syntax" and thus the triadic design of the initiation ritual. The assonant sequence "the eye,/the key,/the second eye" is unquestionably indebted to that ritual's logic as well as to the principles of ideogrammatic writing embodied in the Dogon and Bambara signatures on which I have commented. In addition, there is a link with the epilogue in Ellison's *Invisible Man*, which begins, "So there you have all of it that's important. Or at least you *almost* have it."[77] This connection would admittedly seem tenuous were it only predicated on the fact that the above citation appears at the end of the third long section of part 1 of *Dimensions of History* and may thus be regarded as a kind of epilogue. There is, however, more: The Invisible Man's epilogue refers us back to the novel's beginning, the prologue. Both epilogue and prologue are associated with hibernation, and figures of hibernation occur in very interesting, strategic places in Wright's poem. The first one, in fact, opens *Dimensions of History*: "Brightness is a curse upon the day. /The light has turned the plain cave dark" (*DH*, 7).

The initial juxtaposition of brightness and darkness yields the image of a cave, "the warm pit of auquénidos," which strongly suggests the Invisible Man's underground residence, which he describes as a "warm hole."[78] The figure of the cave, however, recalls not only the Invisible Man's "hole"; it also alludes to Plato's Allegory of the Cave,[79] so that a parallel can be drawn between Wright's concern for seemingly incompatible relationships and images, in this case the relationship between appearance and reality, and what Plato calls an understanding of the "relation of the shadow to the substance." Wright follows the Platonic notion that the ability to see in darkness, to see the "shadows" projected by the light of the fire—Plato's sun; Wright's star—is a particular kind of blindness."[80] According to Plato, "Blindness is of two kinds, and may be caused either by passing out of darkness into light or out of light into darkness." But while Plato deems the blindness caused by passing from darkness into light "blessed," Wright, in contrast, emphasizes that the descent into the cave is a voyage toward insight (or inner sight), toward "the darkness of all light," in which shadows (doubles) assume their own reality. Wright thus inverts one of the fundamental tenets of the Allegory of the Cave by collapsing the difference between appearance and reality. His poet's ability to see in the darkness of all light is clearly an instance of "double vision": the ability to see both shadow and substance and to identify the shadow, that is, the other self, as substance.

The cave is the first image in a series of transformations set in motion by the Ellisonian trope of hibernation, which recurs, at the very beginning of both "The Key That Unlocks Performance" and "The Second Eye of the World," respectively in the form of images of blindness and sleep: "And, as the god relieved you/of the burden of sight" (DH, 17) is a reference to Wright's "Second Conversations" with the blind Dogon sage Ogotemmêli in Soothsayers and Omens; "Anochecí enfermo amanecí bueno" ["I went to bed sick I woke up well"] (DH, 31) will be commented on later in this section. An "exile's scriptorium" for both Wright's poet and Ellison's Invisible Man, the cave is a locus of transformation and as such analogous to the blank spaces representing the incisive power of writing. On the one hand, the cave is a metaphoric space signifying a state of self-imposed exile. On the other hand, the descent into the cave is not simply an act of withdrawal or separation but also a form of immersion, of "understand[ing] the claims the living/owe the dead" (DH, 7). This understanding, in turn, becomes the basis for a special kinship, which, as I have noted, is a figure for a new kind of order. In the space of the cave, which is no doubt suggestive of Williams's Archive and particularly

Carpentier's "Lipsonoteca," the place where the bones of saints are kept, an old order is suspended, held in limbo, as it were, to make it possible for a new order to emerge. What happens in Wright's cave is a change of his poet's (and our) *angle* of perception, a change represented as the ability to sec in the darkness of all light. This "double vision"—to see in the dark as well as see darkness itself—is also a form of internal navigation: the ability to read the contents of the Archive, which is what Wright means by hibernation. This special skill, then, is a state not so much of "double consciousness" but of conscious doubleness. It is best described as "after hibernation," a phrase that signals the extent to which Wright has revised Ellison's trope.[81]

If hibernation, as Ellison defines it, is a "covert preparation for more overt action,"[82] then "after hibernation" is precisely the kind of overt action that not only constitutes a call for a new order but signifies the actual achievement of that order. The difference here is between *indeed* and *in deed*. It must be kept in mind, however, that "after hibernation" by no means designates an actual moment (or period) in a diachrony. Used purely as a metaphor of duration and continuity, "after hibernation" does not announce the end of hibernation and thus closure. Instead, it returns us to the concept of supplementarity, as does Stepto's notion of the "epilogue," which is of course a kind of textual supplement. As Stepto uses "after hibernation" as a trope for postmodernism ("after modernism"), it is instructive to consult his working definition.

> Literary modernism may never end, but there exist in modern literature certain aesthetic as well as historical moments when the modern writer appears to call for a new order. Because it is his call, and because the new set of images demanded is to be in some sense a natural outgrowth of his own figurative language, we may say that the modern writer is prefiguring his epilogue, or at the very least inaugurating a rather specific type of post-modernist expression.... "After modernism" may therefore be discussed as a series of incidents in recent literary history wherein a literary exchange (call and response?) between modern writers yields epilogues (or epilogues to epilogues ...) to the modernist's work.[83]

There is no doubt that *Dimensions of History*, and in fact all of Wright's poetry, constitutes an epilogue to Ellison's novel, an epilogue no less that breaks open the self-confinement of Afro-American literature and literary history represented by the Invisible Man's "hole." It cannot, after all, be overlooked that this kind of self-imposed exile is an evasion of history owing to the reluctance to assert difference that Walcott criticizes in an earlier quotation. The present context of literary modernism and postmodernism brings to mind my initial comments on the relationship between modern literature and anthropology: Wright's poems are to Western literature what anthropology is to Western culture. Put differently, Wright's work is a vast poetic epilogue to the history of Western civilization. Like anthropology, it both voids and supplements the cultural identity and centrality of the West. Wright's concept of New World writing hinges on this idea of supplementarity. The full extent of such poetic supplementation is suggested by the fact that, for Wright, New World writing is not just American and much less United States literature, but a *new* world literature: "Who is my own if not the world?/Were we not all made at Ife?" (*DH*, 21). Stepto declares with good reason that "Wright's art is neither American nor Afro-American in any familiar, provincial sense. The boundaries of the United States, even in this postmodern era of expansion (military and cultural), cannot contain Wright's poet's 'facts of history,' any more than the rhythmic structures of ballads and blues can fully define that poet's ancient cadences."[84] But if Wright's vision, or better, double vision, and the texts it generates go "beyond geography,"[85] that going beyond cannot be understood simply as an act of transcendence; rather, it is a deepening of vision and a sharpening of focus. Wright's poet's acute angle of perception enables him to see things that cannot be found on ordinary maps but which are none the less real for being invisible.

> Now I invoke my map of beads.
> I coil the spirit's veins about my wrists.
> I kneel at Ocumare to worry
> > the saint's bones,
> and rise on the walls of Cumaná.
> Poco a poco,
> I cut my six figures
> on another coast, in a western sunrise.
> In Carolina darkness, I push
> my jaganda into the blessed water.
> I ask now:
> all the blessed means my journey needs,
> the moving past, the lingering shadow

of my body's destination.
I ask my body to be here;
I ask for eyes that can invest
the natural body, the invested land,
the invested star, the natural spire,
landscape of spirit and the spirit's
rise in stone or in the fragile bones
        of the earth's body.
This will be my secular rosary,
my votive map, my guidebook
to the deeper mines of destiny. (*DH*, 93)

The geography mapped here is an inner landscape invested with various manifestations of history and myth, strung together into a "secular rosary" Wright's spiritual landscape recalls Nicolás Guillén's poem "El apellido" with its unmapped "geografia llena de oscuros montes,/de hondos y armagos valles" [geography filled with dark mountains,/with deep and bitter valleys].[86] Guillén's "montes" may be more appropriately rendered as "spaces" or "clearings," since the word also evokes the Afro-Cuban concept of "el monte," a sacred space frequently imaged as a clearing in the forest.[87] There no doubt exists a connection between Guillén's "montes" and Wright's own textual clearings. In addition, Wright's "map of beads" is evidently a metaphoric variation on that "interminable" string of last names Guillén offers at the end of "El apellido" to displace the figure of an umbilical cord and to void, much like Wright himself, the genealogical imperative presumed to connect the Afro-American writer with his or her African origins.

The allusions in the above citation to the poetry of Guillén, as well as Wright's references to the old Venezuelan cities of Ocumare and Cumaná, facilitate the transition from the explicitly African relations of *Dimensions of History* to its elective Latin American/Hispanic affinities. This transition cannot be a complete one, because these two *Kulturkreise* are by no means separate but have a long history of intersection to which the poem appeals throughout. I encounter at this point yet another set of cultural and historical references, which affects the consistency of the poem's texture in ways that make it impossible to conceive of Afro-American literature solely in terms of its African heritage. The figures and images Wright projects become even more aggressively unfamiliar as his "Black limbo" begins to embrace Hispanic American and Amerindian elements. Intent on demonstrating that there is no excuse not to know other cultures, Wright shakes us out of the complacency and indifference that come with familiarity and forces us to experience, in the act of reading, the pain, the anguish, and the restlessness, but also the ecstasy, of knowledge and of the special kinship that knowledge offers. Wright's poems are the reasons of "'a heart that is stirred/from its foundations, and tormented with its/ceaseless conflagrations'" (*DH*, 9). But that heart is also capable of healing its wounds by recognizing the historical necessity of its ordeal: "Anochecí enfermo amanecí bueno" [I went to bed sick I woke up well]. This line is repeated with the first person singular significantly changed into the first person plural to maintain the subject's plurality of identities.

> Still, anochecimos enfermo   amanecimos bueno,
> learning the dwelling-place of the act,
> the spirit holding the understanding
> of our life among ourselves. (*DH*, 33)

All this would seem easy enough if it were not for the fact that "the dwelling-place of the act," the locus of the transformation that brings about both rupture and healing, lies precisely in the gap opened up between "anochecimos enfermo" and "amanecimos bueno." Compressed into this space, this opening or clearing that we have already encountered several times, is an entire poetic geography that attempts to *chart* the way from sickness to health, that is, from exile to kinship. Wright's use of *amanecer* (to wake up, to dawn) and *anochecer* (to go to bed, to meet the night, to dusk) is the key to that "geography"; it explains how the "beads" are strung together into a map.

Both verbs are employed, as Wright remarks in his notes (*DH*, 108), to signal a very subtle Arabic influence on the Spanish language and culture. Since both *amanecer* and *anochecer* have unmistakable Latin roots, this influence is evidently not an etymological one, but, as Américo Castro has pointed out, one that has to do with uses of language. What is unusual about these two verbs in the context of the Romance languages is the adoption of a personal conjugation. for instance, *amanezco* (I dawn) or *amanecí* (I dawned), the past tense Wright uses. Castro explains that "the Arabic is grafted not only on objective notions (*hidalgo*, etc.), but also on inner experience, on the manner of behaving inwardly while expressing the existence of an objective reality. Instead of limiting himself to perceiving the existence of a natural phenomenon (it becomes day, it becomes night), the soul of the person transforms what he perceives into its own creation, into something which happens not only outside, but inside, the person: *anochecí*, the night met me, and I met the night."[88] This notion of an intimate intertwinement of the object with the experience of that object is essential to Wright's idea of historical reality, and it is telling that Castro's comments should invoke J. B. Danquah's remarks on the reconciliation of the given with the experience of the given as one of the bases of the Akan concept of life.

Wright offers *anochecer* and *amanecer* as representative examples of how processes of cultural exchange and synthesis manifest themselves in language, of how they affect the "dwelling place" of a people, a phrase Wright directly borrows from Castro.[89] Wright's insistence on using Spanish instead of an English translation is understandable in light of the semantic poverty of "I went to bed sick   I woke up well," a line totally incapable of retaining any of the historico-cultural resonances and philological depths of the original. To explore those resonances further, it is worth considering the following lines from Octavio Paz's *Piedra de sol* [Sun Stone] (1957), which stand out because Paz, like Wright, employs amanecer in its personal conjugation. I first quote the original Spanish to highlight the turbulences this causes in the English translation.

> cada día es nacer, un nacimiento
> es cada amanecer y yo *amanezco*,
> *amanecemos* todos, amanece
> el sol cara de sol, Juan *amanece*,
> con su cara de Juan cara de todos,
>
> puerto del ser, despiértame, *amanece*,
> déjame ver el rostro de este día,
> déjame ver el rostro de esta noche,
> todo se comunica y transfigura,
> arco de sangre, puente de latidos,
> llévame al otro lado de esta noche,
> adonde yo soy tú somos nosotros,
> al reino de pronombres enlazados.
>
> [Every day is a birth, and every daybreak
> another birthplace and I *am the break of day*,
> *we all dawn on the day*, the sun dawns
> and daybreak is the face of the sun, John
> *is the break of day* with John's face, face of all

gate of our being, awaken me, *bring dawn*,
grant that I see the face of the living day,
grant that I see the face of this live night,
everything speaks now, everything is transformed,
O arch of blood, bridge of our pulse beating,
carry me through to the far side of this night,
the place where I am You, equals ourselves,
kingdoms of persons and pronouns intertwined].[90]

The italicized words in both the original and the translation convey some sense of the semantic range of *amanecer*. Yet, to my mind the best translation of what Paz is trying to accomplish by using *amanecer* in connection with words and phrases such as "nacimiento," "puerta del ser," and "todo se comunica y transfigura" is a concise passage from Wright's *Explications/Interpretations*:

We say each dawn is a bond
of your own beginning,
the ground established for our
movement from dawn to dawn.[91]

For both Paz and Wright, [*to*] *dawn* is a kinetic trope for the process of bringing together elements from different cultures to form a palpitating bridge, an arc of intermingling blood or what Wright calls "a bond/of your own beginning." Dawn is the moment of transformation and transfiguration, the point at which the twi[-]light opens the door of being to become a human gateway. All these figures belong to the tropological cluster building up around that synthetic myth Wright has labeled the "Black limbo."

I have so far been preoccupied with filling the space between "anochecimos enfermo   amanecimos bueno." But it is also necessary to take into account that cultural synthesis "does not necessarily mean plenitude, but a void where elements meet and cancel each other to open up the question of being."[92] This comment is helpful insofar as it enables us to ponder the larger theoretical implications of the kind of spacing Wright practices. The gap in the text, which is elsewhere imaged as fertile whiteness (*DH*, 11), is the starting point for Wright's poet's ontological quest, the point at which it becomes necessary for a self or a culture to define (or redefine) its mode of being. This attempt at self-definition becomes necessary because the clash between the different cultures that meet in this space has brought about a deracination. As the result of a process, during which the old values and beliefs of each of the cultures involved have been unsettled and have become floating signifiers in a new commerce, it now becomes inevitable to create a new order into which those signifiers can settle. But since the exchange never really comes to an end, that settling down into a new order is not a permanent achievement but a temporary resting or pausing: The space must remain open for future exchanges.

The poetic "beads" Wright strings together into a map are precisely such places of cultural exchange and deracination. Another, perhaps even more complex "bead" Wright adds to his "secular rosary" right next to medieval Spain is the Hispanic Caribbean and in this instance Cuba.

> In Cuba,
> Black Melchior caresses the cobra.
> Dahomey dance   Havana Boa
> This Python, sacred serpent of Delphi,
> this Pythia, stretching the dark corners,
> dark herself, caught in darkness,
> sees the fat sin burned on the island.
>
> Upon a Day of Kings,
> these women dressed in white
> group themselves and pirouette
> and become my dawn,
>   my sun,
>   my dawn,
>   my earth,
>   my lamb,
>   my buzzard,
>   my butterfly.
> I live this day through them,
> counting no clock time
> but the blood's time,
> the gentle rise and fall
>   of a donu bird's wings.
> I assert that I am twinned to your light within. (DH, 32)

Wright's invocation of the "Día de Reyes" (the Day of Kings) is vital to this passage. Tellingly, a connection with my previous quotation is already established through the conspicuous recurrence of the textual gap: "Dahomey dance Havana Boa." The significance of the "Día de Reyes" lies in the fact, as Fernando Ortiz has demonstrated, that it was an important ritual during slavery in Cuba, as well as in Brazil.[93] On this day, the black slaves were allowed to act out their desire to be free and symbolically to return to their motherland. Each *cabildo* ("nation," or regional culture group) elected a king for a day and marched, dancing, to their masters' house to request a Christmas bonus. The "Día de Reyes," traditionally celebrated on the day of the Epiphany, was a syncretic ritual, in which the Three Magi (among them, of course, Black Melchior) represented the various groups that make up Cuban culture.[94] The copresence in the above citation of Dahomey, Havana, and Delphi is suggestive of such a syncretism. Commenting on this cultural phenomenon in an essay on Carpentier's *Explosion in a Cathedral*, Gonzalez Echevarría states that "[the ritual's] force, its movement, is given by inversion, by a kind of *retruécano* in which Blacks assume power, even if only mock power, and freedom, even if only for a day, and a fake freedom at best. Neo-African culture in the Caribbean thus appears as a tropological process akin to the one seen as the language of the islands. African culture is the difference that generates, among many other modifications, the time warp, the whirl of dates and rituals, the new, 'deformed,' shape of history."[95]

The Afro-Cuban (and Afro-Brazilian) celebration of the "Día de Reyes" is a symbolic ritual of resistance to slavery that stands for the unsettling effects of black culture specifically on Latin America, but also on the New World as a whole. In *Dimensions of History*, as in Carpentier's *Explosion in a Cathedral*, the presence of this ritual creates a time warp: As the women in their white dresses "group themselves and pirouette," history is no longer measured according to "clock time," but instead becomes "the blood's time," a whirl(wind) of dates freed from chronology. This deformation of history brings about a new "dawn" (*amanecer!*), a fresh beginning at the meeting place of two cultures, the Spanish and the African.

Instances of this kind of ritual displacement and supplementation, which is a sort of cultural modulation, abound in *Dimensions of History*. My following examples are from part 2, "Modulations: The Aesthetic Dimension," and more particularly from the section entitled "Rhythms, Charts, and Changes." This section is fittingly introduced by a Bambara ritual signature announcing the beginning of a new creation (see fig. 2). This ideogram, which Wright also employs in *The Double Invention of*

Komo (55–56), is composed of "God's" immutable and permanent knife"
and "the whirlwind's hook," whose combination announces the fashioning
of a new order after the destruction of the world, from the chaos produced
by the whirlwind.[96]

Unlike the first part of *Dimensions of History*, which is divided into
three long sections, "Rhythms, Charts, and Changes" is composed of a
rapid succession of fourteen relatively brief poems, each of which derives
its title (and its cadence) from a particular musical or poetic form. In some
cases, Wright uses the names of individual musical instruments employed
in a specific dance or ceremony: "Teponaztli" is a pre-Columbian wooden
drum; "Atabaqué" is a set of drums used in the Afro-Brazilian ritual of
candomblé; "Bandola" is a small guitar employed in Caribbean folk music;
"Huehuetl" is a Mexican upright drum, as well as related to the
huehuetlatolli, an Aztec form of ritual speech;[97] "Pututu" is a Quechua
shell trumpet; and "Maracas," I believe, is self-explanatory.[98] The
important thing is that all these various instruments are peculiar to New
World cultures; their origins are, for the most part, Amerindian, Afro-
American, or Latin American. The same holds true for "Joropo," a
Venezuelan folk dance; "Lundú," a Brazilian folk dance held at harvest
celebrations; "Tamborito," a Panamanian-African dance; "Bambuco," a
dance form popular in Colombia and Venezuela; "Vela," a Dominican
semireligious service; "Son," a Cuban song form written in *romance* or
ballad lines;[99] and "Areíto," a *taíno* (Arawak) responsorial chant.
"Villancicos" are a form of fifteenth- and sixteenth-century Spanish verse,
but Wright's allusion is specifically to Sor Juana Inés de la Cruz, who
wrote some *villancicos* in black creole.[100] We need not examine in detail
every single one of the above poems to realize that "Rhythms, Charts, and
Changes" is a complex admixture of elements gathered together from the
different cultures present in the New World in order to "make one music
as before/but vaster," to recall the Tennysonian lines Du Bois cites in *The
Souls of Black Folk*.[101]

There is, however, one poem that is particularly representative of the
mixed cultural congregation evoked in this section of *Dimensions of History*:
Wright's version of the "Son de la Ma' Teodora," which appears as the
third "tuning" of his "Bandola."

> Má lover of god
> Má loved by god
> Má of the sun
> Má of the river

Má of the timber
Má of the wood
Má of the grief
Má Teodora
What source
is in your circle?
Why do you dance with the *palo codal*?
What itch constrains
your orisha limp?
Who is the simp
to arrange your fall?
Má Má Teodora
fifteen sinners
guide you through the berries
of your own exultation.
Fifteen lines and a stick
make a whip
to remind you of the grave.
Fifteen stones and a star
lift you to a cloud beyond my reach.
Má loved by god
you ride your flesh so surely
the gods within the flat drums
keep a tap
upon the earth. (*DH*, 43)

The original "Son," composed and performed by Teodora Ginés, a black Dominican, during the second half of the sixteenth century, goes like this:

—¿Dónde está la Ma' Teodora?
—Rajando la leña está.
—¿Con su palo y su bandola?
—Rajando la leña está.
—¿Dónde está que no la veo?
—Rajando la leña está.
Rajando la leña está.

[—Where is Ma' Teodora?
—She is splitting logs.
—With her staff and her bandola?

—She is splitting logs.
—Where is she that I can't see her?
—She is splitting logs.
She is splitting logs.][102]

Weaving features from Spanish, African, and *taíno* cultures into a responsorial structure that emphasizes the ritualistic aspect of this performance, the "Son de la Má Teodora" is a powerful pretext of Wright's poetic tapestry. Gonzalez Echevarría's comments are particularly relevant to Wright's rewriting of the "Son de la Má Teodora."

> The responsorial structure of the "Son" and the ritual that it evokes are not only African, but also *taíno*. The singing and dancing of Teodora's song is an *areíto*, a *taíno* celebration whose name suggestively means "to dance while remembering," or "dancing to remember." Dancing is a way of keeping the past— tradition, heritage, culture—alive. We can assume from the "Ma'" that Teodora is not only a mother, but also old. She embodies tradition. When she asks, "Where is Ma' Teodora?" she is asking, "Where is tradition?" The mock pursuit of Ma' Teodora is a pursuit of tradition, a spell against its vanishing. Teodora is memory incarnate. The jubilation at the end is the intoxicating recovery of tradition, an immersion in a rhythm that is primordial, that keeps time.[103]

Wright's Má Teodora certainly *keeps time*, and not just by rhythmically *tapping* her African staff (*polo*) on the ground while she dances. More to the point, the rhythm generated by her tapping is an articulation of the thoughts of "the gods within the flat drums," who, like Teodora herself, "keep a tap/upon the earth." Má Teodora is a *keeper* of the rhythm and the music of tradition, of the "language" of those gods in the drums. But this rhythm differs from that of the original "Son." Not only does Wright alter the basic responsorial structure of the *son/areíto* form, he also invests the original figure of Má Teodora with a variety of new, supplementary features, whose enumeration follows the form of Catholic litany. The "constrained orisha limp" associates her with *Eshu-Elegba*, the Yoruba deity who guards the crossroads, while the epitaph "Má of the river" identifies her as Ochún, the Afro-Cuban goddess of the calm waters, who, in turn, is associated with the Virgen de la Caridad del Cobre, the patron saint of Cuba.[104] "Má of the timber" and "Má of the wood," in addition to alluding to "Rajando la leña está," also evokes the image of a carved wooden mask of the kind that is used in a variety of different African divination ceremonies. "Má of the grief," furthermore, stresses that Wright's Teodora, like her original counterpart, is not a "young mother" who has yet to learn "the meaning of another death" (*DH*, 14), but is someone who knows and understands dispossession, that is, the lessons of slavery ("Fifteen lines and a stick/make a whip") as well as the meaning of kinship. Clearly, Má Teodora is the female counterpart of the Dogon sage Ogotemmêli.

Last but not least, we must notice the change from "palo" (staff, stick) to "palo codal," the latter being, as Wright himself explains, a stick hung around the neck as a penance. This alteration is of considerable interest because it evokes a famous figure in Latin American literature: Juan Rodríguez Freyle's Juana García, who appears in *El carnero* (1638). Juana García is the prototype of the black sorceress. At the end of her story, which has been widely anthologized as "Las brujerías de Juana García" or "Un negocio con Juana García," she is punished for her magic transgressions by the Chief Inquisitor of Santafé de Bogotá: Her sentence condemns her to standing on a raised platform with a lighted candle in her hand and a *halter* around her neck.[105] The final image we glimpse of Juana García is suggestive of Wright's Má Teodora, whose "palo codal" signals the ironic transformation of a sign of bondage (the halter) into an emblem of freedom.[106] The connection between Má Teodora and Juana García adds another dimension to the figure of this dancer: Teodora, like Juana García, is "una negra un poco voladora," a kind of sorceress, or to be more precise, someone who has the power to heal and to "fly," that is, to achieve an "angle of ascent" in Hayden's sense. As the embodiment of tradition, Teodora has the ability to heal the wounds of exile by creating, in the form of her "Son" (her own Black limbo), a vital image of a new community, that of the "Orphans of the earth" (*DH*, 52), congregating at the crossroads. These crossroads are a symbolic place of exchange and transformation, which is the inside of Má Teodora's "circle," the "source" of Hispanic Caribbean literature.

> My life
> is in the middle of this dance.
> My heart unfolds
> to accept this cross,
> the stone of our customary light. (*DH*, 62)

The "Son de la Ma' Teodora," like Benjamin Banneker's letter to Thomas Jefferson, is another founding fable of New World culture and writing, another "bead" to be added to the poet's "rosary."

III

> I felt, Sire, as if I were going mad: the compass of my mind had lost its directional needle, my identities were spilling over and multiplying beyond all contact with minimal human reason.
> —CARLOS FUENTES, *Terra Nostra*

Symbolic places of cultural exchange and transformation, of simultaneous deracination and supplementation, abound in Wright's poetry, and many other examples could be cited. More important, however, than any diligent accumulation of additional textual evidence is the fact that Wright frequently associates those historico-cultural spaces with a very specific kind of landscape: that of the city. It is not coincidental, for instance, that Afro-Cuban culture, the realm to which both the "Día de Reyes" and the "Son de la Má Teodora" belong, is, as Fernando Ortiz and others have shown, a predominantly urban phenomenon.[107] In addition, I have already commented, in my introductory discussion of the Benjamin Banneker poems, on the significance of Wright's trope of the city with respect to the foundations of New World culture. It is now necessary to elaborate a broader context for that trope in order to show how and why the founding of cities plays such a major role in *Dimensions of History*.

As Albert William Levi has pointed out in his remarks on Goethe's and Thomas Mann's notion of the *Weltstadt* or *Kulturstadt*, "the city is an *artifact set within nature*, but *not of it*; in short, a work of art, mind taking shape, at once a symbol of physical accommodation and spiritual destiny."[108] In other words, the city is a cultural (as opposed to a natural) landscape, or what Thomas Mann called a "geistige Lebensform" (Levi renders it as "spiritual way of life"), whose artful organization of space suggests a "distinctive metaphysics of order" or disorder, as the case may be. The city has its own peculiar discourse, a kind of body language, which is at once historical and mythical. Wright regards the city as a charged field, constituted by a series of symbolic acts that make up the ritual of founding. What exactly those symbolic acts are and how they manifest themselves in a given language can best be observed in the following quotation from Vico's *The New Science*, which will help us determine the elements that come together in Wright's concept of the city as a figure for ritualistic coherence.

> Even the philologists say the walls were traced by the founders of the cities with the plough, the moldboard of which ... must have been first called *urbs*, whence the ancient *urbum*, curved. Perhaps *orbis* is from the same origin, so that at first *orbis terrae* must have meant any fence made in this way, so low that Remus jumped over it to be killed by Romulus and thus, as Latin historians narrate, to consecrate with his blood the first walls of Rome. Such a fence must evidently have been a hedge (*siepe*) (and among the Greeks *seps* signifies "serpent" in its heroic meaning of cultivated land), from which origin must come *munere viam*, to build a road, which is done by strengthening the hedges around the fields. Hence walls are called *moenia*, as if for *munia*, and certainly *munire* kept the sense of fortifying. The hedges must have been of those plants the Latin call *sagmina*, bloodwort or elder, whose use and name still survive. The name *sagmina* as preserved in the sense of the herbs with which the altars were adorned; it must have come from the blood (*sanguis*) of the slain, who, like Remus, had transgressed them. Hence the so-called sanctity of walls.[109]

This passage contains a cluster of familiar images which make it possible to establish a clear connection between the ritual of founding a city and the excision or circumcision ritual. This connection is vital to Wright's concept of culture and to his perception of the origins of culture in language and in writing.

To found a city is an act of cultivation (from the Latin *colere*) in the sense of cutting the earth with a plough, thus inscribing upon its surface the insignia of human presence. The plough traces the outlines of the city-to-be and thus creates the semblance of a *map* or *charter*, setting down the fundamental laws of the land in accordance with its actual physical boundaries. This initial gesture of breaking the ground already implies, as Vico suggests, an element of ritual sacrifice: The consecration of the first walls of Rome with the blood of Remus is a kind of fortification represented by the bloodwort hedge, whose roots with their red coloring substance penetrate and saturate the soil like the blood of the slain victim. The sacrificial shedding of blood at the very place where the earth has been symbolically and actually "wounded" is an act of cultivation, which also highlights the religious meaning of *colere*: to honor with worship, to protect, which developed etymologically through the Latin *cultus* to the English *cult*. In much the same way that the blood strengthens the foundations of the city, that is, its walls, it reinforces, in another sense, the collective religious beliefs of the community of founders, the "cult." In this sense, the city's walls are like altars, and each symbolic slaying carried out on that spot is a reenactment of that initial ceremonial cut of the plough into the earth. For Wright, as we have seen, the reopening of that fundamental wound is a ritual of kinship.

The link between the cultivation of the land, the founding of ancient cities, and the raising of altars is further supported by Vico's observation that the heroic cities of the Romans were initially "called *arae*, altars, and *acres*, fortresses."[110] To clarify the connection between Vico's philological observations and Wright's poetry, it is necessary at this point to make a leap from *The New Science* to Dogon religious mythology, specifically to Griaule's *Conversations with Ogotemmêli*. Such a leap is justified because Ogotemmêli's remarks about the significance of altars and ritual sacrifice among the Dogon enhance Vico's etymologies in startling ways.

> On the altar the virtue of new, fresh, blood combines with what has been left there by a long series of ritual [killings]: for the altar is a storehouse of forces, of which man draws at the appropriate time, and which he keeps constantly fed. It is also the point of contact between man and the Invisible.... The Dogon word for sacrifice does in fact come from a root which means to "renew life." ... "The altar gives something to a man, and a part of what he has received he passes on to others, said Ogotemmêli, "A small part of the sacrifice is for oneself, but the rest is for others. The forces released enter into man, pass through him and out again, and so it is for all...." As each man gives to all the rest, so he also receives from all. A perpetual exchange goes on between men, an unceasing movement of invisible currents.[111]

Seen in relation to Vico's comments, Ogotemmêli's (and Griaule's) explanations help us apprehend the altar as a symbolic locus of cultivation. The place it marks is one characterized by perpetual communal exchange, a process kept alive through sacrifice as reenactment of the breaking of the ground with the ploughshare. The altar is thus a figure that demarcates the point of transition from nature to culture. Ogotemmêli also points out that "the shedding of the blood in circumcision ... is like the offering of a victim on the altar, and it is the earth that drinks the blood."[112] Like the ritual knife, the altar represents a process of simultaneous destruction and fertilization: The creation of culture requires a violation of nature, and sacrifice is necessary to atone for that violation. But sacrifice is also a form of supplementation: The blood of the slain victim flows back to the wounded earth; it purifies and heals the cut of the ploughshare, which is thus transformed into a kind of scar, signifying the perfection of nature through human grace.

If we recall that this cut-turned-into-scar is a figure of writing, then it may be said that this "perfection" of nature is achieved through the "grace" of language. It follows, then, that culture is the act of perfecting (and supplementing) nature through language, and that the artifact set within nature but not of it, as Levi describes the city, is something created by acts of language. Culture, in short, is a way of imparting language ("the Word," as the Dogon have it) to nature. This idea may be carried even further to reveal the vital connection between culture and *poiêsis*, as Jay Wright himself endeavors in the following citation from "Desire's Design, Vision's Resonance." "*Poiêsis* is not exhausted," he argues, "in the relatively subordinate act of giving a name to some thing. It goes beyond that into real power, that of transformation and action. [Kenneth] Burke clarifies this when he says, there is a sense in which language is not just 'natural,' but really *does* add a 'new dimension' to the things of nature (an observation that would be the logological equivalent of the theological statement that grace perfects nature)."[113] Language adds something to nature; it transforms it by first creating a necessary deficiency—the cut that widens into the blank textual space—which is immediately supplemented by the manifestations of that new dimension, those fundamental scars that grow into altars and city walls. This notion of supplementarity as it defines the relationship between nature and culture inevitably returns us to the relationship between myth and history as well as to Roland Barthes's concept of an artificial, or what I have termed synthetic, myth. A synthetic myth in Wright's sense is a founding fable that evolves from the simultaneous decomposition and supplementation of the classical mythologies of the Old Worlds, meaning Africa and Europe, as they meet again in the New World.

But the New World is more than just a setting that frames the renewed encounter of Europe with Africa. Wright does not regard the pre-Columbian Americas as an environment completely untouched by civilization. This is already quite evident in his version of the "Son de la

Ma' Teodora." We may even go so far as to say that for Wright the destruction of the ancient civilizations that prospered in the New World long before the first Spaniards landed on its shores is an episode in world history equivalent in significance to the decline of the Roman Empire during the first half of the fifth century. While this analogy is valuable to the extent that it restores to those pre-Columbian cultures their proper status within the context of New World cultural history, it does not form a valid basis for assuming that therefore New World history could be divided into periods roughly corresponding in their historical sequence to European antiquity, the Middle Ages, the Renaissance, and so forth, all compressed into the relatively brief span of approximately five centuries. This is clearly not the case. Moreover, such a linear view of history would remain oblivious to a most decisive factor in New World cultural history, one that clearly distinguishes New World history and culture from its European counterparts: This factor is the time warp, brought about by the copresence of what is generally regarded as separate historical periods. To turn the linear phenomenon we call American history into New World history, it is necessary to transform a diachronic into a synchronic system. We must understand that we are confronted with a historical field, where the Spanish Middle Ages and the Italian Renaissance move side by side, and hand in hand, with the French Enlightenment and the modern age, and where the sounds of the Industrial Revolution mingle freely with Quechua and Náhuatl songs as well as with the compelling rhythms of Yoruba and Ashanti drums, echoes from cultures older than Rome and Greece.

Octavio Paz has argued that "[Spanish Americans] are children of the counter-reformation and the Universal Kingdom; [the Anglo-Saxons] are children of Luther and the Industrial Revolution."[114] This may be true enough, but the value of such an astute observation decreases considerably once it is used to reinstate, albeit surreptitiously, the kind of cultural nationalism Paz himself condemns, in the very same essay, as "a moral aberration" and an "aesthetic fallacy."[115] It seems to have slipped his memory that O'Gorman, in *The Invention of America*, appealed to a similar distinction to explain the alleged superiority of Anglo-American civilization over that of its Latin American neighbors. The point, which both Paz and O'Gorman appear to miss at least in part, is not to substitute different historical origins for some pseudoscientific theory of race (as O'Gorman does) but to realize that the totality of these different historical origins, as well as their peculiar simultaneity, is what constitutes the true cultural legacy of the New World writer. Gabriel García Marquez has made that point brilliantly in *One Hundred Years of Solitude*, and this may well be at least part of the reason for the tremendous success this novel has enjoyed. Jay Wright makes the same point, differently but no less brilliantly, in *Dimensions of History* and offers it as "an initiate's fertile/and uneasy/resolution" (*DI* 56).

If New World history is comprehended not simply as a chronology but instead as a space where all previous historical periods also coexist, then it becomes clear that a New World mythology in Wright's sense can draw from an almost inexhaustible and incredibly diverse reservoir, of which Europe's classical myths are only a relatively small part.[116] For Wright, the most important thing is the way in which different myths interact within the context of New World history and how that process of interaction and transformation gives rise to authentic founding fables. The following long citation from *Dimensions of History*, which returns us to the figure of the city as a cultural landscape, is an excellent case in point.

> So Nuño de Guzmán, governor of New Spain,
> employs Tejo, the trader,
> trader of gold and silver,
> bearer of the tales of the Seven Cities.
> Weary at Culiacán,
> he finds four sailors,
> lost in the search for the flowered
> end of things.
> Now, the friar takes the slave
> into the valley, and sends him on above.
> Send me a cross as big as my hands,
> if the land is good.
> If it challenges our new mother,
> send a cross larger than that.
> A day   two days   four,
> and a cross "as tall as a man"
> mysteries of Seven Great Cities
> under the Black man's eyes.
> Following God's candles
> further than the friar will go,
> your light breaks down at Hawikúh.
> Estevan Stephen
> carrying your own stone

into the valley,
victim again of your services,
you lie at the gate of the Seven Cities.
Who will trim your hair and pair your nails
to send your sunsum home?
What sister will shave her hair for your soul?
The friar never approaches the gate.
He stands elevated long enough
to set a cross for Spain.

At that point,
each day, the young priest appears.
He wears the crescent moon embossed
with sun, moon and stars.
He would set the bowl in the friar's tree.
Your 'Nyame dua, father.
Your shrine not anywhere but here.

Friar and the crowned return,
the plumed and mailed blessed ones
search for the gate again.
This is the gate of gold
Gao   Guinea   Hawikúh.
But there is no gold,
only the whisper of the wind
fluting the Black man's liberated bones.

    Into this sound,
    tracking highways, you come.
    Cold morning's return out of the desert.
    Cold metal search in the Golden State
    to return, enchanted again at the gate.
    Not gold. Not the cities' magnificence.
    What the others left at the gate
    you found within, extended,
        "a gateway to the beautiful." (*DH*, 28–29)

Wright offers in this passage his own poetic version of the history of
Hawikúh, a large Zuñi pueblo whose ruins are located in the northern
region of today's New Mexico. Given that Wright himself was born in

Albuquerque, it is not surprising that the history of New Mexico should hold a special significance for him. But above and beyond any personal memories that may resound in the above lines, it ought to be noted that Hawikúh is an important, though neglected, landmark in early American history. Believed to be one of the so-called "Seven Cities of Cíbola" and reputed to be rich in gold and silver, Hawikúh was the prime motivation behind a series of expeditions organized by various Spanish explorers during the first half of the sixteenth century. Nuño de Guzmán, governor of New Spain from 1528 to 1536, was the first to embark, in 1529, on such an exploratory voyage, inspired by the tales of his Indian slave Tejo. The journey, which lasted for two years, was a failure to the extent that the Spaniard did not succeed in locating the mysterious Seven Cities. It did, however, result in the founding of the city of Culiacán, the present capital of the Mexican province of Sinaloa, which then served as a base for conducting slave raids in that area.[117]

Culiacán was also the place reached in 1536 by four members of another expedition, described in detail in the *Relation que dió Alvar Núñez Cabeza de Vaca de la jornada que hico a la Florida* (1542). Cabeza de Vaca and his three companions, among them the black slave Estevan, were the only survivors of an expedition that had initially consisted of four hundred men, who had landed on the west coast of Florida in 1528, whence they turned north in search of El Dorado, "the flowered end of things." The journey failed miserably, and the disappointed Spaniards returned to the Gulf of Mexico, where they constructed several boats, hoping to sail in them along the coastline toward Mexico. Most were killed in a shipwreck, and the few survivors were enslaved by the Indians. Cabeza de Vaca and his three companions managed to escape and traveled on foot across the continent for six years until they reached the province of Sinaloa. During those years, they lived among various Indian tribes, rendering services as healers, so that by the time they arrived in Culiacán, they had literally been stripped of everything that would distinguish a white man from an Indian.[118] The reports of their impressive voyage across the North American continent reinforced the legend of the Seven Cities of Cíbola, and two other expeditions were outfitted, one in 1538 and the other in 1539. Very little is known of the former, but the second one, headed by Fray Marcos de Niza and including, among others, the black Estevan, is what attracted Wright's attention. Fray Marcos, it may be worth adding, had been in Peru at the time when Pizarro looted the Inca treasure and was thus quite susceptible to tales of gold. Having reached the village of Vapaca, Fray Marcos dispatched Estevan toward

the north fifty or sixty leagues to see if by that route he would
be able to learn of any great thing such as we sought and I
agreed with him that if he received any information of a rich,
peopled land that was something great, he should go no farther,
but that he return in person or send me Indians with this signal,
which we arranged: if the thing was of moderate importance, he
send me a white cross the size of a hand; if it was something
great, he send me one of two hands; and if it was something
bigger and better than New Spain ["our new mother"], he send
me a large cross.[119]

Four days later, Estevan's messenger returned with a cross "as tall as a
man" and a message that he had secured information about "the greatest
thing in the world." After the arrival of messengers with a second cross of
the same size as the first one a few days later, the friar hurried after
Estevan, who had disobeyed his instructions and proceeded to enter
Cíbola. When Fray Marcos finally reached the vicinity of Hawikúh, he
was informed that Estevan had been killed by the inhabitants of that city.

The accounts of Estevan's death and the reasons projected for his
murder vary substantially. The following is taken for a letter by Hernando
de Alarcón, who explored the region of the lower Colorado River in 1540.

Your lordship will remember that the negro who accompanied
Fray Marcos had rattles (bells), and feathers on his arms and
legs; that he had plates of different colors, and that he came to
this country a little more than a year ago. I wished to know why
he had been killed. He [the Indian informant] said: "The chief
of Cevola having asked him whether he had other brethren, the
negro replied that he had an infinite number, that they carried
many weapons and were not very far off. Upon this statement a
great many chiefs gathered in council, and agreed on killing the
negro, so that he might not impart any information to his
brethren in regard to the country of Cevola. Such was the cause
of his death. His body was cut into a great many pieces, which
were distributed among all the chiefs, in order that they might
know that he was surely dead."[120]

Having learned of Estevan's violent death, Fray Marcos decided not to
enter Hawikúh, as he was not prepared to fight with the resident Indians.
Instead, he took possession of the region of Cíbola in the name of Spain

by raising a pile of stone and placing on it a wooden cross. He named the new land the "New Kingdom of Saint Francis." Although he claimed in his report to the Spanish emperor that he actually saw Hawikúh, later historians have, for good reason, doubted the truthfulness of that claim.[121] Hawikúh was "officially" discovered and conquered in 1540 by Francisco Vasquez de Coronado, who named the city Granada.[122] However, no substantial amounts of gold were ever found in that region.

My rather lengthy narrative of the history of Cíbola-Hawikúh-Granada is not intended as a substitute for a reading of the above citation from *Dimensions of History*. It is, however, necessary to be at least somewhat acquainted with the main historical facts and fictions that cluster around the legend of the Seven Cities of Cíbola to understand what exactly Wright is doing in that passage. For what we witness in his poetic version of the history of Hawikúh is a series of displacements and supplementations, whose significance would remain largely incomprehensible outside of this historical context.

To begin with, the conception itself of the Seven Cities of Cíbola is already the result of a displacement brought about by the discovery of the New World. The original legend of the "Septe citate" can be traced back at least as far as the years of the Arabic conquest of the Spanish peninsula, and probably even farther to the ancient tales of the Atlantic isles. Interestingly enough, the contemporary source of that legend is itself a tale of exile and thus of displacement: The "Septe citate," at the time identified with the mysterious islands of Antilia, were presumed to be inhabited by a Portuguese archbishop, six other bishops, and a number of Christians, who had sailed there from Spain in 714 to escape the Moorish invasion. Consequently, the Seven Cities were believed to be a place where Hispanic civilization had been preserved in a state of relative purity.[123] Later on, the Island of the Seven Cities became associated with a variety of unknown Atlantic isles, and the discovery of the New World even inspired cartographers to assign it different places on the maps of the American continent. Ultimately, the elusive Seven Cities became localized as the Seven Cities of Cíbola: The Iberian legend had been transformed into a distinct New World fable, a transformation set in motion largely by the tales of the Indian trader Tejo.

For Wright, this transformation is significant far beyond its contemporary historical context. The fable of the Seven Cities of Cíbola constitutes a syncretism at the meeting place of two cultures; the Spanish, as represented by Nuño de Guzmán, and the Indian, as represented by Tejo. A configuration of ideas generated as the result of the contact and verbal interaction between Guzmán and Tejo, the fable of the Seven Cities of Cíbola is paradigmatic of the kind of cultural exchange and collaboration with which Wright charges the figure of the city. Regardless of its actual existence, Hawikúh in its fabulous manifestation is projected here as a figure for the dwelling-place, in Américo Castro's sense, of New World culture. This notion of syncretism is reinforced by Wright's allusion to Cabeza de Vaca, whose 1542 travelogue is, next to the Inca Garcilaso de la Vega's tale of Pedro Serrano, perhaps the most notable account of the kinds of visible deracination and denuding some of the conquistadors experienced in the New World.[124] Cabeza de Vaca's *relación* is a remarkable work because at a time when the Spanish were engaged in a large-scale destruction of Indian cultures all over the New World, it admits to the possibility of *mutual* cultural exchange between Europeans and Indians, as well as between Indians and Blacks, as the example of Estevan shows.[125] If we are to believe Alarcón's report, Estevan was actually bearing the marks left by his former life among the Indians in the form of those feathers and rattles that adorned his body and probably identified him as a kind of healer.

It is not too surprising that Wright should consider the story of Estevan's death at Hawikúh as the most significant dimension of the legend of the Seven Cities of Cíbola. To be sure, the mere fact that a black man was to discover the first "city" on the North American continent is quite sufficient to accord his story the status of a founding fable equal in importance to Benjamin Banneker's participation in the founding of the United States capital. But there is more to the "mysteries of Seven Great Cities/under the Black man's eyes." In a way, we are again accompanying Wright's poet on another walk across a graveyard: The cross Estevan sends to the friar, a cross "as tall as a man," is one that comes to mark his own grave, that is, the place of his death. It reappears, in the second stanza, as the cross Fray Marcos set for Spain, only to be even further transfigured into "the friar's tree" and finally into "'Nyame dua" [God's tree], the triadic altar of the Akan.[126] But most compelling about this transfiguration is that the "young priest," who is said to appear at that point every day, wears the insignia of Thoth, the Egyptian god of learning, writing, and medicine: "He wears the crescent moon embossed/with sun, moon and stars." This most curious aggregation of figures in that quotation's third stanza is the key to the founding fable Wright elaborates.

The appearance of Thoth, the Master of the books and the "scribe of truth," in the very place where the friar, according to his own fictionalized narrative, had erected a cross to take possession of the land consecrated with the blood of Estevan openly announces a transition from the realm of history to that of myth. The figure of Thoth opens up another interpretive dimension, which becomes evident once we look more closely at the characteristics ascribed to that god in Egyptian mythology. Derrida has carefully examined Thoth's attributes in "Plato's Pharmacy," and his findings are quite relevant here.

> In all the cycles of Egyptian mythology, Thoth presides over the organization of death. The master of writing, numbers, and calculation does not merely write down the weight of the dead souls; he first counts out the days of life, *enumerates* history. His arithmetic thus covers the events of divine biography. He is "the one who measures the length of the lives of gods and men." He behaves like a chief of funeral protocol, charged in particular with the dressing of the dead .... This god of resurrection is less interested in life or death than in death as a repetition of life and life as a rehearsal of death, in the awakening of life and in the recommencement of death. This is what *numbers*, of which he is also the inventor and patron, mean. Thoth repeats everything in the addition of the supplement: in adding to and doubling as the sun, he is other than the sun [he is the moon] and the same as it; ... Always taking a place not his own, a place one could call that of the dead or the dummy, he has neither a proper place nor a proper name. His propriety or property is impropriety or inappropriateness, the floating indetermination that allows for substitution and play .... He would be the mediating movement of dialectics if he did not also mimic it, indefinitely preventing it, through his ironic doubling, from reaching some final fulfillment or eschatological reappropriation. Thoth is never present. Nowhere does he appear in person. No being-there can properly be *his own*.[127]

Thoth is a figure for the process of supplementation that Wright engages in this passage. Charged with the dressing of the dead, Thoth is the one who administers Estevan's funeral rites: "Who will trim your hair and pare your nails/to send your sunsum home?" But he also takes the place of Estevan and sets in motion a fascinating play of doublings and substitutions, reincarnating Estevan in a variety of forms and figures and thus preventing his death from bringing about closure. "Estevan

Stephen." It is no coincidence that we should once again encounter this textual gap, signifying in this case the presence (or rather, the absence) of Thoth, who occupies the locus of substitution and supplementarity. It is in that spot that Estevan, the discoverer of Hawikúh, is reincarnated as Carpentier's Esteban in *Explosion in a Cathedral*, Miguel Barnet's Esteban Montejo in *The Autobiography of a Runaway Slave* (1966), and, last but not least, as Joyce's Stephen Dedalus in *A Portrait of the Artist as a Young Man*. That Joyce also evokes Thoth in connection with Stephen Dedalus, a character to which especially Carpentier's Esteban is indebted, further strengthens the link between these figures: "A sense of fear of the unknown moved in the heart of his [Stephen Dedalus's] weariness, a fear of symbols and portents, of the hawk-like man whose name he bore soaring out of his captivity on osier-woven wings, of Thoth, the god of writers, writing with a reed upon a tablet and bearing in his narrow ibis head the cusped moon."[128] That Thoth is also the inventor and patron of numbers alerts us to the textual presence of another mythological being, who is equally entrusted with language: Nummo (or Nommo), the seventh ancestor of the Dogon, who, like Thoth, is the master of the Word.[129] In Dogon mythology, Nommo is represented by the number seven, which appears, in the context of *Dimensions of History*, not only in the *Seven Cities*, but also in the line that represents Estevan's journey to Hawikúh: "A day two days four." The number of days mentioned (four) plus the number of phrases that constitute this line (three) yield another seven, while the textual blanks continue to insinuate the ambiguous presence of Thoth, the absent one, who acts as a catalyst for this play of numbers. Incidentally, the stanza in which Thoth appears in the form of a young priest is the only one in this passage that has seven lines.

Let us look more closely at the mythological significance of that number seven as related by Ogotemmêli.

> The seventh in a series ... represents perfection. Though equal in quality with the others, he is the sum of the feminine element, which is four, and the masculine element, which is three. He is thus the completion of the perfect series, symbol of the total unity of male and female.... And to this homogeneous whole belongs especially the mastery of words, that is, of language.... The others equally possessed the knowledge of these words ..., but they had not attained the mastery of them nor was it given to them to develop their use. What the seventh ancestor had received, therefore, was the perfect knowledge of

a Word—the second Word to be heard on earth, clearer than the first and not, like the first, reserved for particular recipients [the Spirits], but destined for all mankind.[130]

Like Thoth, the seventh Nommo is the author of the second (and secondary) Word. As interpreter of the language of the Spirits (the first Word), he is also the one who introduces difference into language.[131] This difference is the result of the mediation he performs between the realm of the Spirits and that of man, between the living and the dead. Although this Nommo is not directly identified as a scribe, the tale of how he invented the second Word is cast in metaphors strongly suggestive of the act of writing:

At sunrise of the appointed day the seventh ancestor Spirit spat out eighty threads of cotton; these he distributed between his upper teeth which acted as the teeth of a weaver's reed. In this way he made the uneven threads of a warp. He did the same with the lower teeth to make the even threads. By opening and shutting his jaws the Spirit caused the threads of the warp to make the movements required in weaving. The whole face took part in the work, his nose studs serving as the block, while the stud in his lower lip was the shuttle. As the threads crossed and uncrossed, the two tips of the Spirit's forked tongue pushed the thread of the weft to and fro, and the web took shape from his mouth in the breath of the second revealed Word. For the Spirit was speaking while the work proceeded. As did the Nummo in the first revelation, he imparted his word by means of a technical process, so that all men could understand. By doing so he showed the identities of material actions and spiritual forms, or rather the need for their cooperation.[132]

I have mentioned earlier that weaving is one of Wright's foremost figures of writing, one that is of particular significance in his "Second Conversations with Ogotemmêli" in *Soothsayers and Omens*. That there is a close metaphorical resemblance between a woven cloth and a written text is obvious enough, but the link between weaving and writing goes even farther than that and returns us to what I have called the "language" of the city as a cultural landscape. For, as Ogotemmêli also remarks,

The old method of cultivation ... is like weaving.... If a man clears ground and makes a new square lot and builds a dwelling on the plot, his work is like weaving a clot. Moreover, weaving is a form of speech, which is imparted to the fabric by the to-and-fro movement of the shuttle on the warp; and in the same way the to-and-fro movement of the peasant on his plot imparts the Word of the ancestors ... to the ground on which he works, and thus rids the earth of impurity and extends the area of cultivation round inhabited places. But, if cultivation is a form of weaving, it is equally true to say that weaving is a form of cultivation.... The finished web is the symbol of the cultivated field.[133]

The breaking of the ground, then, is clearly a form of writing. It is a process that transforms the natural landscape into a cultural and cultivated landscape, the city, and thus constitutes an act of founding. With regard to the quotation from *Dimensions of History*, which still remains the focal point of my discussion, it is important that the slaying of Estevan symbolically reenacts that fundamental process of cultivation. Estevan's blood fortifies the gate of the Seven Cities, but, more importantly, it mediates between the history of Hawikúh, the myth of the Seven Cities of Cíbola, and the poet who explores the ruins of both. These traces of blood can be said to render the ruins legible; because of them, the ruins of Hawikúh are "enchanted" by "the whisper of the wind/fluting the Black man's liberated bones." Wright's figure of the desert wind fluting Estevan's bones stands for a kind of metaphoric symphony, or transference of spirit, which is also related to the cannibal bone-flute of the Caribs in a way that Wilson Harris's following remarks elucidate: "In the Bone or flute [of the Caribs] is implicit the skeleton wall of a cruel age—the fissures or cracks in the mind or shell of conquest. That shell is no longer the seat of an absolute proprietorship of the globe but is converted into an *organ of memory* through which to sound the invocation of resensitized perspectives of community as a warning against plastering over afresh the mind or shell of empire into a recurring monolith or callous."[134] As a historico-mythical event, Estevan's death produces such fissures or cracks in the text of the poem, openings that make it possible for both poet and reader to penetrate the Procrustean surface of American Culture and sound the mysterious depths of New World (cross-)cultural interaction.

Wright's poet, this postmodern chronicler of the cultural history of the New World, searches not for gold, as the conquistadors did, but for a "gateway to the beautiful." This gateway, or threshold, which extends in the cracks between "Gao Guinea Hawikúh," leads him and us to a locus of transformation where the black slave Estevan sits, liberated, in the company not only of his more immediate literary kin, the other Estebans, but also with Thoth and the seventh Nommo, at the shrine of the Akan god 'Nyame (or Onyame). According to Danquah, Onyame embodies "understanding and also ... extended reality .... he is a unification of all feeling towards being, and in that unity there is a union, a harmony or fruition of the artistic, a pleasing and articulate placidity, gateway to the beautiful."[135] As the textual fissures evolve into such a gateway, Wright's poetic tale of the Seven Cities contracts into an epic (and epiphanic) moment that loudly echoes a passage from *The Souls of Black Folk*, where Du Bois writes,

> I sit with Shakespeare and he winces not. Across the color line
> I move arm in arm with Balzac and Dumas, where smiling men
> and welcoming women glide in gilded halls. From out the caves
> of evening that swing between the strong-limbed earth and the
> tracery of the stars, I summon Aristotle and Aurelius and what
> soul I will, and they come all graciously with no scorn nor
> condescension. So, wed with truth, I dwell above the Veil. Is
> this the life you grudge us, O knightly America? ... Are you so
> afraid lest peering from this high Pisgah ... we sight the
> Promised Land?[136]

Wright's poet's "Promised Land," that dwelling place above the Veil, are the Seven Cities, a place located both within and outside of history, a place that is at once historical fact and myth. Hawikúh-Cíbola is like the inside of Má Teodora's circle: a place at the crossroads, where historical realities are transformed and extended. It is an "enchanted" place in that it is consecrated with the blood of Estevan in the same way that the walls of Rome were consecrated with the blood of Remus. The parallel between these two deaths lies in their ritual significance. Estevan's blood, like Remus's, nourishes the arid soil of the past; it adds to it another dimension: myth. In this sense, the black man's death may be regarded as another form of cultivation. While Estevan's life can be viewed as a process of turning myth into historical reality (of localizing the Seven Cities as the Seven Cities of Cíbola), his death reverses that process and brings about the transformation of that historical reality into a founding fable. This synthetic myth is both other than and the same as the original or originary myth(s) whose place it takes. Its function is not strictly to replace those myths but to displace them and, in the process, open up a space for itself.

To effect such a displacement is the ultimate purpose of Estevan's death, and this is precisely why Wright associates him with Thoth. Because of this association, Estevan's death itself becomes a figure of writing, of that ambiguous acquisition of literacy that subverts historical chronology and inaugurates a new order in the form of a new set of historical and mythological allegiances. Estevan, like Wright's initiate, is "bled/black, in the space/between the lines" (*DI*, 33) of the official chronicles of the history of New Mexico, the *relaciónes* written by Nuño de Guzmán, Cabeza de Vaca, Fray Marcos, and many others. These spaces, representing, as we have seen, deracination as well as plenitude, are the textual dwelling places of cultural exchange and transformation. They localize the play of differences (and of *différances*) on the cutting edge of New World culture.

The textual fissures also ensure the continuation of that play of differences beyond the text in the eyes of the reader and thus prevent the poem from freezing into the shape of an allegedly definitive meaning. The kinetic properties of *Dimensions of History* are best illustrated by the words of another apprentice: the Peruvian novelist and anthropologist José Maria Arguedas. These are the words of Arguedas's young protagonist as he *beholds* (in Stevens's sense) the remnants of the ancient Inca walls of Cuzco:

> The stones of the Inca wall were larger and stranger than I had imagined; they seemed to be bubbling up beneath the whitewashed second story .... Then I remembered the Quechua songs which continually repeat one pathetic phrase: *yawar mayu*, "bloody river"; *yaway unu*, "bloody water"; *puk'tik yawar k'ocha*, "bloody boiling lake"; *yaway wek'e*, "bloody tears." Couldn't one say *yawar rumi*, "bloody stone," or *puk'tik yawar rumi*, "boiling bloody stone"? The wall was stationary, but all its lines were seething and its surface was as changeable as that of the flowing summer rivers which have similar crests near the center, where the current flows the swiftest and is the most terrifying. The Indians call these muddy rivers *yawar mayu* because when the sun shines on them they seem to glisten like blood. They also call the most violent tempo of the war dances, the moment when the dancers are fighting, *yawar mayu*.[137]

The text(ure) of *Dimensions of History* is, in many respects, like that of the old Inca wall, whose ruins provided the foundations upon which the

Spaniards rebuilt Cuzco: The poem is stationary like a wall, but the pattern forming on its surface as the result of Wright's interweaving bloodlines from so many different sources is ever-changing. *To make a stone bleed* is an appropriate figure for investing what is generally considered an inanimate object with its history and to give it, as Lezama Lima would have it, new metaphorical strength.[138] In this regard, a bleeding stone is like a germinating seed. Arguedas's "bloody stone" also recalls the figure of the altar as a place characterized by the commingling of the blood of the living with that of the dead, that is, as a place of ritual exchange and revitalization. Wright visualizes the ruins of Hawikúh as such a place or space, but there are, as we will see shortly, many other stones on which his poet cuts his time. What Arguedas's protagonist finds in Cuzco, Wright's poet now experiences among the ruins of the Aztec city-states in Mexico.

> I lay my pyramids wall upon wall.
> The walls recall the war of Venus and Mars.
> Four days I sat without a sun.
> I build that darkness here.
> And at the top I place my sun god
> and his promise of the years.
> Fifty-two serpents wind the years
> around my knees. The walls contain me.
>
> And so, in fever, I walk the city's wall.
> In the Cathedral, I walk upon
> the distinguished dead.
> Marble, cal y canto, stone,
> cathedral born to Carlos Fifth.
> I name you Santa Catalina Alejandrina,
> I name you the Cathedral of Cartagena de Indias.
> Would the maimed one fill you with light?
> Would your Virgin and your Child fall from cedar?
> Mozarabic crowns of fragile silver
>   would become you. (*DH*, 98)

As Wright points out in the notes, the first stanza of this quotation draws heavily on Aztec (Náhua) mythology. More specifically, it explores the Náhua concept of time and history as manifest in the ancient *Leyenda de los Soles* [Legend of the Suns], which recounts the myth of the creation and subsequent destruction of the world at the end of each of four fifty-two-year cycles. According to Náhua chronology, fifty-two years constitute one century or age in world history.[139] The cataclysm at the end of each cycle is said to be the result of an ongoing struggle for supremacy among the four sons of Ometéotl, the god of duality and principal deity of the Náhuas. The Fifth Cycle of the Sun, presumed to be the present age, is characterized by a harmony between these contending gods, each of whom represents one of the four cosmic forces: earth, water, air, and fire. As long as this balance of forces, in which exactly thirteen years are allotted to each deity, remains undisturbed, the world will not be subject to another apocalypse.

The profound significance the Náhuas attributed to these cycles of creation, destruction, and reconstruction, on which their calendar is based, is also reflected in their architecture. The Aztec temple-pyramids constitute, in Wright's terminology, the "physical dimension" of Náhua historico-mythical thought. "I lay my pyramids wall upon wall" refers specifically to the fact that these temple-pyramids were built by superimposing new levels at the beginning of each fifty-two-year cycle. The same principle underlies Williams's big, square paragraphs in "The Destruction of Tenochtitlán." The best example of that architectural technique is the Pyramid of Tenayuca near Tenochtitlán, the ancient Aztec capital. Archaeologists have suggested that the huge double pyramid of Tenochtitlán, which was almost completely destroyed by Cortes and his men, had been built in the same manner.[140] Wright's allusions to Tenochtitlán are related to the above quotation from *Deep Rivers*: In the same way that modern Cuzco was built upon the ruins of the ancient Inca capital, Mexico City was erected on the former site of Tenochtitlán. Both cities constitute another wall or level superimposed on the previous ones to mark the end of one era and the beginning of another. For Wright, as for Williams, this architectonic phenomenon indicates the super-imposition of one culture upon another, a practice whose visible, physical results inadvertently bear witness to the surreptitious, and subversive, continuation of the Náhua tradition in modern Mexico.

That these "walls recall the war of Venus and Mars" opens our view onto another chapter in Náhua history as well as introduces another series of mythological dimensions. This line is not just a general reference to the above-mentioned struggle between the four gods or cosmic forces but points specifically to the conflict between Quetzalcóatl, the plumed serpent, and Huitzilopochtli, the Aztec God of War. The former is associated with Venus, the "Big Star,"[141] while the latter, who came to replace Quetzalcóatl and inaugurated a reign of bloodshed and warfare (the era of the so-called flowered wars), is frequently identified as the "Mexican Mars."[142] Huitzilopochtli was, in that sense, the eagle (the symbol of war) that "swallow[ed] a [plumed] serpent's heart" (*DH*, 99), which is, furthermore, an allusion to the practice of human sacrifice that escalated among the Aztecs during the reign of the War God and constituted the prime motivation behind the warfare with their neighbors. But there is more: It can be said that, after the mysterious disappearance of Quetzalcóatl, Tenochtitlán became the City of Mars, which is also the name for Rome in the *Aeneid*. Romulus and Remus were, of course, the twin sons of Mars whose city, founded by Romulus and consecrated with the blood of his brother, displaced Lavinium, the city founded by Aeneas, son of Venus. The link Wright establishes here between Rome and Tenochtitlán substantiates my earlier argument concerning the analogy between the decline of the Roman Empire and the destruction of the pre-Columbian cultures in the New World. Both events, almost exactly a millennium apart in conventional historical chronology, mark the beginning of a new era, of a new cycle, which is that of the Fifth Sun, figured here as "Carlos Fifth," who is Charles I of Spain, also known as Charles V of the Empire.

Given that Charles V was the emperor in whose name the conquistadors took possession of the overseas territories, Wright's mention of his name as well as his curious association with the cycle of the Fifth Sun is not surprising, particularly since the Aztecs had initially believed the Spaniard to be a reincarnation of Quetzalcóatl, sending his messengers to restore peace. The "cathedral born to Carlos Fifth" is situated in Santafé de Bogotá. The site for this first cathedral in the New Kingdom of Granada was staked out on the same day (6 August 1539) that Jiménez de Quesada, Nicolás Federmann, and Sebastián de Benalcázar founded Santafé de Bogotá in the name of the emperor. Rodriguez Freyle recounts this event in *El carnero*: "The city they baptized Santafé de Bogotá del Nuevo Reino de Granada: the Granada in tribute to the said Jiménez de Quesada, its first founder, who hailed from Granada in Spain, Santafé because in its setting it resembled the town of that name facing Granada, and Bogotá from its arising on the site of the *cacique*'s [the Indian chief's] retreat."[143] *El carnero* is relevant to our reading of Wright's text not only as a source book that details this and other incidents from the history of New Granada, today's Colombia. It is also the first history of New Granada, which was in addition written by an American (a *criollo*)— incidentally, around the same time that the second volume of the

Comentarios reales appeared in Spain. Both *El carnero* and the *Comentarios* deliberately deviate from the ideal of Renaissance historiography as practiced by the official Spanish court historians. They concentrate on those "spaces" between the lines that were filled, not with heroic deeds, but with stories of everyday events in the colonies; with details, in short, that were either not known to the official chroniclers or considered irrelevant by them. Among these tales in *El carnero* is the story of Juana García discussed earlier. It is this deviant, subversive mode of historiography that Wright's *Dimensions of History* shares with *El carnero*, which may indeed be described, among many other things, as a history of the lives of the "distinguished dead" who are buried in the Cathedral of Bogotá.

It is not without interest, nor entirely without irony, that Wright's poet should dedicate this cathedral to Saint Catherine of Alexandria— "Santa Catalina Alejandrina"—one of the first Christian martyrs decapitated by the Romans and venerated as the patron saint of philosophers, as well as name it "the Cathedral of Cartagena de Indias" in reference to one of the major colonial ports and early commercial centers in the New World. The significance of these names may be sought, and perhaps found, in the fact that the conquest of the New World was a joint venture of church and state, combining the missionary spirit of the Catholic church in Spain with the obsession of the Spanish Empire to enhance its "Mozarabic crowns of fragile silver" with the splendor of "gold and emeralds" from the New World. The "Mozarabic crowns" also evoke the Arabic elements that continued to influence Spanish architecture in the New World, specifically in New Granada (the old Granada with its famous Alhambra was the last Muslim stronghold on the Iberian Peninsula).

But the most remarkable part of the second stanza is the line "Marble, cal y canto, stone," which repeats the Nerudean thrust of "I lay my pyramids wall upon wall": "Piedra en piedra, el hombre, dónde estuve?" [Stone upon stone, and man, where was he?] Neruda exclaims in his *Heights of Macchu Picchu* (1945).[144] The following lines from the same poem constitute a sort of answer to this question, but, more importantly, they help us understand the full significance of the figure of the city as a coherent cultural landscape.

> Pero una permanencia de piedra y de palabra,
> la ciudad como un vaso se levantó en las manos
> de todos, vivos, muertos, callados, sostenidos

de tanta muerte, un muro, de tanta vida un golpe
de pétalos de piedra: la rosa permanente, la morada:
este arrecife andino de colonias glaciales.

Cuando la mano de color de arcilla
se convirtió en arcilla, y cuando los pequeños párpados se
cerraron
llenos de ásperos muros, poblado de castillos,
y cuando todo el hombre se enredó en su agujero,
quedó la exactitud enarbolada:
el alto sitio de la aurora humana:
la más alta vasija que contuvo el silencio:
una vida de piedra después de tantas vidas.

[Yet a permanence of stone and word,
the city like a bowl, rose up in the hands
of all, living, dead, silenced, sustained,
a wall out of so much death, out of so much life a shock
of stone petals, the permanent rose, the dwelling place:
the glacial outposts on this Andean reef.

When the clay-colored hand
turned to clay and the eyes' small lids fell shut,
filled with rugged walls, crowded with castles,
and when man lay all tangled in his hole,
there remained an upraised exactitude:
the high site of the human dawn:
the highest vessel that held silence in:
a life of stone after so many lives.][145]

Macchu Picchu, Cuzco, Tenochtitlán—lives of stone, stone petals, bloody stones—are permanent, not because they are monuments frozen in time, but because they continue in silence the movements of the lives they embody. They are solid—"cal y canto"—yet they move. Wright's use of "cal y canto" has the same kinetic effect as Arguedas's "bloody stone." In the same way that the semantic properties of "bloody stone" are deeply entrenched in the Quechua language, "cal y canto," although a Spanish idiom, recaptures one of the most distinctive rhetorical features of the Náhuatl language: the practice of *difrasismo*: "[Di frasismo] is a procedure in which a single idea is expressed by two words, which in a way complement one another, either because they are synonymous or because they are placed next to each other. Several examples in Spanish will more suitably illustrate this: 'a tontas y a locas' [recklessly]; 'a sangre y fuego' [by blood and fire]; 'contra viento y marea' [against wind and tide; against all odds]: 'a pan y agua' [on bread and water]; etc. This mode of expression is rare in our languages, but quite common in Náhuatl."[146] Wright's "cal y canto" is a figure for infusing solidity with movement, for creating, as Neruda has it, "a permanence of stone and word," or in other words, a city. *Difrasismo*, according to Garibay a characteristic expression of the fundamental dualism that lies at the heart of Náhua thought, can be described as the art of *thinking in twos* ("We dream in twos,/strict destiny, the two in one" [*DH*, 24]), of making two different things cohere by placing them next to one another and charting the manner in which they interact. This process is at once subversive and supplementary: *Canto* (song), for instance, is clearly not synonymous with *cal* (mortar) but supplements it by creating a deficiency (*cal* alone does not mean "solidly"), a space that has to be filled in order for the idiom to attain its full meaning. But in the process, *canto* also achieves a certain degree of synonymity with *cal*, and vice versa, which is particularly relevant in the context of the above citation from *Dimensions of History*. If mortar is a substance that literally fills the spaces between the individual stones in a wall (or between marble and stone, as the case may be), that joins them together, then "song" accomplishes the same on the metaphoric level. Song, that is to say, poetry (which the Náhuas, in another *difrasismo*, call "flower and song"), is Wright's mortar, that which holds the textual construction together. It is the way in which the "stones" are put together that determines the architecture of Wright's cities and thus the degree of their "enchantment." "Cal y canto" is another one of Wright's figures of writing, which is best translated as "enchanted mortar."

Architecture, like poetry, translates temporal (that is, historical) relations into spatial configurations. This analogy is particularly applicable to the final section of *Dimensions of History*. The most notable formal aspect of "Landscapes: The Physical Dimension" is the way in which the poetic text is strewn with passages that read like encyclopedia entries. Each of these five passages, which vary in length, lists some of the main geographical, economic, and historical features of one particular New World country: Venezuela, Colombia, Panama, Mexico, and the United States, respectively. Between these block entries, which represent what I have previously termed the Library, the text of the poem winds like a vast stream of images, filling the spaces between these curious "stones" with an intricate web of relationships far beyond the reach of the collections of topographical data they embody. The layout of this section leaves no doubt that these extended spaces between the encyclopedic "stones," frozen into questionable objectivity, are far more important to the poet than the individual "stones" themselves. They belong to a complex whole that is clearly larger than the sum of its parts.

As parts of Wright's poetic landscape, the encyclopedic monoliths formally represent what Wilson Harris has called the "enormous *callouses* and conceits of power in our age," in the midst of which "there continues a complex descent into forces of conscience." Harris continues, "That complex descent into the modern age is less than 500 years old. It scarcely yet possesses criteria of evaluation though I would suggest such criteria must accept the deep fact that all images (or institutions or rituals) are partial, are ceaselessly unfinished in their openness to other partial images from apparently strange cultures within an unfathomable, and a dynamic, spirit of wholeness that sustains all our hopes of the regeneration of far-flung community in an interdependent world."[147] Harris, like Auerbach before him, calls for a mobilization of all the rich tensions each individual is capable of accommodating within the diverse layers of his or her cultural personality. Both Harris and Wright demand that these tensions and frictions be articulated and experienced as something positive, rather than being subjected to, and at least partially leveled by, the kind of intellectual and emotional censorship that comes with the extension of political nationalism to the sphere of culture. Cultural nationalism, as useful and as necessary an ideological tool as it may have been to reinforce the desire for political independence in the Third World, must give way to a vision of cultural interdependence in order to counteract what Harris has aptly termed "illiteracy of the imagination." That illiteracy may be defined as a narcissistic inability (or unwillingness) to experience cultural cross-fertilization through an active probing of the depths of otherness that lie beneath the shallow surfaces of the Ego. Wright's poems, it is safe to say, are figures of a *literate* imagination, taking the form of a language generated by the poet's acute experience of self-division (or hyphenation) as a gift. That gift enables him to remain open to all the different and conflicting aspects of the New World's complex cultural heritage. It also enables him to intuit and articulate mutuality between cultural spaces miles and centuries apart, yet present in the living strata of his exterior and interior geography. In *Dimensions of History*, as well as in *The Double Invention of Komo* and *Explications/Interpretations*, this fundamental openness is manifest in the ceaseless play of substitutions representing an amazing proliferation of cultural identities or, again in Harris's words, "a visualization of roots beyond roots, a visualization of unfathomably rich potential that torments yet overjoys."[148] To achieve a creative coexistence of those manifold cultural identities, is, for Wright, the major "task in a new land" (*DH*, 20). The fulfillment of this momentous task is what liberates him and his language from the intellectual and emotional strictures of institutionalized culture. At the same time, this freedom is what lends authority to his writing.

Dimensions of History shows with utmost clarity that Wright envisions New World literature as an "accumulation/of all that we have suffered and won" (*DH*, 12). Losses and gains figure equally in the articulation of this new cultural space, opened up by exile as a form of geographical, historical, and mythological displacement. Since the inevitable result of such a violent act of displacement is, as we have seen, a kind of deracination, or razing, it is understandable that, especially in Afro-American literature, this new space was frequently visualized as a sort of no man's land, a barren desert and a perilous wilderness. It is this (limbo) area of uncertainties that Wright sets out to cultivate: "all the powers lying dead,/with no one to transform them" (*DH*, 33). His method of cultivation is a process of threading the fragments of countless myths dispersed by history into a new tapestry, a map that charts the New World's cultural and literary tradition of exile. This dynamic construct is a mythological *field* constituted by clusters of tropes that merge into, and emanate from, one master trope: that of the city. Wright's city as a cultural landscape is "blood given bodily form" (*DH*, 12), the physical embodiment of tradition, whose architecture is also an *arche-texture*: a rainbow arc (as in Harris) or a palpitating bridge (as in Paz) extending across ideological divides that segregate so-called cultural majorities from minorities and one ethnic group from another.

This arc or bridge as a figure for mutuality culminates at the end of *Dimensions of History* with the poet's arrival at the ancient Mayan city of Labná.

> And I return now to my city at Labná.
> It has been a long march.
> I am half-naked.
> I retain no more than a band
> about my head, and a band about my waist,
> my sandals on my feet,
> my home-spun mantle and a pouch

for the gods' bones.
But I am victorious.
I march from the humble
to the sacred side of the city.
I enter where I return.
I return again to the land of the star.
There is peace in this elevation.
You come, if not to God,
near to yourself.
It is a star land, a golden land, our dark and true light,
the image of our life among ourselves. (*DH*, 103–4)

Unlike Tenochtitlán, Cuzco, Macchu Picchu, Cartagena, and Bogotá, Labná is not fortified; it has no walls. Curiously enough, however, it does have a gate in the form of a triumphal arc, which formerly linked the two parts of the city. The Great Gate of Labná synecdochically suggests the existence of a wall that joins rather than divides, and it is this gate that Wright offers as his final "image of our life among ourselves." Redressed as a gateway to the beautiful, this triumphal arc is Wright's ultimate "emblem of the ecstatic connection" (*DH*, 34). Celebrating the triumph of Wright's synthetic approach to New World writing, this emblem embodies a profound poetic dialogue at the crossroads of various Western and non-Western cultures, a dialogue that includes Williams's *In the American Grain* and Guillén's *El diario*. Wright's is a poetic voice that speaks, paradoxically but most effectively, "without song," and in doing so, it brings about "sea-changes" that are "waterless."

NOTES

1. Wilson Harris, *Explorations: A Selection of Talks and Articles, 1966–1981*, ed. Hena Maes-Jelinek (Mundelstrup, Denmark: Dangaroo Press, 1981), 5.

2. John Hollander, "Poetry in Review;" *Yale Review* 74 (November 1984): xvi.

3. Charles H. Rowell, "The Unravelling of the Egg: An Interview with Jay Wright," *Jay Wright: A Special Issue, Callaloo* 19.6 (Fall 1983): 6–7. Wright has also published several plays, among them "Love's Equation," *Callaloo* 19: 39–75, and "The Death and Return of Paul Batuta: A Play in One Act," *Hambone* 4 (Fall 1984): 61–110. Given its focus on Wright's poetry, this study will not consider these plays.

4. The term is Michael S. Harper's; see "High Modes: Vision as Ritual: Confirmation," in *Images of Kin: New and Selected Poems* (Urbana: University of Illinois Press, 1977), 177–78.

5. Included in my definition of cultural groups of a non-European origin are not only Afro-Americans, Asian-Americans, and Native Americans but also Latin Americans. The rather ambiguous position Spain has occupied in European cultural history since the Middle Ages because of her intense contact with the Arabic world justifies this inclusion. See Américo Castro, *The Structure of Spanish History*, trans. Edmundo L. King (Princeton: Princeton University Press, 1954), which was first published in 1948 as *España en su historia*.

6. Erich Auerbach, *Gesammelte Aufsätze zur Romanischen Philologie* (Bern: Francke Verlag, 1967), 223.

7. Auerbach, "Philologie der Weltliteratur," in ibid., 310.

8. Jay Wright, Afterword, *The Double Invention of Komo* (Austin: University of Texas Press, 1980), 114. All further references to this edition are identified in the tact as *DI*.

9. Jay Wright. "Desire's Design, Vision's Resonance: Black Poetry's Ritual and Historical Voice," *Callaloo* 30 (Winter 1987). Page numbers refer to the manuscript.

10. Harris, "The Native Phenomenon," in *Explorations*, 52–53.

11. Williams, "The Poem as a Field of Action," in *Selected Essays of William Carlos Williams* (New York: New Directions, 1969), 285.

12. Robert B. Stepto, *From Behind the Veil: A Study of Afro-American Narrative* (Urbana: University of Illinois Press, 1979).

13. My use of the term *origin* is indebted to Walter Benjamin's comments in *Der Ursprung des deutschen Trauerspiels* (19631, where he writes: "Origin [Ursprung], although an entirely historical category, has, nevertheless, nothing to do with genesis (*Entsiehung*). The term 'origin' is not intended to describe the process by which the existent came into being, but rather to describe that which emerges from the process of becoming and disappearance. Origin is an eddy in the stream of becoming, and in its current it swallows the material involved in the process of genesis.... Origin is not, therefore, discovered by the examination of actual findings, but it is related to their history and their subsequent development." (*The Origin of German Tragic Drama*, trans. John Osborne [London: NLB, 1977], 45–46.)

14. See Melvin Dixon, "Singing a Deep Song: Language as Evidence in the Novels of Gayl Jones," in *Black Women Writers (1950–1980): A Critical Evaluation*, ed. Mari Evans (Garden City, N.Y.: Doubleday-Anchor, 1984), 236.

15. For a discussion of the extent to which African slaves in the Americas refused to abandon their linguistic ties with their homeland see John W. Blassingame, *The Slave Community: Plantation Life in the Antebellum South*, rev. and enl. ed. (New York: Oxford University Press, 1979), 24–30.

John Blassingame and Mary Berry cite a 1740 South Carolina state law as a representative example of the early institution in North America of a pattern of compulsory ignorance designed to ensure the continuation of slavery: "That all and every person and persons whatsoever, who shall hereafter teach, or cause any slave or slaves to be taught to write, or shall use or employ any slave as a scribe in any manner of writing whatsoever, hereafter taught to write; even such person or persons shall, for every offense, forfeit the sum of one hundred pounds current money" (*The Long Memory: The Black Experience in America* [New York: Oxford University Press, 1982], 261–62). No such legal restrictions on the education of slaves were found in the *Recopilación de las leyes de los reynos de las Indias* (1680) or in the Spanish slave codes of 1789 and 1892. See Franklin W. Knight, *Slave Society in Cuba during the Nineteenth Century* (Madison: University of Wisconsin Press, 1974), 121–36.

16. See, for instance, Stepto's discussion of such "passes" in connection with Frederick Douglass's 1845 *Narrative* and Ralph Ellison's *Invisible Man* (1952); *From Behind the Veil*, 172–73. For an extensive bibliography of Afro-American slave narratives see John W. Blassingame, ed., *Slave Testimony: Two Centuries of Letters, Speeches, Interviews, and Autobiographies* (Baton Rouge: Louisiana State University Press, 1977).

17. See Lawrence W. Levine, *Black Culture and Black Consciousness: Afro-American Folk Thought from Slavery to Freedom* (New York: Oxford University Press, 1977), and Stephen Henderson, *Understanding the New Black Poetry: Black Speech and Black Music as Poetic References* (New York: Morrow, 1973).

18. See Jacques Derrida's critique of Saussure in *Of Grammatology*, trans. Gayatri Chakravorty Spivak (1967; Baltimore: Johns Hopkins University Press, 1976), especially pt. 1, "Writing before the Letter."

19. The splendid contradictions in a passage from Charles Olson's "Human Universe" corroborate this: "Logos, or discourse," he writes, "so worked its abstractions into our concept and use of language that language's other function, speech, seems so in need of restoration that several of us go back to hieroglyphics or to ideograms to right the balance" (quoted in Lazlo Géfin, *Ideogram: History of a Poetic Method* [Austin: University of Texas Press, 1982], 92; my italics).

20. Baraka is quoted in Kimberly W. Benston, *Baraka: The Renegade and the Mask* (New Haven: Yale University Press, 1976), 110.

21. Jay Wright, *The Homecoming Singer* (New York: Corinth Books. 1971), 75. All further references to this edition are identified in the text as *HS*.

22. Ralph Ellison, *Shadow and Act* (New York: New American Library, 1964), 147. Also Robert Stepto, "Study and Experience: An Interview with Ralph Ellison," in *Chant of Saints: A Gathering of Afro-American Literature, Art, and Scholarship*, ed. Michael S. Harper and Robert B. Stepto (Urbana: University of Illinois Press, 1979), 453.

23. See *Christopher Columbus: Four Voyages to the New World: Letters and Selected Documents*, bilingual ed., trans. and ed. R. H. Major (Gloucester: Peter Smith, 1978), 49–50; also *Hernando Cortés: Five Letters, 1519–1526*, trans. Bayard Morris (New York: Norton, n.d.), 17–18.

24. See Juan Rodriguez Freyle, *El carnero* (1638; Bogota: Editorial Bedout, 1976). Parts of this book have been translated by William C. Atkinson as *The Conquest of New Granada* (London: Folio Society, 1961). See also Kutzinski, "The Logic of Wings: Gabriel García Márquez and Afro-American Literature," *Latin American Literary Review* 13 (January–June 1985): 133–46.

25. For details see Perry Miller, *Errand into the Wilderness* (Cambridge: Harvard University Press, Belknap Press, 1956), and Sacvan Bercovitch, *The American Jeremiad* (Madison: University of Wisconsin Press, 1978).

26. Silvio Bedini, *The Life of Benjamin Banneker* (New York: Scribner, 1972), 104–3. Banneker's letter is reprinted on 152–56.

27. One of the most prominent examples is Aimé Césaire's *Cahier d'un retour au pays natal* (*Notebook of a Return to the Native Land*) (1939). The most recent translation of this poem is included in *The Collected Poetry of Aimé Césaire*, trans. Clayton Eshleman and Annette Smith (Berkeley and Los Angeles: University of California Press, 1983), 34–85.

28. Afro-Americans, that is, those who were United States citizens, were excluded from the Exposition: Frederick Douglass, ironically enough, attended the fair as a representative of Haiti. Despite a petition, signed by Douglass, Dunbar, and others, no exhibit was arranged to show the contributions of blacks to American life. A compromise was reached by setting aside 25 August 1893 as Colored Americans Day. See Benjamin Quarles, *Frederick Douglass* (New York: Atheneum, 1968), 346–47. Details on Douglass as Haiti's representative can be found in Frederick May Holland, *Frederick Douglass: The Colored Orator*, rev. ed. (New York: Haskell House, 1969), 398; Philip S. Foner, *Frederick Douglass* (New York: Citadel Press, 1969), 360; and Nathan Irving Huggins, *Slave and Citizen: The Life of Frederick Douglass* (Boston: Little, Brown, 1980), 168. For details on the Exposition itself see Alan Trachtenberg, *The Incorporation of America: Culture and Society in the Gilded Age*, especially chap. 7, "White City." 208–34.

29. More detailed references to the Haitian Revolution can be found in *Dimensions of History* (Santa Cruz: Kayak, 1976), 20–22. All further references to this edition are identified in the text as *DH*. See also C. L. R. James's *The Black Jacobins: Toussaint l'Ouverture and the San Domingo Revolution*, 2d ed., rev. New York: Random House, 1963 [1938]).

30. Alejo Carpentier, *The Kingdom of This World*, trans. Harrier de Onis (1949; New York: Collier Books. 1910 [1957]), 178.

31. *Selected Poetry of Amiri Baraka/LeRoi Jones* (New York: Morrow, 1979), 23.

32. Jay Wright, *Soothsayers and Omens* (New York: Seven Woods Press, 1976), 27. All further references to this edition are identified in the text as *SO*.

33. Bedini, *Life of Benjamin Banneker*, 158–201.

34. Joseph N. Riddel, "Decentering the Image: The 'Project' of 'American' Poetics?" in Josué Harari, ed., *Textual Strategies: Perspectives in Post-Structuralist Criticism* (Ithaca: Cornell University Press, 1919), 357.

35. Charles Olson, "Projective Verse," in *Selected Writings of Charles Olson*, ed. Robert Creeley (New York: New Directions, 1966), 15–26.

36. Riddel. "Decentering the Image," 344–45.

37. See Olson, *Human Universe and Other Essays*, ed. Donald Allen (New York: New Directions, 1967), 19.

38. See Germaine Dieterlen and Marcel Griaule, *Le renard pâle*, vol. 1, *Le mythe cosmogonique* (Paris: Institut d'Ethnologie, Université de Paris, 1965).

39. Paul de Man, *Blindness and Insight: Essays in the Rhetoric of Contemporary Criticism*, 2d ed., rev. (Minneapolis: University of Minnesota Press, 1983), 185. See also Eugenio Donato's insightful comments on memory and representation in "The Ruins of Memory: Archeological Fragments and Textual Artifacts," *PMLA* (French issue) 93 (May 1978), especially 579–80.

40. See my discussion of the Seventh Nommo in Pt. 2, Sec. 3. Compare this to Allen Ginsberg's notion of "basketweaving" in connection with *The Fall of America* (quoted in Géfin, *Ideogram*, 124).

41. D.T. Niane, *Sundiata: An Epic of Old Mali* (London: Longman Drumbeat, 1979), 1; my italics.

42. R.G. Collingwood, *The Idea of History* (1956; reprint, London: Oxford University Press, 1982), 113.

43. de Man, *Blindness and Insight*, 165.

44. Roland Barthes, *Mythologies*, trans. Annette Lavers (1957; New York: Hill & Wang, 1919), 112.

45. Jacques Derrida, "Structure, Sign, and Play in the Discourse of the Human Sciences," in *The Structuralist Controversy: The Languages of Criticism and the Sciences of Man*, ed. Eugenio Donato and Richard Macksey (Baltimore: Johns Hopkins University Press, 1972), 260.

46. Rowell. "Unravelling of the Egg," p. 12.

47. See, for instance, Vladimir Nabokov's *Ada or Ardor: A Family Chronicle* (New York: McGraw-Hill, 1969) and *Pale Fire* (1962, reprint, New York: Putnam, 1980); Ishmael Reed's *Mumbo Jumbo* (New York: Avon Books, 1972); and Augusto Roa Bastos's *Yo el supremo* (Buenos Aires: Siglo Veintiuno, 1974).

48. Mikhail Bakhtin, *The Dialogic Imagination: Four Essays*, ed. Michael Holquist, trans. Caryl Emerson and Michael Holquist (Austin: University of Texas Press, 1987).

49. One of Wright's earlier poems entitled "The Neighborhood House" (*HS*, 36–37) was in part inspired by Guillén's "El apellido" [My Last Name], a poem preoccupied with this process of effacement. I shall return to this text, as well as to the literary relationship between Wright and Guillén, in Pt. 3, Sec. 1.

50. See Wande Abimbola, *Ifa Divination Poetry* (New York: NOK Publishers, 1977); L. O. Sanneh, *The Jakhanke: A History of an Islamic Clerical People of the Senegambia* (London: International African Institute, 1979); also Franz Rosenthal, *A History of Muslim Historiography* (Leiden: E. J. Brill. 1968); J. B. Danquah, *The Akan Doctrine of God: A Fragment of Gold Coast Ethics and Religion*, 2d ed., rev. (London: Frank Cass, 1968 [1944]).

51. Derrida, "Structure, Sign, and Play," 251.

52. Roberto González Echevarria, "*Cien años de soledad*: The Novel as Myth and Archive," *MLN* (Hispanic Issue) 99 (March 1984): 364.

53. The term "ideogrammatic writing" has not been adopted here to suggest an indebtedness of Wright to Pound's poetics. It has to be noted, however, that while Wright is hardly a self-confessed Poundian. Pound's notion of the ideogram

is relevant to Wright's poetics, an influence that could possibly be traced through Olson. See Géfin, *Ideogram*, for a lucid analysis of Pound's method.

54. Claude Lévi-Strauss, *The Savage Mind* (1962; Chicago: University of Chicago Press, 1969), 264.

55. Michael Houseman, "Les artifices de la logique initiatique," *Journal des Africanistes* 54:1 (1984): 41–63.

56. See W. E. B. Du Bois, *The Souls of Black Folk* (1903; reprint, New York: New American Library, 1969), 45.

57. Harris, "History, Fable and Myth in the Caribbean and the Guianas," in *Explorations*, 25–28.

58. Octavio Paz, "A Literature of Foundations," in *Triquarterly Anthology of Latin American Literature*, ed. José Donoso and William A. Henkin (New York: Dutton, 1969), 4.

59. See Dieterlen and Griaule, *Le renard pâle*, 252–53.

60. See Germaine Dieterlen, *Les âmes des Dogons* (Paris: Institut d'Ethnologie, 1941); Geneviève Calame-Griaule, *Ethnologie et langage: La parole chez les Dogons* (Paris: Gallimard, 1965).

61. See Dieterlen and Griaule, *Le renard pâle*, 253, 475–76; also Wright's notes in *Dimensions of History*, 105.

62. These underlying connections may he effectively compared to Esteban's meditations on celestial constellations in the epigraph of Carpentier's *El siglo de la luces* [Explosion in a Cathedral], trans. John Sturrock (1962; New York: Harper & Row; 1979), 7–8. Carpentier's double image of the guillotine as "a doorway opening on to the immense sky" and as "a gigantic instrument of navigation," which is suggestive of Wright's "gates" in the quotation below, accentuates the dangers and ambiguities involved in the passage toward self-knowledge on which both Esteban and Wright's poet embark.

63. See Césaire's poem "Le verbe marronner/a René Depestre poète haitien" (*Noria*) in *Collected Poetry*, 368–71. The poem was initially entitled "Réponse à Depestre poète haitien" and first appeared in *Présence Africaine* (April–July 1955). See also A. James Arnold's comments on that exchange between Césaire and Depestre in *Modernism and Negritude: The Poetry and Poetics of Aimé Césaire* (Cambridge: Harvard University Press, 1981), 181–83.

64. John Deredita, "Vallejo Interpreted, Vallejo Traduced," *Diacritics* 8 (Winter 1978): 17.

65. See Wright, "Desire's Design, Vision's Resonance"; also Stepto, *From Behind the Veil*, to which this part of my discussion owes much.

66. Robert Hayden, *Angle of Ascent: New and Selected Poems* (New York: Liveright, 1971), 10.

67. Gabriel García Márquez, "Un senor muy viejo con unas alas enormes," in *La incrédible y triste historia de la cándida Eréndira y de su abuela desalmada: Siete cuentas* (Caracas: Monte Avila, 1972), 11–20. A translation of this story by Gregory Rabassa is included in *Leaf Storm and Other Stories* (1972; New York: Harper & Row. 1979), 105-12. See Kutzinski, "Logic of Wings," 143–44.

68. See Calame-Griaule, *Ethnologie et langage*, 32.

69. W.B. Yeats, "Among School Children," in *The Variorum Edition of the Poems of W.B. Yeats*, ed. Peter Allt and Russell K. Alspach (New York: Macmillan, 1977), 446.

70. Calame-Griaule, *Ethnologie et langage*, 25.

71. Frederick Douglass, *The Narrative of the Life of Frederick Douglass, An American Slave: Written by Himself* (1845; New York reprint, New American Library, 1968), 43.

72. See Du Bois, *Souls of Black Folk*, 45.

73. This is quoted from the *Egyptian Book of the Dead*. "I am the great Bennu [Phoenix] in Annu [Heliopolis]. I am the Former of Beings and Existences." See Charles H. S. Davis, ed., *The Egyptian Book of the Dead: The Most Ancient and Most Important of the Extant Religious Texts of Ancient Egypt* (New York: Putnam, 1894), 54.

74. Wright's fire images here also evoke the ancient Arawak/Macusi creation myth of "The Tree of Life in Flames," which is discussed in connection with Guillén's inner geography in "El apellido" in Pt. 3, Sec. 1.

75. See Griaule and Dieterlen, *Le renard pâle*, chap. 3.

76. Danquah, *Akan Doctrine of God*, 75–76.

77. Ralph Ellison, *Invisible Man* (New York: Random House, 1952), 432.

78. Ibid., 5.

79. *Republic*, 514–21. References are to *The Dialogues of Plato*, vol. 2, trans. B. Jovett (Oxford: Clarendon Press, 1953).

80. See also Ellison's second epigraph in *Invisible Man*, which is from Melville's *Benito Cereno*: "'You are saved,' cried Captain Delano, more and more astonished and pained, 'you are saved: *what has cast such a shadow upon you?*'" (my italics).

81. The phrase is Robert Stepto's; see "After Modernism, After Hibernation: Michael Harper, Robert Hayden, and Jay Wright," in *Chant of Saints*, 470–86.

82. Ellison, *Invisible Man*, 11.

83. Stepto, "After Modernism: After Hibernation," 470.

84. Robert Stepto, "'The Aching Prodigal': Jay Wright's Dutiful Poet," *Callaloo* 19 (Fall 1980): 82.

85. See Frederick Turner, *Beyond Geography: The Western Spirit against the Wilderness* (New York: Viking Press, 1980).

86. Nicolás Guillén, *Obra Poética, 1920–1970*, ed. Angel Augier (Havana: Instituto Cubano del Libro, 1974), I: 395; my translation.

87. See Lydia Cabrera, *El monte: Igbo finda ewe orisha, nfinda: Notas sobre las religiones, la magia, las supersticiones y el folklore de los negros criollos y del pueblo de Cuba* (Havana: Ediciones C.R., 1954; reprint, Miami: Colección del Chichereku, 1971).

88. Castro, *Structure of Spanish History*, 234.

89. Ibid., chap. 2.

90. Octavio Paz, *Piedra de sol* (Mexico: Tezontle, 1957), 39–40; my italics. *Sun Stone*, trans. Muriel Rukeyser (New York: World Poets Series, New Directions, n.d.), 45.

91. Jay Wright. *Explications/Interpretations* (Lexington: University of Kentucky Press, Callaloo Poetry Series, 1984), 1.

92. Roberto González Echevarria, "Literature of the Hispanic Caribbean," *Latin American Literary Review* 8 (Spring–Summer 1980): 10.

93. Fernando Ortiz, *La antigua fiesta afrocubana del "Dia de Reyes"* (1925; reprint, Havana: Ministerio de Relaciones Exteriores Departamento de Asuntas Culturales, División de Publicaciones, 1960).

94. For further details about the "Dia de Reyes" see my discussion of Guillén's "Sensemayá," in Pt. 3, Sec. 1.

95. Roberto González Echevarria, "Socrates among the Weeds: Blacks and History in Carpentier's *Explosion in a Cathedral*," in *Voices from Under: Black Narrative in Latin America and the Caribbean*, ed. William Luis (Westport, Conn.: Greenwood Press, 1984), 51.

96. See Germaine Dieterlen and Youssouf Tata Cissé, *Les fondements de la société d'initiation du Komo* (Paris: Mouton, 1972), 91.

97. See Todorov, *Conquest of America*, 79–81.

98. For further details see *DH*, 108–9.

99. Nicolás Guillén was the first to develop the *son* into a distinctive literary form, the *poema-song*. See Pt. 3, Sec. 1.

100. See Alejo Carpentier, "America Latina en la confluencia de coordenadas históricas y su repercusión en la música" (1977); reprinted in *Ese músico que llevo dentro, Selección de Zoila Gómez* (Havana: Editorial Letras Cubanas, 1980), 3:336.

101. Du Bois, *Souls of Black Folk*, 209.

102. Quoted by González Echevarria in "Literature of the Hispanic Caribbean," 7.

103. Ibid., 8.

104 See Lydia Cabrera, *Yemayá y Ochún* (Madrid: Colección del Chichereku en el exilio, 1974).

105. Rodriguez Freyle, *El carnero*, 143.

106. See Kutzinski. "Logic of Wings," 137–38.

107. Fernando Ortiz, *Hampa afrocubana: Los negros brujos: Apuntes para un estudio de etnologia criminal* (Madrid: Editorial América, 1917). See also Cirilo Villaverde's novel *Cecilia Valdés, or Angel's Hill*, trans. Sydney G. Gest (1882; New York: Vantage Press, 1962), and Nicolás Guillén, *Prosa de Prisa, 1929–1972* (Havana: Arte y Literatura, 1976), 3:288–99.

108. Albert William Levi, "Culture: A Guess at the Riddle," *Critical Inquiry* 4 (Winter 1977): 315.

109. *The New Science of Giambattista Vico*. 3d ed., abr.. trans. Thomas Goddard Bergin and Max Harold Fisch (1744; Ithaca: Cornell University Press, 1961; reprint, 1970), 149.

110. Ibid.. 138 and 241.

111. Marcel Griaule, *Conversations with Ogotemmêli: An Introduction to Dogon Religious Ideas*, intro. Germaine Dieterlen, a translation of *Dieu d'eau* (1948) (New York: Oxford University Press, 1975), 131–37.

112. Ibid., 158.

113. Wright, "Desire's Design, Vision's Resonance," 11.

114. Paz, "A Literature of Foundations," 5.

115. Ibid.. 3.

116. See Alejo Carpentier's concept of the Baroque and of the "stylelessness" of Latin American reality in "De lo real maravilloso américano," in *Tientos y diferencias* (Montevideo: ARCA, 1967), 102–20; also relevant to this is my later discussion of Guillén's recasting of the Latin American Neobaroque as "algarabia en lengua de piratas y bozales" (*El diario*) in Pt. 3, Sec. 2.

117. See Frederick Webb Hodge, *History of Hawikúh, New Mexico. One of the so-called Cities of Cíbola* (Los Angeles: Southwest Museum, 1937), 3–4.

118. See *Cabeza de Vaca's Adventures in the Unknown Interior of America*, trans. Cyclone Covey (Albuquerque: University of New Mexico Press, 1983). An earlier translation of the original *relación* by Frederick Hodge ("The Narrative of Alvar Núñez Cabeca de Vaca") is included in the *Original Narratives of Early American History: Spanish Explorers in the United States, 1528–1143* (New York. Scribner, 1907), 3–126.

119. "Narrative of Fray Marcos," in Cleve Hallenbeck, *The Journey of Fray Marcos de Niza* (Dallas: University Press in Dallas, 1949), 18. Other translations of that narrative are included in *Discovery of the Seven Cities of Cíbola*, trans. and ed. Percy M. Baldwin (Albuquerque: Historical Society of New Mexico Publications, vol. 1, 1926), 3–59, which also has the Spanish text; Henry W. Haynes, "Early Explorations of New Mexico," in *Narrative and Critical History of America*, ed. Justin Winsor (New York: Houghton Mifflin, 1887), 2:473–503; A. F. Bandelier, *The Gilded Man (El Dorado) and Other Pictures of the Spanish Occupancy of America* (New York: Appleton, 1893), 125–257.

120. Quoted in Hodge, *History of Hawikúh*, 25–26. See also John Upton Terrell, *Estevanico the Black* (Los Angeles: Westernlore Press, 1968), 144.

121. For details see Hodge, *History of Hawikúh*, 28, 112; Cleve Hallenbeck is convinced that the friar was a liar (*The Journey of Fray Marcos de Niza*); so is John Upton Terrell, who gives Estevan full credit for discovering Hawikúh (*Estevanico the Black*, 144).

122. See George P. Hammond, *Coronado's Seven Cities* (Albuquerque: U.S. Coronado Exposition Commission, 19440); "Coronado's Letter to Mendoza" (3 August 1540), in *Old South Leaflets* (n.p., n.d.), 1:20; J. H. Simpson, *Coronado's March in Search of the Seven Cities of Cíbola and Discussion of their Probable Location* (Washington, D.C.: U.S. Government Printing Office, 1871).

123. See Hodge, *History of Hawikúh*, 1–2; also Terrell, *Estevanico the Black*, 64; Stephen Clissold, *The Seven Cities of Cíbola* (London: Eyre & Spottiswoode, 1961), 24–33. Aileen Nusbaum, *The Seven Cities of Cíbola* (New York: Putnam, 1926), a collection of Zuñi folktales, presents a slightly different version (3–8).

124. See Garcilaso de la Vega, el Inca, *Royal Commentaries of the Incas and General History of Peru*, trans. Harold V. Livermore (Austin: University of Texas Press, 1966; reprint, 1970), 1:27–30.

125. Todorov's portrait of Cabeza de Vaca is somewhat different. It is perplexing that he ignores Estevan's presence (*Conquest of America*, 196–200).

126. Danquah, *Akan Doctrine of God*, 53.

127. Jacques Derrida, *Dissemination*, trans. Barbara Johnson (Chicago: University of Chicago Press, 1981), 92–93.

128. James Joyce, *A Portrait of the Artist as a Young Man: Text, Criticism, and Notes*, ed. Chester C. Anderson (1916; reprint, New York: Viking Press, 1974), 225.

129. See also Janheinz Jahn, "Nommo: The Magic Power of the Word," in *Muntu: An Outline of New African Culture*, trans. Marjorie Greene (1958; New York: Grove Press, 1961), 121–55.

130. Griaule, *Conversations with Ogotemmêli*, 27.

131. See Derrida, *Dissemination*, 88.

132. Griaule, *Conversations with Ogotemmêli*, 27–28.

133. Ibid., 77.

134. Harris, *Explorations*, 53; my italics; for further details on this Carib ritual see Harris, *The Womb of Space: The Cross-Cultural Imagination* (Westport, Conn.: Greenwood Press, 1983), 24–26.

135. Danquah, *Akan Doctrine of God*, 131.

136. Du Bois, *Souls of Black Folk*, 139.

137. José Maria Arguedas, *Deep Rivers*, trans. Frances Horning Barraclough (1958; Austin: University of Texas Press, 1981), 6–7.

138. See José Lezama Lima, "Imagen de América Latina," in *América Latina en su literatura*, ed. César Fernández Moreno (Paris and Mexico: Siglo Veintiuno for UNESCO, 1972).

139. A translation of the ancient Náhuatl text narrating the "Legend of the Suns" is provided by Miguel León-Portilla in *Aztec Thought and Culture: A Study of the Ancient Náhuatl Mind*, trans. Jack Emory Davis (1963; Norman: University of Oklahoma Press, 1975), 38–39.

140. See ibid., 51; also Hans Helfritz, *Mexican Cities of the Gods: An Archeological Guide* (New York: Praeger, 1968; reprint, 1910), 43–44.

141. It is worth recalling here the previous discussion of "anochecimos enfermo amanecímos bueno." Venus, as Octavio Paz points out in his notes to *Piedra de sol* (43–44), appears in the sky twice every day: at dusk and at dawn. It is both the Evening Star and the Morning Star, and therefore embodies the universe's

essential ambiguity and duality. Fuentes clarifies this in *Terra Nostra*: "Quetzalcóatl, Venus, Hesperia, Spain, identical stars, dawn and dusk, mysterious union, indecipherable enigma, but cipher for two bodies, two lands, cipher for a terrible encounter" (485).

142. León-Portilla, *Aztec Thought*, 51, and Helfritz, *Mexican Cities*, 44.

143. Rodriguez Freyle, *El carnero*, 93.

144. Pablo Neruda, *Canto General* (Buenos Aires: Editorial Losada, 1955), 1:36. The translations are from John Felstiner, *Translating Neruda: The Way to Macchu Picchu* (Stanford: Stanford University Press, 1980), 231. Felstiner's translation is, in many respects, superior to the standard translation by Nathaniel Tarn (1966; New York: Farrar, Straus & Giroux, 1983).

145. *Canto General*, 32–33; *Translating Neruda*, 219.

146. Angel Maria Garibay Kintana, Llave de Náhuatl: Collección de trozos clasicos, con gramática y vocabulario, 2d ed., rev. and enl. (Mexico: Porrúa, 1961), 115.

147. Harris, *Explorations*, 99, my italics.

148. Ibid.

ROBERT B. SHAW

Selected Poems of Jay Wright:
Review

Reviewers are likely to treat this book in a gingerly manner. The selection it offers from Jay Wright's five books of poetry comes sandwiched between an introduction by Robert B. Stepto and an afterword by Harold Bloom, and this in itself may make some readers impatient or quizzical: can't the work speak for itself? But leaving aside the prose, the poetry here is hard to get a grip on. Anyone whose hackles are raised by the walk-on appearances of the critics may wish after some attempts to penetrate the poetry that they had not just offered encomiums but footnoted the more forbidding passages. Jay Wright is a difficult poet who makes few concessions to readers uneducated in the sources upon which his work has increasingly relied. These sources are anthropological. Wright's extensive knowledge of West African and Latin American cultures informs the structures and imbues the substance of many of his more elaborate pieces. As a black American born in New Mexico, Wright is well situated to explore cultural diversity, and as a poet he is equipped as well with a wide array of rhetorical skills. He seems in many ways a belated High Modernist; certainly his appropriation of myth and some of his particular kinds of stylistic density put one in mind of Eliot or, even more, Hart Crane, as the critics in this volume both note.

From *Poetry* 152, no. 1 (April 1988): 45-47. © 1983 by *Poetry*.

I have found in this book some poems I was moved by, a great many more I was intrigued by, but not many that I am certain I understand. It is typically Wright's earlier poems which I accept (and enjoy) with fewer questions. These include some mordant descriptions of Mexican scenes, and some subtle, incisive attempts at self-definition. In these latter pieces Wright adds something of his own to the strong tradition of American poets seeking, questioning, and embracing their vocation. The dream vision at the end of "The Homecoming Singer" is one of the more eloquent evocations of an American muse that I have read:

> I kneel before her. She strokes my hair,
> as softly as she would a cat's head
> and goes on singing, her voice shifting
> and bringing up Carolina calls,
> the waterboy, the railroad cutter, the jailed,
> the condemned, all that had been forgotten
> on this night of homecomings, all
> that had been misplaced in those livid arteries.

In the later work, roughly the second half of the book, the content is frequently more esoteric and the rigor of the style does not relax to provide a helpful context in which references might be understood. When I read

> My own darkness
> gives me
> back
> to Yuri and Dya,
> to the burnished darkness
> of my blind saint

—I assume Wright's cultural explorations lie behind what is being said, but I have no ready means of identifying Yuri or Dya, and so what is being said remains obscure. A rhapsodic chant like

> Má lover of god
> Má loved by god
> Má of the sun
> Má of the river
> Má of the timber

Má of the wood
Má of the grief
Má Teodora What source
is in your circle?

may immediately capture attention, but it is doubtful whether it can long
hold it, since no aid is given the uninitiated who would like to move
onward from sound to sense. My distrust of the oracular increases year by
year, and yet I do not wish to dismiss these poems. I would like to suggest
that judgments of their value will be hard to form without the benefit of
more commentary. Here I feel an opportunity has been missed in the
present volume. I wish that Stepto and Bloom had given us some detailed
explications of certain key poems rather than limiting themselves to their
shrewd comments on the poet's background and literary affinities. And
(dare one say it?) I wish this book had included a glossary, so that Yuri,
Dya, Má, Zando, Mousso Koroni, and their ilk would be able to shed some
of their opacity. I take it that the aim of this selection was to introduce
Wright's work to a broader audience than it has previously reached. I am
not sure that all which might usefully have been done to secure that
objective has been done. As things stand I shall not feel comfortable
evaluating much of this work until I have the leisure to steep myself in
some large library's Folklore section. But just when that will be, Má only
knows.

ISIDORE OKPEWHO

From a Goat Path in Africa:
An Approach to the Poetry of Jay Wright

In attempting to gloss the poetry of Jay Wright, I am aware what risks I run. For one thing, poetic composition since the modernist vogue has steadily attenuated the communication line between the poet and his reader/audience. Even when the poet chooses a familiar phenomenon or communal experience as the subject of his creative reflection, the constitutive images of such a subject are so severely refracted in the prism of the private vision that the language of the poem has an inevitably self-reflexive ring to it. Although many a modern poet makes a candid effort—as I believe Wright does—to capture within the texture of his statement the complexity of the world he conceives, the critic of modern poetry has gradually come to accept the severe limitations to his role as midwife charged with delivering the message from a mind grown inevitably less accessible.

For another thing, Wright has himself warned against any confident readings of his statement. In the few occasions when he has volunteered some clues to his intentions, he has taken care to stress that his poetry is a self-contained statement which—as he tells us in the Afterword of *The Double Invention of Komo*—"does not encourage paraphrase or substitution" (*Komo* 109). At the end of *Dimensions of History*, Wright does volunteer about eight pages of notes to various references in the text; but

From *Callaloo* 14, no. 3 (Summer 1991). © 1991 by *Callaloo*.

these are hardly more helpful than directions given to a visitor which guide him only as far as the barred gate to a house he wishes to enter. "The notes could have been more extensive and more detailed," says Wright. "I have given only so many because I must, ultimately, rely on the good will and intelligence of the reader" (*Dimensions* 105).

It is all very well to trust the intelligence of the reader. But recent tendencies in critical praxis have shown that certain kinds of intelligent reading take us no further beyond the gate than the poet does. Wright has no doubt flown a kite by declaring himself a "bookish poet" (*Komo* 109) and by displaying, in several volumes of his poetry, such an intricate intertextual tapestry as to leave the impression, on some readers, of a cultural decenteredness if not an outright lack of a sustaining *ethnos*.

I think that Vera Kutzinski has done tremendous service to American literary scholarship by projecting a poet like Wright, whom the average reader, or even critic, would rather not strain his or her mind on, by focusing attention on a wide-ranging variety of documents which both constitute the sources from which the poet may have drawn and mirror the variegated cultural landscape that he has evidently traversed. But Kutzinski may have taken her deconstructive exertions a little too far by representing Wright as a "writer, whose cultural heritage does not *per se* constitute a unified whole" and his polymythic unity as "a structure without a center in that it is not founded on, and is thus not reducible to, a single absolute frame of reference" (*Against the American Grain* 72). Such a position, I am afraid, subtly attenuates the line between a sustaining *ethnos* and a guiding *ethos*, if it does not go so far, indeed, as to question the basis of that cultural fusion which we may concede to be Wright's poetic agenda.

And yet in 1983 Wright told an interviewer how his creative (and cultural) vision had grown since the more conventional themes of his first real volume of poetry, *The Homecoming Singer*. At that point, he said, he had begun to take account of his "developing black African-American life in the United States" as a basis for constructing a larger cultural identity (Rowell 6). He goes on to say: "from my second book, *Soothsayers and Omens*, onward, I have plotted and carried out books as books, not as collections of poems which just happen to make a book. I had the end of a series in mind. *The Double Invention of Komo* closes that phase." Pressed to state the sequence of his work, Wright says: "My books should be read in the following order: *The Homecoming Singer, Soothsayers and Omens, Explications/Interpretations, Dimensions of History, The Double Invention of Komo*" (Rowell 7).

A careful look at these books will reveal that the sequence is in a fundamental sense propelled by Wright's progressive acceptance of a guiding African(ist) sensibility, an ever-tightening embrace of a cultural something that he felt he needed as a dependable beacon in his continuing explorations through cultural history. This is why, in *The Double Invention of Komo*, there is a proportionally larger space devoted to African images than there is in the earlier books, with a corresponding reduction in the non-African images. In fact, the non-African forays are severely circumscribed by a controlling African sense of purpose, which provides a mooring-base that the much buffeted voyager must return to again and again, and finally.

Perhaps because of this stabilizing factor, *The Double Invention of Komo* has a recognizably neater structure. The poet, now reasonably certain where he started his journey, has taken care to (re)trace his steps and to recreate his voyage of self-knowledge and self-discovery against the canvas of a well-defined cosmology and within the format of a sequence of ritual seances whereby the native son takes his proper place within the culture. In this essay, I shall be identifying both the cosmology and the ritual suggesting in what ways the symbolisms relative to them have been woven into the intricate autobiographical portrait that Wright has painted in his poetry.

I

Wright was not, of course, the first Afro-American writer to reach out and touch Africa in his work. The process began as far back as the eighteenth century, when enterprising ex-slaves acquired literacy and endeavored to evoke the homeland, now distant both in time and space, through dim and often warped memories. For instance, Phillis Wheatley, who was taken away to America at the tender age of seven or eight, seeks to appeal to the sanctimony of her Christian audience by representing Africa as a "pagan" and "benighted" race from which she was redeemed by her merciful captors (18). Olaudah Equiano does better in his *Interesting Narrative*. Although motivated by the author's sometimes overzealous convictions of the "inestimable Benefits of Christianity," the book admirably evokes positive memories of the traditional African setting and culture of the "Eboe" (Igbo) homeland from which Equiano had been kidnapped at age eleven.

But even Equiano's recollections have long proven so problematic for a proper placement of his roots that, despite the chauvinistic claims of more recent researchers like Catherine Acholonu, it has not been established beyond doubt that he was even an Igbo man.[1] Indeed, as time further passed, the idyllic glow that illuminated Equiano's reminiscences began to dull in the minds of later generations of freed slaves. It is true, of course, that in various aspects of their cultural and religious life the slaves, as Blassingame has lucidly documented; sought to keep alive their links with ancestral forms. It is true, even, that the sporadic revolts across the New World were motivated as much by the slaves' rejection of their holders' estimation of their origins as by a gored sense of justice. But some of the testimonies by later freedmen were already echoing the conventional propaganda about Africa as a land where men lived on trees, knew no agriculture, "didn't know anything 'bout singing," ate wild game (and even human beings) raw, and generally lived "jes' like wile Injuns" (Mellon 50–51).

However, the glow was not to die. For by the turn of the century, a good number of freedmen and especially the children of freedmen had acquired a respectable degree of education that led them to question the ideologies of race on which the whole enterprise of slavery had been supported. The researches and writings of scholars like W. E. B. Du Bois, Martin R. Delany and Carter G. Woodson sought to highlight the ancient civilizations of Africa—Egypt, Ethiopia, and Sahelian kingdoms, etc.— and African traditions both as evidence of the innate capabilities of the Black race and as part of a concerted program for the emancipation of the subjugated nations of Africa and, especially in Du Bois' case, the projection of a proud pan-African identity. Institutions of higher learning had also been set up to promote the ideals of black self-hood as well as offer conventional instruction along liberal and technological lines; in a notable article published in 1924, "Apropos of Africa," Alain Locke urged blacks to conscientiously educate themselves about Africa by all means, including travel and an exchange of students and publications.

Many of these efforts coincided with the growth of a strong black consciousness in those earlier years of this century generally referred to as the Harlem Renaissance or—when the consciousness moved beyond that black metropolis in New York—Black Renaissance. Alain Locke's recommendation on travel was not taken lightly. At a time when a gateway already existed with the settlement of Liberia as a homeland for freed slaves and the enthusiastic participation of black Americans in a variety of missionary and civic work in Africa, here was a chance for the writers to visit the continent and nourish their genius with the cultural wealth of the race and be the cultural standard-bearers of the New Negro. But, on the whole, it does not appear as if the writers of the age achieved a sufficiently deep cultural empathy with Africa. Perhaps because the arguments for the emancipation of the black race were being conducted in a largely chauvinistic idiom, similar in many respects to the jingoism of the European nations, the perception of Africa by the major Negro writers did not rise beyond a romantic celebration of the physical qualities of the continent.

Du Bois apparently led the way in this. Some of his imaginative pieces about Africa published in *The Crisis* between 1908 and 1924 have a predominantly romantic strain to them: the poem "A Day in Africa" (*Creative Writings* 17) celebrates the luxuriance and rapturous beauty of the landscape; "The Story of Africa" (97–98) evokes the majesty of the three great rivers of the continent in generously heroic imagery; and "Little Portraits of Africa" (130–32) is a collection of vignettes which paint glowing portraits of the lush vegetation and the people in their habitation, work, and recreation, with an interesting emphasis on their well-formed bodies (though "the face is not so lovely"). It is possible that Du Bois was too heavily engaged with the lofty political business of emancipation and too little with the actual lives of the Africans he encountered: "riding on the singing heads of black boys swinging in a hammock" (131), like the disreputable European colonizer, was certainly no way to get close to the intimate cultural lives of a people.

Langston Hughes did get close. In his autobiography, *The Big Sea*, he reports a visit to the Nigerian delta town of Burutu: in the company of a shipmate, he walks through the town where he hears *juju* drum sounds and pays a call to a local vendor of odds. Perhaps he never stayed long enough on the ship's stops at these West African coastal communities, because his poetry reveals little intimacy with Africa;[2] for him it is largely a "far away" land "that history books create," a land of drumbeats and haunting, impenetrable melodies (*Selected Poems* 3); he evokes "ancient, dusky rivers" like the Congo and the Nile (4), again encountered only in books; and again and again he summons images of dancing girls and tom-tom music and the dark depths of a continent that lives mostly in the romantic imagination.

This lack of cultural empathy should not, one must stress, be held against the writers of this generation. It was an intensely political moment in the history of a race in pursuit of self-affirmation, and perhaps the choices available to the writer were bordered within two extreme positions. He could, as Countee Cullen in "Heritage," admit that he was too long removed in time "from the scenes his fathers loved" to form any dependable judgments, and had rather "Quench my pride and cool my blood, / lest I perish in the flood" of confounding thoughts about Africa (*Color* 36–39). Or he could adopt the supreme romantic posture of Melvin Tolson much later in the period; appointed "poet laureate" in 1947 to celebrate a centennial Liberia that he had never visited, he carefully avoided the well-known social problems of the country—e.g., the growing division between the descendants of American settlers and the indigenous groups—and instead "chose to celebrate the democratic aspirations inherent in its founding ideals and its potential role in a brotherhood of nations seeking to realize a universal democratic dream" (Farnsworth 165).

In expressing some doubt and ambivalence about Africa, Countee Cullen was at least closer to the disturbing realities of the continent. These realities gradually dawned on Afro-American writers of the next generation as they observed African nations caught in the feverish agitation for emancipation from colonial rule. Visiting the Gold Coast on the eve of self-government, Richard Wright took some time to see the country and discuss its problems with a cross-section of the people. Although at this time he had grown disenchanted with the aims and methods of world communism, he left Ghana with so much disdain for "an Africa beset with gummy tribalism" (344), "a fetish-ridden past," and "mystical and nonsensical family relations that freeze the African in his static degradation" (348) that he strongly urged Kwame Nkrumah to run a fully "militarized social structure" (348) as the only solution to his people's problems. Lorraine Hansberry has also been able to capture some of the agitation in *A Raisin in the Sun*. In a subplot which mirrors the tragic illusions of independence with as much prophetic insight in 1959 as Wole Soyinka was to show a year later in *A Dance of the Forests*, she foresees a whole pageant of "crooks and petty thieves and just plain idiots who will come into power to steal and plunder the same as before—only now they will be black and do it in the name of the new independence" (Hansberry 84).

Not that the black American writers were not sympathetic to the aspirations of their African kin. It is on record, for instance, that the Negritude movement of Francophone writers, which flourished mostly in the forties and fifties, received a great deal of inspiration and encouragement from the writers of the Harlem Renaissance. Langston Hughes, indeed, was one of the early celebrators of the African literary re-awakening at the dawn of political independence, by publishing two anthologies—*An African Treasury* (1961) and *Poems from Black Africa*

(1963)—which brought to light some of the oral traditional poetry as well as a judicious spread of older (e.g., Senghor, Adali-Mortti) and younger (e.g., Soyinka, Rive) poets of the continent. Clearly, the black American poet was beginning to catch the pulse of libertarian sentiment from the land of drumbeats and haunting melodies. Sentiments like the following from "Independence," translated from a sarcastic Yoruba *ewi* chant by Adebayo Faleti of Nigeria:

> Let us rejoice with the slave.
> The one whose life has never been pawned
> Does not know the hardship of work before dawn
> > *(Poems from Black Africa* 102)

or these from the Ghanaian F. E. Kobina Parkes:

> Our God is black
> And like a goddamned god
> Guiding when loving
> Killing when angered (53)

must have enjoyed an endorsement in the heart of a poet who straddled the Black Renaissance and the sixties when black Americans were becoming increasingly impatient about who they were and where they belonged.

This shared predicament between blacks of the homeland and the Diaspora became quite evident at the September 1956 Conference of Black Writers and Artists in Paris, France, which was attended by notable figures like Richard Wright, James Baldwin, Mercer Cook, and Claude McKay from the United States, Aimé Césaire and George Lamming from the West Indies, and Leopold Senghor, Alioune Diop, and Cheikh Anta Diop from Africa. Baldwin has reported the proceedings of this conference and confesses being disturbed at hearing Senghor, amid the general feeling of brotherhood as well as sincere (and often turbulent) soul-searching contained in the various speeches, invoke Richard Wright's Black Boy as one of the major *African* autobiographies. There were many things at the conference which forced Baldwin to wonder whether a mere history of oppression was "enough to have made of the earth's black populations anything that can legitimately be described as a culture." But he found ample reason, within the general thrust of Senghor's speech, to be certain what this link was:

What they held in common was their precarious, their
unutterably painful relation to the white world. What they held
in common was the necessity to remake the world in their own
image, to impose this image on the world, and no longer be
controlled by the vision of the world, and of themselves, held
by other people. What, in sum, black men held in common was
their ache to come in to the world as men. And this ache united
people who might otherwise have been divided as to what a
man should be. (Baldwin 28–29)

Baldwin's generation of writers may not have been immediately
impelled to pursue these cultural ties, because there was urgent business
at home. The intense social and political sensitivities let loose in the self-
confident twenties had waxed bolder through the decades—what with
protests, marches, and court actions aimed at desegregation—until they
achieved explosive proportions in the sixties. But other forces were
operating at this time which made the connections inevitable. President
Kennedy's Peace Corps program brought many black American teachers
and other professionals to live and work in several African towns and
villages, where they had an opportunity cultivate and accumulate an
empathy with the cultures they encountered. Others were making their
own independent visits and taking up private employment; in the general
climate of political independence, they could now mix freely with the local
populations, free from any surveillance or menace from the erstwhile
colonial machine. Black American artists—visual artists, musicians, and
others—were also going over to Africa to explore the indigenous forms
and even participate in them: notable among these were the participation,
by jazz artists Ornette Coleman and Archie Shepp, in cultural festivals in
Nigeria (1965) and Algeria (1968) in which they actually recorded
performances with local traditional ensembles.

Malcolm X had visited Nigeria in 1963 and been christened
Omowale, "the homecoming child." I was an undergraduate at the
University of Ibadan when he gave a spellbinding lecture at Trenchard
Hall, at the end of which many black Americans living in the area went up
to him to be identified.[3] "Where do you come from?" he asked one lady.
She mentioned somewhere in Mississippi. "That's not where you come
from," Malcolm said, smiling. "Where do you come from?" Everyone,
including the lady, laughed off the mild embarrassment. A dozen years
later, however, it was no longer a laughing matter. For Alex Haley, who
had helped Malcolm to shape his *Autobiography*, was able to identify
Juffure in the Gambia as the home of his ancestors.

The discovery marked the end of questions which had racked his mind ever since as a youth he had been hearing first Grandma and later Cousin Georgia tell the haunting story of the stubborn slave "Kintay" who to the last was determined to return to Africa. And it "was significant, as Haley tells us towards the end of *Roots*, that Cousin Georgia "passed away within the very hour that I walked into Juffure village. I think that, as the last of the old ladies who talked the story on Grandma's front porch, it had been her job to get me to Africa, then she went to join the others up there watchin'" (682).

II

We could safely say, then, that by the sixties, what Kilson and Hill saw as "the romance of Africa" among Afro-American leaders had consolidated into a reasonably firm umbilical connection. The connection was aided, to a large extent, by the shift in ethnological scholarship from the romantic speculations on the origins of culture—indulged by European evolutionists by whom scholars like Delany and Du Bois had been influenced—to more empiricist investigations of individual societies encouraged by social or cultural anthropologists like Malinowski, Radcliffe-Brown, and Boas. American anthropologists and folklorists like Melville Herskovits and William Bascom were joining their European counterparts as well as indigenous African scholars in conducting detailed investigations of individual African societies, and so helping to uncover the vast mosaic of cultures and outlooks as well as the underlying homogeneities on the continent. It is from such researches that African-American writers like Paul Carter Harrison and Jay Wright have derived some of the controlling metaphors of their work.

When Wright says that *The Double Invention of Komo* "closes that phase" of his poetic development which began with *The Homecoming Singer*,[4] he is obviously referring to a growth in awareness in which he felt obligated to seek security in a specific frame of reference. It is true that he was born in New Mexico and spent his early youth there; but whatever cultural images had taken root in his psyche must have been forced to suffer a recontextualization in the light of his "developing black African-American life in the United States." The pleonasm in the phrase "black African-American" is no accident, for it bears witness to that underlying drive toward the affirmation of a black cultural outlook—as the pivot of everything else—which reaches a culmination in *The Double Invention of Komo*.

"I have," Wright tells us in the afterword to the book, "been the beneficiary, for some fifteen years of my life, of one of the most remarkable cooperative intellectual efforts in contemporary times. My major texts have been those assembled by the group of French anthropologist's; associated with Marcel Griaule, on an expedition to Dakar and Djibouti beginning in 1929 and subsequent expeditions to Mali, Chad, and Cameroon. Michel Leiris, Solange de Ganay, Genevieve Calame-Griaule, Deborah Lifchitz, André Schaeffner, Denise Paulme, Germaine Dieterlen, and Griaule have nourished those fifteen years, as well as this poem" (109). Wright acknowledges other African and non-African sources of influence in his work. But there is no doubt, as we read through his poems up to *The Double Invention of Komo*, that he has found his greatest concentration of images in the corpus of myths and rituals which Griaule and his team have brought to light from the Dogon and Bambara of Mali. Let us first explore the parallel (or twin) cosmologies of these groups as they emerge in the team's publications.[5]

First, the Dogon, about whom Marcel Griaule had been writing since 1938. Dogon myth has it that the world existed out of nothing, but was encapsulated in a timeless egg which both contained and constituted the godhead of the creator, Amma. This egg was itself made up of four smaller eggs referred to as "clavicles" which were "prefigurations of the four elements"—water, air, fire, and earth. "Thus, all the fundamental elements and future space were present in the morphology of the primordial 'egg'" (*Pale Fox* 81). Note that this entire structure was conceived in the mind of Amma who was himself the egg, and that within the morphology of the four "clavicles" Amma had already accounted for every creature and every object in the world that was going to be created from any of the four base elements.

The cross-section of the Amma-egg was designed as a double placenta, and in the middle of the entire structure was a spiral whose vibrations, under the driving force of Amma's *word* or speech, touched off the various acts of creation undertaken by Amma. The first of these, the creation of the primordial plant (*sene na*), followed by the emergence of two thorns pointing toward each other and representing the heavens and the earth, was rejected by Amma as a false start. When Amma resumed the act of creation, it was signaled by an explosion which opened up the egg and released a whirlwind, in the wake of which emerged a nuclear grain— the *po* or *fonio*, i.e., the *digitaria exilis*-at the heart of the matter. The wind was both the initiary speech of Amma and Amma himself; and inside the grain was contained the principle of human and all other life. Thus life, we are told, "developed at the same time as its means of support made of the blended elements" (*Pale Fox* 135).

After the *fonio*, Amma proceeded to create seven other forms of grain by the simple movement of the spiral propelled by his whirlwind-speech. At this point, however, it is important to grasp one principle which underlies the whole act of creation and on which Wright has conceived his entire poem. This is the principle of *doubling* or *twinhood*: Amma, the creator-god, is composed of a twin sexuality (male and female), and so is every one of the eight originary grains and everything else in creation. In this principle of sexual matching, the female element is of the order of 4, while the male is of the order of 3. I can see no other way of explaining this matching than as an effort by this culture to conceptualize the fundamental harmony of things in the universe and the coherence of the human components of the social structure.

Like the eight originary grains which served as the basis of its support, the human universe started from a nucleus of eight ancestors called *Nommo*. There is a minimal discrepancy between the version of the tale that Marcel Griaule collected in 1946 from the old Dogon sage Ogotemmêli (in *Conversations*) and the one which emerged from further elaborations recorded later from other Dogon by Griaule and Germaine Dieterlen (in *The Pale Fox*). In the earlier version, God (Amma) had a forced intercourse with the female Earth. whom he had created from clay. The issue from this unwarranted union, a jackal, was rejected and cast out, but not before he had caused some disorder in the nascent universe by committing incest with his mother, Earth, and stealing away the "word" of divination which he later taught to men. In his next intercourse with the Earth, Amma sired the first Nommo twins, half-human, half-serpent autochthons who were of the essence of water (i.e., as their life-force), emitted copper rays of light, and were each both male and female. This twin Nommo—frequently referred to as a single godhead Nommo—generated other twins who ultimately brought the number to eight. To the original Nommo is credited the invention of speech as known by man today and the various forms of technology (e.g., smithery and weaving), agriculture, cultural and religious life, and even the disposition of the cosmic and social orders. But the consummation of these elements of human civilization came only after the Nommo ancestors had escaped from heaven with, essentially, a piece of the copper light of the sun (for fire),[6] the celestial granary containing the signs or symbols that prefigured everything in creation—plants, animals, social space, etc.—and the eight elementary grains needed for human survival (*Conversations* 41–46).

The story of the creation of the world as it appears in *The Pale Fox*, succinctly summarized by Genevieve Calame-Griaule in her ethnolinguistic study of Dogon society, emphasizes the primordial rupture as well as Amma's speech as the organizing principle of all creation:

> The actors in the drama of creation are: Amma, the creator-god, "father" of all creatures; the "mother," represented by the "egg of the world" ..., composed of a double placenta fertilized by the "speech" of Amma; the first created beings, two androgynous twins, one of whom forms the figure of a rebel against paternal authority and the other a savior who by self-sacrifice reorganizes a world disturbed by the agitations of the former (the most serious of which was incest with the Earth, as a result of his taking a piece of the original placenta with him in his premature descent). Put to death, then resuscitated, the savior, Nommo, descended to the earth with an ark bearing the first humans, as well as all the animals and plants destined to populate the universe. Meanwhile, his enemy-brother was turned into a type of fox and condemned to lead a miserable life. His abominable influence is forever in conflict with that of Nommo, with the contradictory principles that they embody causing a division in the world and among mankind.
>
> The first ancestors who descended on earth with the ark were eight: four pairs of twins, whose marriages and those of their immediate descendants are given as a charter for the system of marriage operating in present-day Dogon society ... Amma eternal and uncreated, is the absolute master of all beings and things; to him belongs the *word* and all creation; it is by his speech that he forms the original placenta and fertilizes it. Perhaps at this divine level, we should construe this "speech" as "internal," or "thought-up," so to speak, or else unformulated, but taking shape in the object which invents it. Amma being the sky, his speech represents air among the four elements. (*Ethnologie* 93–95)

Out of the seven other grains originating from the *fonio* in the primordial placenta, Amma created seven different worlds (including the one that the eight Nommo ancestors later descended to), again by the force of his whirlwind-speech operating on the double placenta. Once again, the logic of the number 7 is based on the combined valency of the constitutive male and female elements (3 and 4 respectively) in every order of existence. And again, by the logic of doubling, the number of worlds created by Amma actually comes to 14 (i.e., 7 x 2), since the heavens and the earth are seen as twin worlds. Hence, "when one invokes Amma during ceremonies performed on the family altar consecrated to him, one says, 'Aroma, seven above, seven below, he spun 14 worlds'" (*Pale Fox* 193–94).

The cosmology of the Bambara is in some ways strikingly similar to what we have outlined for the Dogon above: whether this is due to cultural diffusion or to the fact of the two peoples originating from the same Mande stock (Dieterlen, *Essai* xiii; *Pale Fox* 27), it is not easy to say. As with the Dogon, the universe of the Bambara originated from nothing or an absolute void (*fu*): from this nothing the twin figures of the Earth (Pemba) and the Sky (Faro, who also rules over the waters) were already existing in an equipoise, shaped into existence by a "primordial vibration" (*Essai* 1). Of the two, Pemba was the creator-god, and was responsible for the existence of the element of generation of all things in the universe. This element, called *gla*, connotes perpetual movement and vitality, and by generating its own double (*dya*) established the principle of twinhood and thus of perpetual self-multiplication in all things. A primordial contact between the *gla* and its twin (*dya*) resulted in an explosion which saw the release of signs prefiguring every object—animate or inanimate, concrete or abstract—destined to exist in the universe: in other words, everything in creation was already prefigured, *ab initio*, by its own sign (4). We shall return to this grammatology which underlies both Dogon and Bambara culture and which features as an organizing principle in the poetry of Jay Wright.

Pemba was also plagued by two convulsions at the dawn of creation. The first came from the female essence of the earth which he had created, given a life-force (*ni*), a double (*dya*), and a name, Mousso Koroni, and taken as wife. Intercourse between them (though not necessarily sexual) results in the birth of plants and animals (the first of which is a panther) and of human beings; every one of these creatures was also provided with a life-force and a double.[7] But Pemba was not satisfied with one wife and began do have intercourse with the daughters born to him by Mousso Koroni. Knowledge of this threw her into a rage; in revenge she began to disclose to men the secrets entrusted to her by Pemba, and tore up everything in sight, causing much bloodshed.[8] Pemba gave chase, and Mousso Koroni fled through the earth and across the sky. Faro, whose aid Pemba had sought, finally apprehended Mousso Koroni and demanded capitulation; but she refused to yield and insisted on her freedom. Faro let her go, but after a long life of misery and misadventure, she died in distress and neglect. In the process she did learn how to overcome hunger, thus teaching mankind the secrets of survival through the cultivation of the earth (18–19); which is why today her fortunes are gratefully commemorated in ritual songs and mimetic rites performed at harvest-tide (*Essai* 39–40).

Pemba's second trouble came from Faro. Having created the principle of generation (*gla*), Pemba entrusted it to Faro's keeping while he busied himself with affairs in the terrestrial world. These turned out to be deleterious. The major earthly manifestation of Pemba was a phallic tree, *balanza*, which lived by sucking up the blood and powers of human beings who bowed to him in worship. Faro did not like this; to counter the powers of Pemba, he taught men how to rejuvenate themselves with vegetable juices. Armed with this virtue, men survived but still continued to worship Pemba. Obviously feeling spurned, Faro responded by setting conditions for the supply of water—an element indispensable to life and over which he presided—and demanded that the entire practice of nourishment by blood should cease. Pemba knew he was in for a big fight, which Faro was likely to win. He prepared for the fight anyway, and was defeated by Faro (*Essai* 24–25).

Having overcome Pemba, Faro proceeded to reorganize the universe in the following ways: he established the four cardinal points; divided the universe into seven corresponding heaven/earth twin worlds, establishing his seat in the middle (i.e., fourth) world from which, by turning his copper spiral, he ensured the perpetual revolution of the entire universe; established the domains of water (seas, rivers, and the restitutive or purificatory rain), his main area of influence; classified all living thins (men, animals, and plants) into the four cardinal points; identified the major sources of nourishment as well as taboos for both animals and men; and finally taught men the science of agriculture by giving them, through the medium of heaven-descended smiths, the eight original grains of cereals "created at the same time as man, but remaining secretly in the sky" (*Essai* 26–30).

We must stress here that all these activities and their resultant effects had earlier been *prefigured* in the signs released, as we mentioned above, in the primordial explosion between the atom of generation (*gla*) and its double (*dya*). Faro embarked upon his job of cosmic organization only after he had descended form his original seat, the sky, to an earth he had effectively usurped from Pemba. This descent was effected by Faro first putting all the primordial signs in a boat (or ark) and sitting in it with an oar (*pembele*) in his hand; the boat was then let down from heaven, by a "long chain," onto a pool and held stably on its surface by the teeth of a crocodile. Let us now examine this system of signs, an area in which the Dogon and the Bambara demonstrate considerable agreement.

Both groups are agreed in affirming that these signs were conceived and created in the primordial void by the creator-god (Amma, Pemba), and contained the nuclei of everything that was to constitute the material and nonmaterial universe known to man, as well as the totality of knowledge available to man: astrology, religion, agriculture and the other arts, the disposition of the social structure, and all else besides. Both groups are also agreed, that there is a total of 266 signs in the cosmic system, but this number has been attained by slightly different paths of computation. For the Dogon there are first 2 "guide" signs representing the primordial Nommo twins; then there are 8 "master" signs, formed from a doubling (thanks to the parallel male and female elements) of the four axes or clavicles of Amma's egg; and finally the 256 "complete" signs of the world. The 10 (i.e., 2 plus 8) earlier signs provide the base for the "soul and life force" given to everything, while the 256 impart qualities like form, color, and substance (*Pale Fox* 85).

The Bambara have taken a more complex "cosmo-biological" route in their reckoning. This system is based on the human vertebral column, which is said to have 33 vertebrae (foreshadowing the 33 stages of philosophical instruction in the Komo cult). Each vertebra is also said to be structured into four segments. Again, by the principle of doubling, the 4 segments add up to 8; multiplying this 8 by 33 vertebral steps, we get the 264 basic signs prefiguring everything in the universe. Another way to derive the 264 would be to see each of the 33 vertebrae as bisexual, which in effect gives us 66 vertebral steps; multiply this by the 4 segments of each of these, and you get 264. The remaining two signs are said to be prefigurations of the leader of the Komo, the society which guards this sacred primordial system, and the masked dancer, described as "the foundation" of the Komo institution (*Fondements* 22).

Both the Dogon and the Bambara are emphatic that the original 266 signs are by no means final: they are simply the first series in a system of perpetual self-generation (best summed up perhaps in the Bambara concept *zo*). What this involves is that, as the universe expands and each new being is created or new thing (animate or inanimate) is added to man's conceptual space, a fresh set of 266 signs is brought into existence. "Thus," we are told, "the signs proliferate to prefigure, in the abstract, all the beings and things which come to form the universe. And the bonds which unite them—the universe being considered as a unit—are transformed by the classifications and correspondences established between all these sets, correspondences which are seen as designed to promote the functioning of this universe such as the Bambara conceive it" (*Fondements* 25; cf. *Pale Fox* 94–95). In other words, each time anything new is added to the universe, the latter becomes newer and stronger as it adjusts itself to accommodate the newcomer.

What we have then, in this West Sudanic system of signs, is a coherent and self-contained nucleus of ideas enabling man's apprehension of the world in which he lives. It is important indeed to grasp the man-centeredness of this system. The seemingly abstract idiom in which it presents itself, and the emphasis laid on prefiguration, would leave the impression that this is a closed system in which mans creativity or choice is utterly precluded. On closer reflection, however, it becomes clear that this system mediates the respective claims of destiny and creativity. For by continuously giving birth to fresh generations and by engaging in occupations designed to improve the quality of life in the world in which he lives, man is responsible for the perpetual reduplication of the original 266 signs in a more fundamental way than the other beings—plants and animals—with whom he came into the universe.

It is therefore not without logic that the entire world-system is symbolically structured in the outline of the human anatomy. Here I refer to that most dramatic scene in Griaule's *Conversations with Ogotemmêli*, in which the dead Nommo (Lébé), dancing, back to life from under the earth to the rhythm of the Nommo-smith's strokes on the anvil, first swallows the smith, then regurgitates him in a welter of *dougue* stones laid out in the form of a prostrate skeleton. "He organised the world," Ogotemmêli tells us, "by vomiting the *dougue* stones in the outline of a man's soul" (*Conversations* 49–50). We are told by later Dogon elaborators of the concept of prefiguration that, although "the sign precedes the thing signified, it is dependent upon the conscious and active mind" of man to give it perceptible shape (*Pale Fox* 92). And the Bambara echo the same idea when they hold that, "More than anything else, the human personality is the living expression of the 266 basic signs of creation" (*Fondements* 81). We are in the final analysis face to face with a traditional system in which man is an active and a conscious partner in the determination of his future.

This complex body of knowledge, contained in the matrix of 266 signs, is closely guarded in every community in this region by a cult, headed by a cult leader who is a smith. The Dogon have their cults, but we are going to restrict the rest of our discussion to an examination of Bambara cults, especially the Komo, since this forms the substratum of Wright's volume, *The Double Invention of Komo*. There are altogether six cults in Bambara society: N'dono, Tyiwara, Komo, Kono, Nama, and Kore. The Kore is the finishing point of the seemingly interminable system of instruction built upon the 266 primordial signs; in effect, it is a society of elder citizens or aged men. But the Komo is considered the all-embracing society open to all the circumcized citizens (only women and griots are excluded), the one sanctioned by the ancestors as the sanctuary and the library, as it were, of the symbols of knowledge created by Pemba and entrusted to Faro.

What is the origin of Komo? As we mentioned above, Faro descended from the sky in can ark suspended from a chain, and landed in a pool of water, his favored element, taking with him in the boat the 266 signs. Somewhere in the course of his cosmic reorganization, he undertook to impart the secrets of creation and of universal wisdom to the creatures—men and animals—whom Pemba had earlier created in the terrestrial world. Of all these creatures, only three proved attentive and assiduous in acquiring the secrets contained in the signs: the hyena, the vulture, and a smith. According to the myths, the hyena got particularly close to Faro and, in his voracious curiosity, was in the habit of rustling about in Faro's pool to fish for the signs concretized there in the various parts of the water lily. From this activity, the hyena acquired its name *ko mo suruku*—viz. *ko* (pool), *mo* (fish), and *suruku* (splasher)—"the rustler who fishes in the pool," a name which was later given to the society as *Komo* (*Fondements* 26).

For their diligence, these creatures were awarded various virtues and powers by Faro. Although in the folklore the hyena emerges, rather deceptively, as naive and a dupe of smaller animals like the hare, from Faro he received patronage of the "black knowledge" such as the secrets of motherhood, living, agricultural yield, songs and dances, and other arts. To the vulture, "bird of heaven," was imparted the secrets of the "white knowledge" such as the arts of divination, priesthood, royalty, war, hunting, even death. But the smith made away with the key prize. He was so attentive to Faro's instructions that he even mastered the art of transforming himself into other creatures, including the hyena. For this spectacular assiduity, as well as his rather politic submission to Faro, the smith (as representative of humans) was awarded three very special gifts: thought or reason, speech, and a power or authority which enabled him to address himself directly to God and to gain mystic control of the universe including the animals. He was also charged with the foundation of the Komo cult in which the other creatures (hyena and vulture) would nevertheless enjoy a special regard. To inaugurate the cult, he raised the first altar to Faro, which he constructed out of a meteorite (thunder-stone) in the shape of an anvil. The smith was the first priest of the Komo cult (*Fondements* 27).

Historically, however, the establishment of the Komo cult is credited by a rather old tradition to a group of seventeen smiths called "the seventeen men of the first Komo," whose names or actual geographic provenience is lost to memory. A later tradition, however, gives the credit for establishment to certain smith families—Doumbia, Sissoko, and Koromaka—acting under the impetus of their ancestor Fakoli, warrior, smith, and priest (*Fondements* 15–16), a key ally and general of the thirteenth-century monarch Sunjata in the latter's war against Sumanguru for the control of Mali. Whatever the historical genesis of the cult, however, the important thing to note here is the prominence enjoyed by the smith in the cosmologies of the Western Sudanas well as the special mention which he gets in the poetry of Jay Wright.[9]

In any Bambara community, the Komo enclave is usually situated in a wood or forest on the outskirts of town. Among the stable property of the cult are a shrine-house or sanctuary (often a mud-hut), decorated with black, white, and red lines and certain geometric designs taken from the *gla* complex; within the hut, an altar built in a semicircular shape, indicating thereby that its other half (or *double*) is under the earth, contains certain objects like meteorite (from which the smith built the first altar) and some gold (one of the metals worked by the smith); and the cult's estates which are traditionally portioned into three for the cultivation of (a) *fonio* and other grains, (b) other "purificatory" plants, and (c) ritual tobacco.

The "movable" property of the cult, which is situated in the various locations of the enclave, include a large wooden board on which the 266 signs are engraved; a wooden trough, also engraved with the 266 signs and representing the ark or canoe in which Faro came down from heaven, bearing the signs of the *gla*; a wooden block (*pembele*), also engraved with the signs, and representing the paddle of Faro's boat (they are usually placed together); an iron chain of 17 links, representing the 17 founder-smiths of the cult as well as being a piece of the "long chain" by which Faro let down his ark in the primordial void (the chain is also claimed to symbolize the umbilical chord which a child loses on the seventh day after its birth); musical instruments like whistle, bells, rhombus, wooden drum, trumpet, etc., called "instruments of speech"; certain portable altars (theoretically 266 in number) which contain special items of the cult like grains, a crucial element in Faro's baggage; and finally a double-faced mask, made of *kapok* wood, and bearing on one side the face of a hyena and on the other the face of a crocodile, two animals connected with Faro's career. The mask is seen as central to the entire collection of sacred items, because the masquerade's dance is believed to invest these items with a dynamic force, to "make the objects speak," and so "disseminate the wisdom contained in the signs represented by the objects" (*Fondements* 53).

The process of belonging to the Komo cult begins[10] from infancy. Three days after the birth of a boy, his father dedicates him to the Komo offering to the god certain condiments (*boli*) that he has provided for the ceremony and chanting certain verses (*Essai* 154). But the induction of the child actively begins at age five or six, when he is introduced to the first cadre of initiation (N'domo) along with boys of his age set. Here, he is put through a program of instruction in a variety of things: games; songs both religious and historical, and tales; the construction of various objects featuring the cosmic myth, such as the "great net" symbolizing the idea of "fishing for wisdom" (as the hyena did in Faro's pool) and the "great bird with four wings" which is the vulture; and the drawing of a large chart of signs taken from the *gla*. The child is still not circumcised, and goes on in his N'domo apprenticeship until the age of seven.

From age seven until age ten the boy and his age-mates, still members of the N'domo group, are taught a secret ritual language as well as other games (e.g., Bambara wrestling) which are more violent than the previous ones and are designed to "steep their bodies, liven their thoughts, and enlarge their souls" (*Fondements* 57). From age ten the boys become members of the Tyiwara group, where they are made to participate in functions like farm-work and village vigilante, and are taught various prayers and chants relating to the dancing *tyi wara* mask and to the mythic hyena and vulture. The ritual language they have learned will be forgotten as soon as they graduate from the Tyiwara.

The final segment of the apprenticeship in the Tyiwara is the period of circumcision, which is seen to confer certain spiritual and other privileges on the patients. At this point, the boys are sequestered in a bush outside the village for seven weeks. After the circumcision, carried out by the officiating smiths or by "house slaves," signs are traced on the ground or on the walls of the enclave and the boys are given a whole range of lessons. These comprise (a) lessons in good manners, such as proper ways of eating, sleeping, and dressing as well as injunctions against lying and duplicity, calumny, stealing, and so on; (b) physical exercises, such as long walks in the wood, hunting, fishing, swimming, and other games aimed at paramilitary formation of the youths; (c) sexual education, carried out with songs filled with sexual references but without a pornographic intent. These songs, which should not be sung outside of this context, are aimed at instilling a decent regard for sexuality and its fundamentally generative role; (d) religious education. This is the final stage of the induction and involves the actual initiation into the Komo society.

Since the process of initiation forms the subject of Wright's poem, I shall postpone discussion of it until the next section. But at this point it is important to establish the acknowledged aims of the initiation and the role that the Komo society plays in the lives of the initiated Bambara. There is no doubt that, as the guardian of the "great signs" (*ti baw*), the 266 signs which Faro is said to have brought into the world, the Komo is the depository of the entire body of knowledge recognized by the Bambara, the compendium of their ethical conduct, the charter for the organization of their entire life, and the insurance of the survival of Bambara civilization as it unites all generations past, present, and to come. Every facet of Bambara life—childbirth, marital and agrarian rites, justice, recreation, collective decisions on war and political issues, even funeral rites—is superintended by Komo. The knowledge acquired during the initiation is secret and potent. It is a knowledge that comes from God, designed to help the initiate know himself and his place in the scheme of creation, "to move beyond himself, to move beyond life so as to raise himself towards nothingness and towards God" (*Fondements* 18). The cult thus guides life on earth but also transcends it, hence we are told; "When life ceases to exist on Earth—whether of men, animals or plants—the Komo will awaken the souls of dead things over which it has eternal charge" (*Essai* 165).

III

The sketch which we have given so far of Dogon and Bambara mythology and ritual will have served to establish the semantic backgrounds to the vast body of symbols that Wright has utilized in *The Double Invention of Komo*; so that, when we encounter references to the whirlwind, smith, the god, pool, boat, copper, gold, kapok, stone, vulture, jackal, and other creatures and images, we are no longer at a loss to know what is their relevance to the poet's quest for self-knowledge. It now remains for us to follow the sequence of the initiation as here specially defined by Wright in his "search in these Americas for a breaking of the vessels, for a redefinition of personality, and for new areas of creative experience" (*Double Invention* 111).

Before examining Wright's poem, it will be useful to state the basic sequences of the initiation ceremony so as to see in some relief the liberties that Wright has taken in the poem.[11] The ceremony begins with a council held by established members of the cult. On the morning of the meeting, the Komo leader traces on the ground certain figures which mark the positions of the respective members attending the session, and of the Komo objects to be displayed on the occasion. Then begins a period of deliberations which are usually broken by intervals, some of which are taken up by the playing of musical instruments and other affairs. The ceremony of "the coming out of Komo," which comes early in the sequence, involves the formal bringing out of the various Komo objects—the wooden board, the wooden trough, (i.e., Faro's boat), the staff (i.e., his paddle), the chain, tunic, mask, portable altars, musical instruments, etc. These are cleaned and redecorated, and the shrine repainted especially with the design of the red, white, and black stripes and geometric designs. After this purificatory activity, the masked dancer (Komo medium) puts on the tunic and the mask and winds up this section with a brief dance and chant which offers the Komo signs for divine blessing and renewal.

The next sequence is called the "descent into the pool," during which the members of the cult go to the sacred pool of the village, seat of Faro, singing a chant. An interlude of music and singing hails on the hyena (patron of the cult) and Faro the "keeper of the black gold" or "black knowledge" which he imparts to various mystic animals. Still singing, the members descend into the water, where they undress as a sign of humility, wash their faces, and pray to Faro for protection. Then the various Komo objects are dipped in the water. At sundown, the procession moves back to the shrine-house in the enclave, accompanied by further music and singing. This whole sequence is aimed at the purification and revivification of the signs and renewal of the process of creation.

At about 8 o'clock in the evening, the actual initiation of the circumcized boys begins. This is again preceded by a session of music and chanting of prayers, followed by the three essential phases of the initiation. The first phase involves the ritual death of the initiates, when they lie on the floor before the officiants and elders. Next is the slaughtering of the animals which the parents and relatives of the initiates have brought on their behalves: fowls and goats, but more often fowls. The initiates are then "revived" by the officiants sprinkling on them water fetched from the village stream or pool. On waking they are asked a variety of questions, to which they give the symbolic answer: "I don't know my name or my parents' name; I don't know where I come from or where I am going; I don't know how to tell left from right, front from back; show me the path to the race of my fathers." This session of interrogations also includes the administration of an oath of total allegiance to Komo and a pledge of total secrecy: a whole range of horrible deaths is threatened on any violation of this oath.

Next, the initiates are fed from the cooked entrails of the slaughtered fowls. They are also made to drink the blood of a sacrificial goat, designed to instill in them the forces of Komo and to seal their oath. They are then taught the operations of the society in great detail, the need for the hierarchy of grades and for respecting the taboos and prohibitions of the cult. They are also given moral instruction on the need to lead an honest life, to avoid duplicity and bad faith. They are told the story of what happened to the first members who violated these laws. In the final stage of the ceremony, the initiates are made to prostrate themselves before the altar and the Komo articles. After this, they are presented with cult emblems which confer on them full membership of the society: they are now reborn with a new spiritual life and asked to "open your eyes to Komo." The ceremony ends with the Komo leader welcoming them to the life of "true Bambara" charted by their ancestors, and charging them further to lead honest lives.

As we begin our analysis of *The Double Invention of Komo*, it is necessary to take seriously what Wright says in his afterword (114–15) about the multiple voices on which the statement rides. The initiate speaks in his own ceremonial voice but also in the voices of the several personalities that inhabit the larger cultural space that he traverses: African, European, and American. But there is more than that. Wright reveals in this poem a pervasive sense of "the Other" in terms both of the Bambara concept of personality and of the poem itself as a performative enterprise. When, therefore, the initiate says

> Brother, I take your woman's heart into my head.
> Already, I am four.
> I double myself and double you (4)

or later

> Brother, I have spoken in your voice
> My initiate's love, afflicts you (34)

he is addressing both his "double" (*dya*)—with whom he holds constant debate in the poem—and the reader of the poem who may well reflect some of the complex personality of the poet. In following the sequence of the poem, it is also important to heed Wright's warning that the poem is far less "a point-for-point presentation of Komo's rite" than "an imaginative apprehension of the facts and values embodied in Komo."

The Double Invention of Komo begins with an "Invocation" taken from a purification ceremony designed to cleanse a world troubled by the misfortunes of Mousso Koroni.[12] Chants regularly begin the annual rites of the Komo society; but Wright has appropriately chosen one that proclaims his total humility in his quest ("desire," often also called "love") for self-knowledge and self-fulfillment. The invocation is therefore both a statement of the project and an effort to purify the enclave where the ceremony will take place.

The next section, titled "Prefigurations" (3–8), is interesting because it is not are actual stage of the ceremony. In fact, the actual rites which precede the initiation do not come up until page 23 ("The First Return ... "). The entire portion up to page 23 marks an introduction of the personality of the initiate into the field in which his future career will operate. "Prefigurations" prepares the embryo-soul of the initiate for its journey into the world, dressing this idea of inception in well-chosen images from the creation myths of both the Dogon and the Bambara and especially Faro's career:

Walk in the light of copper
By an egg's radiance I arrange my soul's baggage
Age over age, my bones thicken and flex
I am adept in the god's boat. (3)

Before he begins the journey, however, he must proclaim the Komo credo: "I profess / one master / one creator / one power / one king / one cult / one submission" (3–4). The embryo journeying with its baggage of signs now approaches the Komo enclave (the "clearing" in the "wood" 5) wherein is located the shrine house decorated with "black, white, red" and a "simple design." At this point he is able to "figure" himself, to identify what configurations in his baggage of signs will determine his future character. So now he ceases to be an embryo-soul living a prefigurative life, and is transformed into a fetus in the womb of a "mother" (who, for all practical purposes, may be seen as the initiate's guide or sponsor for the rites).

Note that this figural journey is simultaneous with the meeting of Komo members in the enclave, prior to the initiation rites. The figural fetus, traveling as a "shadow in the god" through their tobacco-scented session (6), continues its journey across the village "pool" around the enclave as a passenger in Faro's boat. As he nears the end of his journey, however, he is gripped by anxiety about the character allotted to him in his baggage of signs. "What child am I?" he worries (7), and although his "mother" tries to reassure him by figuring him in the image of a dutiful child, he is truly worried as the boat approaches the threshold to the descent into the world (8).

"It is night," says the anxious fetal initiate, "yet it is morning" (8). With this we can safely assume that the initiate and his group have arrived at the scene of the ceremony (which, as we pointed out above, begins about 8 p.m.). The arrival of the fetal initiate is now seen in the light of childbirth, but this is filtered through the imagery of Faro's descent into the world with a chain:

> Yes, this is the chain of descent
> Like you, the world unwinds from a body
> Umbilical, it waves through every heaven
> > on every day.

When the child finally arrives in the world—which here enjoys a figural equivalence with the ritual enclave of Komo—he activates the protective altars of the clan which themselves harbor the signs the child has brought with him. This brings us to the next section of the poem, "The Eleven Altars Dance in the Wood" (9–21). Dieterlen and Cissé tell us (*Fondements* 19) that these eleven altars—*dyibi* (or *dibi*), *makari, nene, sele, sukodyi, se, sinikle, buaba, furaba, dyako*, and *tro* (short for *ntoro*)—represent the names of the known Komo societies of the Bambara; each alter is identified by the element (gold, sand, water, wood, charcoal, etc.) that formed a crucial part of its composition. The altars now dance to welcome the initiate or celebrate his arrival in their sphere of influence.

The dance of the altars prefigures the initiate's future history, a history characterized by a fusion of traditional African sensitivity and sobering experiences in foreign lands. True, the initiate bears within him the seeds of his people's cosmic history stamped deep within his psyche:

> You undo the smallest grain.
> Your breath shapes a red clavicle.

> I am beside you.
> I am in you. (14)

True, whatever future associations he forms and whatever other quests he undertakes, he will remain bound by the traditional ties that connect the individual with forebears and posterity:

> Down below the love bed,
> the knit bones of the dead
> cock their conch ears
> to another soul's implosion. (13)

Here, too, the signs figure the harrowing experience of an African soul in the Arab slave trade:

> My camel bags token
> a long ride
> through the black oil of the desert ...
> I complete this figuration
> of the one element
> tale of a Berber's journey,
> the one star's buttress and vault,
> by the soul's compulsion
> in death's drum (15)

and offer intimations of the transatlantic middle passage:

> I see you, a sailor shucked
> On a yellow cliff, finger
> the boat in the dream. (11)

But the destiny is not so rigidly enforced, in the sense that, although its bare outlines have been drawn within the figuration of the signs, the individual is nevertheless allowed to enter into a dialogue with divinity in the determination of his future path. There is room, that is, for a cooperative alliance between divinity (or tradition) and the individual will:

> Within this space,
> Your soul contests its own making.
> Here,

> the tongue dips
>   into its own craving ...
>   In this nexus of exchange,
>   the god will license you
>   to navigate his pool. (9)

Such a prospect is obviously attractive to a nascent American personality. Hence, after the dancing altars have declared with all due excitement the predetermined outlines of the soul's history, the latter seizes the opportunity, in the next section of the poem—"The double argument concerning the altar dance" (21–23)—to engage its "double" in stressing both the South American component of his historical experience ("*cuatro* voice," "papaya mornings," "mariachi spangles" 22) and, even more forcefully, the steady progress of the black American selfhood from slave labor to hard-won freedom:

>   my shackled body's
>   rising
>   into cotton heat
>   my rebel voice
>   the craft of my slow
>   arrival on a politic ground,
>   my stick   and gun
>   on freedom's ground.
> I am a battered body with a care for belonging. (22–23)

It is a persuasive argument, and the initiate's double accepts its implicature even as he prepares to be exposed to his field of experience:

> I accept this argument.
> Contain and free me. (23)

The Komo ceremony now actively begins. In "The First Return, the First Presentation of Instruments" (23–25), the Komo objects are brought out from the shrine-house and altar and laid out in the clearing before the established members sitting in session. The objects are recognizable enough in the mantic roll-call: boat, board, tunic (which the leader will wear during the ceremony), mask, anvil, chain, and various musical instruments. This brief epiphany of the instruments inspires intimations both of knowledge that predates the initiate's experience ("These you may not know") and of experiences that will define his future sociopolitical life ("What may be known").

"The Opening of the Cycle of Redemption" (25–52) is a long sequence which fits into the early part of the Komo ceremony. But it significantly extends the ambiance of that ceremony so that the soul of the initiate is allowed to test itself in number of adventures across time and space, and to return again to the enclave to consolidate the wisdom gained in these trials. Before the soul begins its journey, it pays its respects to the patrons of the Komo cult (the parallelism of "black" and "white" in the first two lines of this section represent the twin patronage of the hyena, keeper of the "black knowledge" and the vulture, keeper of the "white knowledge"), asking for guidance ("Light") in its explorations through the dark recesses of its lonely quest ("hermit heart"). The first journey takes the soul through locales in the United States ("San Pedro/Los Angeles" 26–29). Here the soul encounters scenes of urban rage and armed violence which severely cut short human life ("I book / my days fourscore / by reason of my wrath"), and does not derive much joy from the prospect that it encounters ("There/ is / no / comfort in this picture of you" 27).

A second journey, this time to Frankfurt, exposes the soul to some of the harsher, more unsavory history that it must accommodate in its multicultural personality. This journey proves a signal failure, because the soul finds it painfully difficult to exorcise the bloody career of Hitlerian Germany from the American personality being nurtured under the divine tutelage of Faro:

How can I now will
Your redemption is His will,
Or soothe you with the water vowel of peace?
How can I take your rose stain into my heart?
This that I set down is the mind's
perception of what it will not hold. (36)

The soul's third journey in this section takes it to Rome (49–52). It is a most chastening experience, because here the soul learns the virtues of patience, charity, humility, and submission in the quest for wisdom. These are, of course, virtues that Komo teaches, and it is comforting to find that the virtues which the initiate is obliged to cultivate have their analogues in the Christian faith, complete with "a well spring / of living water" (49). The soul of the voyager (*peregrinus*) is now tiring and aging with the many contradictions it is continually having to resolve. But listening here to the teachings of the fathers of the Church—Augustine, Ambrose, and others—it learns that there is a virtue even in constant tribulation and the attendant self-renewal ("the falling / and rising up"); in the Christian miracle of the Resurrection, the soul is glad to derive the lesson that one who truly desires knowledge need not fear to fall into error again and again:

> I step into the form three times,
> to know that I die with the world,
> am buried, and rise again.
> Brother,
>> Thus let us enter together,
>> in the path of charity,
>> in search of Him ...
> in search of the act,
> in search of the meaning of desire. (52)

In between these journeys, the initiate's soul returns to the Komo enclave, the sanctuary of its enlightenment. The ceremony of initiation is scarcely under way; but it seems essential for the soul to address itself to influences outside itself and its immediate cultural ambiance and thereby understand or *know* itself in the context of the Other, since the nascent personality of the initiate is going to comprise various (seemingly) disparate backgrounds.

After the soul's American excursion (26–29), we return to the Komo enclave. The sequence titled "Komo *enfant* / Komo *mère*" is inspired by this particular cult's duty to acknowledge its obligation to the cult from which it received its franchise, and here the still timorous initiate seeks further reassurance and guidance in the demanding experience it is to go through:

> Consecrated one,
> I must take my strength
> From your name, a bit of foam
> spun from god's hull.
> If I dress my apprehensive foot
> in the pool, I trust your seaman's skill. (29)

The uncertainty is to be expected, because the initiate has not quite grasped the dualities of his personality. The excursions and the return to the sanctifying presence of the cult objects—mask, the tunic worn by the priest, etc.—gradually lead him to appreciate, albeit timorously, that "I am gifted with my own / division" (31) and that the entire ceremony is designed to endow him, under the superintending light of the god in the pool, with "the wisdom / of being set free / in the wood of another's desire" (34).

The interlude after the soul's excursion to Germany is marked by an even more severe self-questioning. Apparently, this exposure to the Hitlerian world has filled the soul with severe doubts about the validity of the presence of *the Other* in its scheme of consciousness, and somehow leads it to wish there was no statutory allowance for unsavory elements in its composition. This rather long section (38–49) is thus riddled with ambivalences, not the least of which is the opposition between *presence* and *absence*. The almost rebellious argumentativeness of the soul earns it a reprimand:

> An idiot initiate is evil's shaft of light.
> If you go from the certainty of oneness
> into solitude and return,
> I must divest you of your double
> and twin you in love's seclusion. (39)

But good sense ultimately prevails. The initiate's soul is guided to reflect on the good fortune of the forebears of the race who benefited from the twin patrons of Komo (42),[13] and is reminded that even his Mande ethnicity is linked with others ("Asante" 43). The soul is gradually subdued, and appeals to Mousso Koroni, the Dogon world's arch-rebel, to guide it to accept to be duly inscribed with a destiny appropriate to it (48). This section ends with the voice of the soul's double—or possibly the Komo leader, the smith as a repository of Komo wisdom, representing the voice of Komo—asserting the will of God (Faro) in the determination of the composition of the initiate's personality (48–49).

The subjugation of the soul at this point is an apt preparation for the journey to Rome, where it learns the salutary lessons of humility and charity. Of course, the soul will be subject to further stresses as the initiation gets well under way: the search for and acquisition of knowledge is, after all, a life-long process and leads even "towards death, / the unknown, / the nothing, / the creator" (43). What is important is that the soul achieves progressive chastening through this process of doubt and illumination.

After Rome, the soul, now reasonably illumined, is ready for the due inscription. The next section of the poem is titled "The Initiate Takes His First Six Signs, the Design of His Name" (53–58), and here the basic outlines of the destiny of the initiate are sketched. The elements from which this destiny is figured are reflections in one way or another of the material (e.g., gold, knives) or immaterial (air, voice of birds) essences of cult wisdom; in their various ways they prefigure a personality that is destined to find its place in a wider, complex milieu, beyond the limited confines of the Dogon-Bambara world. The first sign, *Sanu*—symbolizing gold which is a base material of the protective altars of the cult—"is fear's destroyer," and so guarantees the survival of the identity and the spirit of the initiate in a difficult world. *Ma-muru-fla*, the twin knives for male and female circumcision, preserve the boon of that primal sexual balance enshrined in the composition of the godhead and of all things in creation. *Mako*, the "whirlwind music [which] liberates all things, and directs all things to God," will guide the initiate through his ambiguities and facilitate his full perception of his place in the world he inhabits. *Doo*, of the essence of air, is designed to "comprise / an initiate's fertile and uneasy resolution" (56): the emergent personality will be a complex, uneasy one, but therein lies the potential for creative strength (fertility). *Dyee* symbolizes "union" and prepares the initiate to absorb the non-African elements of the emergent American personality: as the initiate's soul declares,

> Voices of the universe find their higher pitch in me.
> I extend my clan's wall
> > and unfold the limits
> > > of the body I inhabit. (57)

Finally, in *Kono ka* the initiate's soul recognizes the burden he will bear of continually seeking to define himself in his world; "A twin, condemned / to holy ignorance" (58), he will forever be driven to redefine himself in the context of the ever deepening complexities of his selfhood.

The soul continues to be put through some salutary lessons, not the least of which is learned in an excursion to the high intellectual culture of Paris (60–61). Here the pretensions of scientific exactitude are held against the proposition that a respect for the imperceptible and the numinous has its merits:

> Nothing compels God to uncover
> this heart's love of light.

Nothing compels the initiate,
sitting under the spark,
to acknowledge his mind's power.
It is not fitting to confine
this power to the sensible thing. (61)

Such a lesson is particularly apt, because the initiate is being groomed for
life in a highly materialistic culture which places a high premium on
temporal benefits, whereas the highest wisdom that Komo imparts takes
us beyond mortal life:

If the perfect passion holds us,
we will live in the clarity
of being set free to expire. (61)

The actual ceremony of initiation finally begins on page 61. It follows
the essential sequence as we described it earlier. But it is significant that
now the soul or spirit of the initiate undertakes more journeys than it did
before (six as against four). It would appear that, as the poet-initiate's
effort at self-examination winds towards the end, his spirit feels an
increasingly stronger need for due chastening and consolidation. The
consciousness grows even stronger that this is the soul of an "alien
initiate" (66), and journeys take on a much greater significance as the
proper crucible for the emergence of a personality that must marry the
African element solidly with the cultural Other.

We have seen journeys in Wright's earlier volumes of poetry,
especially *The Homecoming Singer* and *Dimensions of History*; the journeys
in *The Double Invention of Komo* are of a piece with those others in stressing
what Wright conceives as the peregrine imperative in the emergent
African-American personality. The journeys in this book, however, are
more than a random sample of the cultures and nationalities that
ultimately define the American cultural landscape. What Wright has done
here is to identify what may be considered the best advertised or perhaps
the most representative element in the places he visits, and to let his
initiate's spirit engage with it in a dialectic that will determine the
acceptability or otherwise of that element or trait within the character that
the signs have set up for the initiate.

In Albuquerque (77–78), a black man's social rage and a hurt sense of
pride almost get the better of his paternal duty, but good sense prevails in
the end to let "the ritual fire of the moon / illuminate the dark hand / of

the man's love for his son" (78). In Bad Nauheim (86–87), the initiate's spirit is still contending with the Hitlerian complex and still rejects it:

> But I am not that boy,
> perpetrator of a strange act.
> My art is in sponging
> those who can be saved
> into wholeness. (86)

In the end, however, the spirit learns to accommodate the "Germanic gabble" and seek its redemptive potential ("Let the new water subject me / to the danger of forgiving your injury" 87). Berlin (89–90) presents an outlook of cold militarism ("barbed wire / and the shine / of silver in snow"), increasing noncompromise ("this city / of sealing sutures"), and isolationism ("the bottomless and shapeless / tankard of self-love"), and it would appear that here again—as in Germany generally—the spirit is a little ill at ease. In Florence (93–95), a Dantesque survey of the city's turbulent civil history yields an accommodating sense of fellowship and a heightened feeling of regeneration:

> Fellowship asserts the spirit's freedom,
> the seal of divinity ...
> You have entered the wood;
> you turn, out of the holy waves,
> born again,
> even as trees renewed,
> pure and ready to mount to the stars. (94–95)

Venice's (97–99) architectural history reveals an ugliness that nevertheless turns to beauty ("*Formosa deformitas*") in the eyes of the beholder, who opts to "cultivate open arms / to receive the blue water" (98) threading through the city. The soul's excursions finally bring it homeward, to Mexico City and Consolapa (a little village in Mexico 104–06). At this point we are drawing towards the end of the initiation ceremony; the initiate has learned to "elevate the trinity of races in my blood" (105)—the African, the European, and the Native American—and a romantic encounter with a woman whose "voice and body / have been turning above the name of my house" (106) gradually reunites him with his double, so that he is ready to wake up from the ritual death.

Something further needs to be said about this concept of the double, because I think that not fully grasping its implications has led some scholars into a misapprehension of the autobiographical personality in Wright's poetry, and especially in a work like *Double Invention*. Although she is referring particularly to Wright's notes and afterwords, I think that Vera Kutzinski takes her deconstructionist zeal a little too far when she suggests that Wright has succeeded in decentering the figure of himself in these poems (*Against the American Grain* 71). An even more serious underestimation is contained in Philip Richard's analysis of *Double Invention* in his entry on Jay Wright in the *Dictionary of Literary Biography, Volume 41*. "At too many places," says Richard, "the poet simply fails to sustain developed characters. And as a consequence, in the course of the poem, continuity, dramatic force, and clarity are lost. Wright's many voices simply lack the sharp distinctiveness which characterizes the many voices of Eliot's *The Waste Land*, a successful long poem with which Wright's later works have a number of affinities" (359).

The essential thing to grasp in the dialectic of the poem is that it is all happening within the personality of the initiate: there is never any doubt in our minds that we are dealing with the initiate as the mouthpiece of the poet Jay Wright. Richard seems to read "the identity of the ritual celebrant in the poem," and this is where I think he begins to misread the dialectical structure of the poem. Ritual celebrants in the Komo initiation ceremony—or any other, for that matter—do not engage in arguments with initiates. They mostly teach them the lessons and rules of the cult; after the initiates wake from the ritual death, they are asked standard questions to which they provide standards answers ("I forget my name, I forget my parents' names," etc.). The complex dialectic—the conundrous sequence of questioning and debating—that we find in the poem is simply an effort within the initiate to rationalize the choices made for him by his combination of signs in a way that balances the (contending) claims of destiny and the individual will.

That internal rationalization is possible because the soul or spirit of the initiate has a double which engages it in the calculation of the risks and benefits of the choices made for it. Although the protagonist/initiate in this poem is not specifically named, his "name" is inscribed in those six signs elected for him before the final rites of initiation actually begin (53–58). He does not go through those seances without an identity. Indeed, in a gesture which I suggest may be Wright's *signifying* revision of the nihilism of Ellison's Invisible Man, the constant counterplay of the figures of "absence" and "presence," and of "denial" and "affirmation," throughout the poem—especially in that sequence during which the initiate is lying in ritual death—is a way of affirming the consciousness of the initiate's personality in the subliminal contests between his spirit and its double.[14] For a male poet, the double will, obviously, have to be female. It would appear that the initiate's double guards the prostrate personality of the initiate while the spirit is at large in its peregrinations; which is why, when the spirit encounters a female in that romantic episode in Consolapa, it is forced to return to its double as having reached the limit of its self-educating vagrancy.

There are two elements in the actual initiation ceremony which deserve special attention. First, we will notice that the ceremony is conducted within the framework of the 33 stages in the acquisition of Komo knowledge relative to the group to which the initiate belongs. These stages "correspond one on one to the 33 human vertebrae; comprise the 266 theoretical categories representing the 266 fundamental signs of creation; these signs, in their turn, correspond one on one to the portable altars of Komo, and above all to the attributes of the creator-god. The point of all this is, that there exists a connection between all things here, 'that all things in the universe are interconnected' (are interpenetrated), to use a favorite Bambara expression" (*Fondements* 217). This initiation ceremony has therefore been designed to equip the initiate with a level of wisdom relevant to the cultural environment for which his signs have destined him.

It will also be observed that, halfway through the ceremony, the initiate acquires four additional signs (91–93). There are three ways of explaining this phenomenon. The first is that the initiate, who is still in a state of ritual death and so has been "living in my body's ruins. / Under the earth," is gradually approaching the termination of that sequence and so needs the necessary apparatus for his "movement from ruins to beauty." Secondly, it would appear that, coming immediately after the initiate's unconscionable encounter with Berlin, this movement is intended as a further act of purification of the spirit. But there is a third reading which puts the signs within the larger framework of, this time, Dogon cosmology. "The more signs a man possesses," we are told, "the more learned he is; the knowledge of the elements of creation consists not only of the knowledge, but of the elements that compose it" (*Pale Fox* 100). For a "bookish poet," nothing can be more apposite than the acquisition of more learning; indeed, the spirit's excursions to such centers of culture and learning as Paris and Florence are well within this urge toward a comprehensive erudition. In acquiring four signs in addition to the earlier six, the initiate has achieved the number of signs in Amma's egg—i.e., ten, made up of two "guide" signs for the original Nommo and eight "master" signs for the first ancestors—

which give "soul and life force" to everything in the world and from which the 256 other signs of the universe originate. In achieving ten signs, therefore, the initiate has been equipped with an organic totality that prepares him for all possible experiences and insights within his universe.

The actual ceremony of initiation follows the main lines of the traditions as we outlined them earlier on. First (61) the Komo objects are brought out, for "the exhibition / of sacred things, to be washed / past the dangers of impurity," to the accompaniment of music and the dance of the mask. Next, the initiates are led to the village pool (62), where

> Naked,
> we cup our hands
> into the water seven times
> exalt the water seven times,
> > cleanse
> our unmasked faces,
> linger in the mud.
> We gather lotus and thick, fleshy roots,
> > openings
> of an unaccustomed speech. (64)

When they return from the pool, the initiates are treated to more music and the masked dance which provides a chastening access to self-knowledge ("The, dance is a way of going forward, / and a way of foreshadowing the return" 65).

It would seem that the experience of ritual death begins on page 66 ("Halfway through my darkness," etc.). In this state, and with his double protecting his prostrate body, the spirit of the initiate experiences all kinds of sensations, self-questioning, and rationalization of the configurations of his destiny, and undertakes the journeys meant to prepare it for its future existence. Further configurations of the middle passage prepare the soul for a life that engenders "the trinity / of sensations in my body, / the grammatical and just insistence of the other lives I carry in my body" (73). This state of ritual death highlights the cohabitational stresses between the soul and its double (79–80), stresses which are captured in a comic parody of the overworked concept of "absence":

> When my double comes,
> My soul runs away.
> You see, again, my talent for being absent. (80)

The double, however, is saluted as "my soul's trace into itself / the prefiguration / of my responsive spirit": it is the "mother" whose "child" the soul is. The image of mother forces an associate link with the story of one of proud Mousso Koroni's unfortunate experiences,[15] which yields lessons of submission and humility (81–85).

In between its excursions the spirit returns again and again to debate with its double the virtues of these experiences on which its growing wisdom is honed. For instance, the spirit absorbs the lesson of the complementarity and continuities between life and death ("the dead child / is an awakened child, his own / beginning, sketch of his own end," 95); accepts that true existence involves an accommodation of Other ("As I will be born, / I will know myself in your eye" 102); and learns that wisdom, in the final analysis, involves having to begin again and again the entire process of the quest for truth, as though one knows nothing at all ("I shall forever assume the contradiction / of returning to the ground I burn to free my god" 104; "I forget my name," etc. 108).

In the final stages of initiation, the sacrificial fowl brought by the initiate's mother is slaughtered, the blood sprinkled on the earth (104); the soul of the initiate gradually rejoins his body, as the pool water is sprinkled on the latter (107–08); he is interrogated, and gives the standard response of self-denial and humble submission; he is fed; takes the final bow to the earth; is presented with the cult emblems; is welcomed "into a new life," and his "eyes open to Komo" (108). Although these final stages are concentrated at the end of the poem, they are prefigured so many times much earlier on that they leave on the poetry a certain stamp of redundancy. But this impression may be excused on the grounds of both ritual structure and the double composition of the initiate's personality, which forces a projection of images on two complementary lenses.

The redundancy, and indeed the general sense of dislocation and complexity which commentators have frequently felt, especially in *The Double Invention of Komo*, may again be explained by the ritual context of this performance. The poem can hardly be seen as the statement of a persona speaking in the language of normal consciousness. What we have here are the more or less mantic articulations of a vision made all the more complex by parallax projections on a double lens. Images are inevitably spliced one on top of another and the poet, speaking as the medium (as it were) of a twin spirit, describes a complex figural terrain through which the reader must tread carefully by the aid of suggestive clues dotted along the way. Which is precisely why Wright has warned that the poem "does not encourage paraphrase or substitution."

IV

In conclusion, let us pose ourselves two questions that may be considered central to the very conception of *The Double Invention of Komo*. First, what purpose is served by the concept of doubling or twinhood? Although Wright has derived the greatest inspiration for his poetry from his readings in Dogon and Bambara cosmologies, he has nevertheless acknowledged an indebtedness to other traditional African systems in which twinhood may constitute a feature in the conception of key divinities but does not inform the logic of personality to the extent that we find among the Dogon and the Bambara.[16] It would seem, therefore, that the paradigm has been employed in the interests of a personality that must contain and accommodate a cultural Other, somewhat in the same sense as what Du Bois has called "this double-consciousness, this sense of always looking at one's self through the eyes of others" but clearly without that streak of self-pity by which Du Bois sees the black American as a victim of "a world that looks on in amused contempt and pity" (*Souls of Black Folk* 3).

For there is abounding self-assurance in Wright's double-ego, making a confident survey through history and cultural space and deciding which qualities to accommodate in the elemental composition of the black American in terms of "two warring ideals in a dark body, whose dogged strength alone keeps it from being torn asunder"; but the double-consciousness, in a personality for whom the future cultural environment had already been prefigured, certainly provides a dependable resource for coping with the stresses of the union. At any rate, the spirit of the "alien initiate" can already see, under the sacred tutelage of the protective powers of the race, the entire tableau of tribulations he will be subject to and the changed cultural circumstances in which he will come to live:

> The mask has heard the stichomythic
> camel walk from one dry well to another
> has heard the lamentation in our
> every anvil, the exaltation
> in our every abandonment,
> and, where the real heart ladders
> a new house in the air,
> the mask has heard
> our bible mouths atone
> for my Bambara absence,
> my Dogon withdrawal
> my Yoruba and Asante abscission. (68)

The double is that stable element in the personality that ensures it survives those stresses wherein something (e.g., a name, whether personal or ancestral) gets lost.

This leads us back to the question that we broached earlier in this paper: What, really, is Wright's cultural constituency or base? In other words, what weight do we give to Wright's dependence on African cosmological systems within the context of his identity as an American writer? And how seriously can we take Vera Kutzinski's ascription to Wright of "a structure without a center" or Robert Stepto's claim that Wright's poetry "does not readily align itself with any one culture or cosmology—it is not a homing pigeon sure of its cage or sure that the cup of water and that of seed promiscuously placed therein is worth the price of incarceration" ("The Aching Prodigal" 82)?

Perhaps I should state quite categorically here that I consider Wright an American rather than an African or any other kind of writer. Although there are a few African poets with whom the shares this sense of selfhood construed against a mythologic or cosmologic backdrop—Christopher Okigbo and Wole Soyinka, with whose work Wright shows much familiarity,[17] come easily to mind—there is no doubt that he has continued to address himself, in every volume of his poetry, to concerns that are peculiarly American in the broadest sense and may not necessarily appeal to the imagination of an African writer.

There is something cannily revealing in the following observation which Baldwin, reflecting on Senghor's speech before the 1956 gathering of black writers and artists in Paris, makes about the differing backgrounds which the African and the (Afro-)American writers bring to the articulation of the interconnectedness between art and "that energy which is life":

> The distortions used by African artists to create a work of art are not at all the same distortions which have become one of the principal aims of almost every artist in the West today. (They are not the same distortions even when they have been copied from Africa.) And this was due entirely to the different situations in which each had his being. (25)

I consider this statement—especially that portion of it in parentheses— revealing because, in a subtle way, Baldwin may be read as much against a black writer like Jay Wright as against a European artist like Pablo Picasso. Indeed, the revelation in the statement may be further seen in the fact that, while both Okigbo and Soyinka are readily classed as African poets even when they drag their traditional mythologies into semiological union with foreign ones, Wright is judged a decentered mythmaker when he does precisely the same thing with Dogon and Bambara mythologies.

And yet, however American and however cosmic Wright may be, he has made it abundantly clear that these African cosmologies are for him the starting point not simply of his forays into cultural history but indeed of his prospect on culture generally. We see this in the images of the poems, which are lavishly steeped in his readings into the ethnographies of various (mostly) West African peoples. We also see it in his increasing use of Bambara ideograms and ideographic metaphors, the cryptic symbols of an otherwise oral culture by which this African-American poet has endeavored to inscribe the African sources of his people into the American cultural soul. When Wright tells Rowell that *The Double Invention of Komo* closes one phase of his poetic output, he is referring to that phase in which he felt obliged to establish the sources of his black consciousness by a careful and steady archaeology of knowledge. Hereafter, everything else is a footnote or an extension of that consciousness.

We should be careful, therefore, how we read Wright's symbols and lines. Consider the following passage which closes *Dimensions of History*, a volume that is profusely dotted with Bambara and Dogon cult designs:

And I return now to my city at Labná.	[1]
It has been a long march.	[2]
I am half-naked.	[3]
I retain no more than a band	[4]
about my head, and a band about my waist,	[5]
my sandals on my feet,	[6]
my home-spun mantle and a pouch	[7]
for the god's bones.	[8]
But I am victorious.	[9]
I march from the humble	[10]
to the sacred side of the city.	[11]
I enter where I return.	[12]
I return again to the land of the star.	[13]
There is peace in the elevation.	[14]
You come, if not to God,	[15]
near to yourself.	[16]
It is a star land, a golden land,	[17]

our dark and true light,   [18]
the image of our life among ourselves   [19]
                                        (*Dimensions* 103–04)

In her discussion of this passage at the end of her study of Wright, Kutzinski is so convinced of the Euro-American sources of the references in it that she makes only the faintest reference to the African sources of Wright's poetic thought. Putting the poem within the historical context of Spanish colonization of American Indian land, Kutzinski tells us:

> Unlike Tenochtitlán, Cuzco, Macchu Picchu, Cartagena, and Bogotá, Labná is not fortified; it has no walls. Curiously enough, however, it does have a gate in the form of a triumphal arc, which formerly linked the two parts of the city. The Great Gate of Labná synecdochically suggests the existence of a wall that joins rather than divides, and it is this gate that Wright offers as his final "image of our life among ourselves." Redressed as a gateway to the beautiful, this triumphal arc is Wright's ultimate "emblem of the ecstatic connection" (*DH* 34). Celebrating the triumph of Wright's synthetic approach to New World writing, this emblem embodies a profound poetic dialogue at the crosswords of various Western and non-Western cultures, a dialogue that includes Williams's *In the American Grain* and Guillén's *El diario*. Wright's is a poetic voice that speaks, paradoxically but most effectively, "without song," and in doing so, it brings about "sea-changes" that are "waterless." (130)

I have enormous respect for Kutzinski's study of Wright's work in this book, but it leans rather heavily on her researches into the Euro-American sources of the poet's imagery and acknowledges the African sources only when they become too obvious to be side-tracked. And yet it is easy enough to break up this passage into so many images that are derived from the Dogon-Bambara matrix that has steadily informed Wright's imaginative thought. To start with, the entire "Landscapes" sequence in the book (*Dimensions of History*) which that passage concludes is prefaced by an astral symbol which Wright explains in his notes as "Sirius and the Sun, as they appear on the Lébé altar. Dogon" (112). Also, Wright's poetic imagination could hardly have missed the sound associations between *Lébé* and *Labná*, so that the return to Labná must have carried for Wright images of a pilgrim/initiate's expiatory visit to an ancestral sanctuary.

The rest of the passage could indeed be read against the background of Dogon and Bambara lore and rite as we have encountered them in this study. The image of the almost naked votary (lines 3–6) no doubt resonates the ritual of the "descent into the pool" of Faro in the Komo initiation ceremony. In lines 7 and 8 there are echoes of Dogon traditions relating to the veneration of the dead and the perpetuation of the ancestral spirit. The "home-spun mantle" is not unconnected with the ceremonially woven cloth of black and white squares which "serves as a pall to cover the dead"; the weaver of the cloth, we are told, "sings as he throws the shuttle, and the sound of his voice enters into the warp, adding to and taking along with it the voice of the ancestors. For the weaver is Lébé ..." (*Conversations* 73–74). The "god's bones" may also be read as the covenant-stones connected with the establishment of Lébé altars by Dogon migrating from their land to found (or colonize) other settlements. The first such migrants did this by opening Lébé's grave and discovering there his remains in the form of covenant-stones which they took away with them on their journey (*Conversations* 117); thereafter, it became the standard tradition for Dogon to pass on covenant-stones as a symbol of the perpetuation of the ancestral line or spirit (*Conversations* 125).

Lines 10–17 once again rehearse familiar themes from Bambara ritual, although these are now married with non-Bambara symbols. The star obviously recalls the guiding star/Star of David by which the voyager traces his journey through the "Landscapes" sequence, but Wright himself has already prefigured this with the Dogon astral symbol. The movement "from the humble / to the sacred side of the city" traces the progress of the initiate to the Komo enclave; the images of entering and returning mirror that continual, endless quest for the wisdom invested in the Komo cult, the ideal of which is to lead one beyond oneself "toward death, / the unknown, / the nothing, / the creator" (*Double Invention* 43). The last three lines again rest on symbols that are evocative of Bambara cosmology. Gold, we will recall, is the base metal of the altars of most Komo cults (the altar in the cult shrine-house must certainly harbor one), and the altar is of course the repository of the secret wisdom ("dark light") of the cult under the patronage of the hyena, "keeper of the black knowledge." It is "true" wisdom, because it reflects everything that sustains the race as a unified entity ("the image of our life among ourselves").

Without, therefore, questioning the integrity of Kutzinski's Euro-American derivations for Wright's imagery, we are clearly on firm, legitimate ground in locating Wright's explorations of cultural history within the body of African symbols which he has acknowledged as nourishing fifteen good years of his growth as a poet. What we have in these explorations is the figure of an "aching prodigal" who knows all too well "what it means to spring from the circle, / and come back again" (*Homecoming Singer* 28). The circle begins from Africa, though like all good circles it is too intimately bound with cognate contiguities for us to notice any breaks in the union. All this is no doubt a credit to the genius of Jay Wright, who "among Afro-American poets ... has made the most ambitious attempt to respond with images of macrocosmic proportions" (Stepto, "After Modernism" 480). But it is important to grasp the starting point of this cosmic vision. In plotting his personal trajectory through cultural history, Jay Wright succeeds in chronicling his people's rites of passage, not "without song," but as "a dark and dutiful dyeli" (*Dimensions of History* 36) with a firm sense of direction who, as he traces the journey back, knows better than his fellows that "The Dixie Pike has grown from a goat path in Africa" (Toomer 10).

NOTES

1. See Paul Edward's introduction to *Equiano's Travels* (xi) and Catherine Acholonu's *Igbo Roots* (2n).

2. Milton Meltzer has pointed out that, although Hughes formed a generally happy impression of Africa during his visit, certain things he saw there touched rather sore spots in him. For instance, his experience of a young mulatto boy in Dakar, who was rejected both by the colonial authorities and his fellow Africans because of his complexion and was consequently sad, inspired Hughes to write poems like "Cross" and the play *Mulatto*. See Meltzer (45).

3. Malcolm X refers to his Ibadan University lecture in his *Autobiography*.

4. Wright had earlier published *Death as History* (1967), a chapbook of 15 poems (in 22 pages) some of which he later included in *The Homecoming Singer*.

5. The following works by members of the team have been used in this synthesis: Griaule, *Masques Dogons*; Griaule, *Conversations with Ogotemmêli*; Griaule and Dieterlen, *The Pale Fox*; Dieterlen, *Essai sur la religion bambara*; Dieterlen and Cissé, *Les fondements de la société d'initiation du Komo*; and Calame-Griaule, *Ethnologie et langage*. To avoid the confusion of names and titles, further references to these works in this study will be by title only.

6. Copper is considered the elemental essence of fire and the force behind creation (*Pale Fox* 153). We are also told (ibid.) that the word for copper (*menu*) comes from the same root word *me* that designates the placenta in which Amma's egg subsists.

7. As with the Dogon, the principle of twinhood or the double applies here, with the male element having the valency of three and the female, four.

8. Again, as in the Dogon evidence, this rupture is explained as the origin of the experience of menstruation among women.

9. On the place of the smith in the worldview of societies in the Western Sudan, see further Dieterlen, "Contribution" and Okpewho, *The Epic in Africa* (116–17).

10. I have used the present tense throughout in discussing the practice of initiation, but one can only point out that it is hardly carried on with the same consistency today as in the past; in many cases, in fact, the practice has been completely abandoned. The idea that things are no longer the way they used to be may be seen in *Conversations* (97, 112) and especially *Pale Fox* (74).

11. Here, I am synthesizing ideas taken from both *Essai* and *Fondements*.

12. See *Fondements* (210–11).

13. In *Fondements* (28–29) Dieterlen and Cissé cite a myth (recorded by C. Monteil) which mentions the hyena, vulture, and other creatures as important figures encountered and consulted by Dinga and other ancestors of the Sarakolle in their search for a proper place of settlement. "The hyena and the vulture," we are told, "appear clearly in the different versions of the legend of Ouagadou ... as the best agents and the most outstanding symbols of the traditional knowledge regarding divination. Besides, the patriarch Dinga bore, right up to the steps of Dya, the title of 'leader of the smiths.'"

14. On naming in Wright, see further Benston, "I Am What I Am." On the absence of "distinctive" voices in Wright's poetry, it is interesting that, whereas in the traditional Komo pledge the members also dedicate themselves to a "single voice" (*Fondements* 18), Wright omits that line from his version (*Double Invention* 3–4), no doubt because he has opted for an all-inclusive format that embraces many voices. In his Introduction to Henry Dumas's *Play Ebony Play Ivory* (xxii), he defends Dumas's use of the same technique.

15. For the story of how Mousso Koroni lost, by an unfortunate act of indiscretion or "deceit," the twins given her by the *kapok* tree, see *Fondements* (207–09).

16. In various African societies—notably among the Yoruba and the Azande—twins were considered manifestations of divinity and, in some cases, exposed soon after birth. For a myth of a twin divinity as the ancestors of a people, see the story of the White Bagre in Jack Goody, *The Myth of the Bagre*. Wright cites Goody as one of his influences (*Double Invention* 110), and certainly in the Bagre myth one finds the same profusion of dual symbolisms that we find in Wright's poetry.

17. See particularly *Double Invention* (110) and "Desire's Design."

Works Cited

Acholonu, Catherine O. *The Igbo Roots of Olaudah Equiano*. Owerri: Afa, 1989.

Baldwin, James. *Nobody Knows My Name: More Notes of a Native Son*. New York: Dial, 1961.

Benston, Kimberly W. "'I Am What I Am': Naming and Unnaming in Afro-American Literature." In *Black Literature and Literary Theory*. Ed. H. L. Gates, Jr. New York: Methuen, 1984.

Blassingame, John W. *The Slave Community: Plantation Life in the Antebellum South*. New York: Oxford UP, 1972.

Calame-Griaule, Genevieve. *Ethnologie et langage: la parole chez les dogons*. Paris: Gallimard, 1965.

Cullen, Countee. *Color*. New York: Harper, 1925.

Dieterlen, Germaine. "Contribution a l'etude des forgerons en Afrique Occidentale," *Annuaire 1965–66* 5:5–28.

———. *Essai sur la religion bambara*. Paris: Presses Universitaires de France, 1951.

——— and Y. Cissé. *Les fondements de la société d'initiation du Komo*. Paris: Mouton, 1972.

Du Bois, William E. B. *Creative Writings*. Ed. H. Aptheker. White Plains: Kraus-Thomson, 1985.

———. *The Souls of Black Folk*. Ed. H. Aptheker. White Plains: Kraus-Thomson, 1973.

Equiano, Olaudah. *Equiano's Travels*. Ed. P. Edwards. New York: Praeger, 1966.

———. *Interesting Narrative*.

Farnsworth, Robert M. *Melvin B. Tolson, 1989–1966: Plain Talk and Poetic Prophecy*. Columbia: U of Missouri P, 1984.

Goody, Jack. *The Myth of the Bagre*. Oxford: Clarendon, 1972.

Griaule, Marcel. *Conversations with Ogotemmêli*. Tr. R. Butler. London: Oxford UP, 1965.

———. *Masques Dogons*. Paris: Institut d'Ethnologie, 1938.

——— and G. Dieterlen. *The Pale Fox*. Tr. S. C. Infantino. Chino Valley: Continuum Foundation, 1986.

Haley, Alex. *Roots*. New York: Doubleday, 1976.

Hansberry, Lorraine. *A Raisin in the Sun*. New York: Random, 1959.

Hughes, Langston, ed. *An African Treasury*. New York: Pyramid, 1961.

———. *The Big Sea: An Autobiography*. New York: Hill and Wang, 1940. ed.

———, ed. *Poems from Black Africa*. Bloomington: Indiana UP, 1963.

———. *Selected Poems*. New, York: Knopf, 1959.

Kilson, Martin and Adelaide C. Hill, eds. *Apropos of Africa: Afro-American Leaders and the Romance of Africa*. Garden City: Anchor, 1971.

Kutzinski, Vera M. *Against the American Grain: Myth and History in William Carlos Williams, Jay Wright, and Nicholas Guillén*. Baltimore: Johns Hopkins UP, 1987.

Locke, Alain. "Apropos of Africa." In *Apropos of Africa*. Eds. Martin Kilson and Adelaide C. Hill. Garden City: Anchor, 1971. 411–18.

Malcolm X. *The Autobiography of Malcolm X* (with Alex Haley). New York: Grove, 1965.

Mellon, James, ed. *Bullwhip Days. The Slaves Remember: An Oral History*. New York: Avon, 1990.

Meltzer, Milton, *Langston Hughes: A Biography*. New York: Thomas Cromwell, 1968.

Okpewho, Isidore. *The Epic in Africa: Toward a Poetics of the Oral Performance*. New York: Columbia UP, 1979.

Richard, Philip M. "Jay Wright." In *Dictionary of Literary Biography, Volume 41: Afro-American Poets Since 1955*. Eds. T. Harris and T. M. Davis. Detroit: Gale, 1985.

Rowell, Charles H. "'The Unraveling of the Egg': An Interview with Jay Wright." In *Jay Wright: A Special Issue*. *Callaloo* 19.6 (1983): 3–15.

Soyinka, Wole. *A Dance of the Forests*. In *Five Plays*. London: Oxford UP, 1964.

Stepto, Robert B. "'The Aching Prodigal': Jay Wright's Dutiful Poet." In *Jay Wright: A Special Issue*. *Callaloo* 19.6 (1983): 76–84.

———. "After Modernism, After Hibernation: Michael Harper, Robert Hayden, and Jay Wright." In *Chant of Saints: A Gathering of Afro-American Literature, Art, and Scholarship*. Eds. M. Harper and R. B. Stepto. Urbana: U of Illinois P, 1979. 470–86.

Toomer, Jean. *Cane*. New York: Liveright, 1975 (1923).

Wheatley, Phillis. *Collected Poems*. Ed. J. C. Shields. New York: Oxford UP, 1984.

Wright, Jay. *Death as History*. New York: Poets Press, 1967.

———. "Desire's Design, Vision's Resonance: Black Poetry's Ritual and Historical Voice." *Callaloo* 30.10 (1987): 13–28.

———. *Dimensions of History*. Santa Cruz: Kayak, 1976.

———. *The Double Invention of Komo*. Austin: U of Texas P, 1980.

———. *The Homecoming Singer*. New York: Corinth, 1971.

———. Introduction. In Henry Dumas, *Play Ebony Play Ivory*. New York: Random House, 1974.

Wright, Richard. *Black Boy*. New York: Harpers, 1954.

RON WELBURN

Jay Wright's Poetics:
An Appreciation

Since the mid-sixties Jay Wright has intensely pursued an absorbing study of West African cosmologies from which he has extrapolated metaphysically the intangible qualities that make an impact on the New World's multifarious cultures and also how we look upon them. In the interview editor Charles H. Rowell conducted with him for the special Jay Wright issue of *Callaloo* in 1983, we encounter the artist-maker, intellect and poetical theorist confident about the criteria of his discourse and the aims of his art. Whatever rationalizations one may advance to explain his relative obscurity as an American poet, his stature as a creative intellect deserves periodical appreciation to remind us of his work's magnitude. My intention in this essay is not to indulge in an exhaustive critical study of Wright's poems and their nuances—Vera Kutzinski's discussion of *Soothsayers and Omens* and *Dimensions of History* demonstrates an astute assessment of those works (*Against the American Grain* 45–130); and Gerald Barrax's essay about his early poems, published in the *Callaloo* special issue, is also well worth reading. I will, however, retrace this ground to offer another perspective on the historical and metaphysical codes that energize his poetry. If I appear to take his later collections, *Elaine's Book* (1986) and *Boleros* (1991), for granted, this is not intentional although it will prove obvious that Wright in these is moving around in

From *MELUS* 18, no. 3 (Fall 1993). © 1993 by *MELUS*.

Mexico and other places in the Americas with the sensibility he attained as the initiated in the remarkable book-length poem, *The Double Invention of Komo* (1980).

Any attempt to discuss Jay Wright's poetics must sooner or later confront the matter of audience. As an American poet of color, self-referred as a "black African-American" (see Rowell), Wright endures being dismissed or challenged in ways all too familiar at one time to Ralph Ellison and to Derek Walcott, when members of their communities of origin have variously accused them of being "too intellectual" if not sociopolitically uncommitted. While Wright may have eluded some such public challenges, he could easily be describing himself in a 1987 essay where he mentions Robert Hayden, several of whose problems he finds to "instruct, delight and lift us":

> Hayden's exemplary historical imagination appears and works, as it must for a poet, in his language, which is a most virtuous arrow of analysis and criticism. Hayden's language has led many of his younger contemporaries to talk down to him. Their language is supposed to be public, "Black" and "of the people"; his is reputedly private, inaccessible and wholly western. We should by now have seen enough of these opinions to see through them. (17)

Wright is a contemporary of Amiri Baraka and Sonia Sanchez, leading expressionists in the Black Arts Movement of the sixties and seventies. Hardly any of his poems are about the urban topicality of experience. Going to the African source of his sensibility never became lip service and posturing rhetoric. His poems are fully detailed as they embrace historicism's inquiries, perceptual fusions involving Africa and the New World, and international voices. Jay Wright's poems are historically and mythically expansive. They dispense with temporal limitations through a language that contains the past and the present while offering scenarios for prospective circumstances. Wright's technique freely indulges in temporal-historical references active in simultaneous locations. His point of view predates postmodernism's multiple voices, for he simply reaffirms indigenous tribal ways of thinking and seeing. On one level his points of view, shifting around between personae, are of a kind familiar to Native American waters like Leslie Silko, Gerald Vizenor, and in recent poetic discourses of length, Maurice Kenny and Ray Young Bear. Hayden and the West Indian poet Edward Brathwaite also use this technique successfully in what amounts to poetic drama and meditation achieved through transcultural and transhistorical ontology.

The personae in Wright's poems are unconfinably peripatetic and intervocally adaptable, carrying large souls through New Mexico, Spain, Harlem, Mexico, West Africa, the Caribbean and other places in Latin America, and they celebrate the connections they make with one another across historical space. His canon suggests also his having moved beyond temporal distinctions. *The Double Invention of Komo*, the poem that completes his four-part cycle as motion toward self-realization, represents the apotheosis of his metaphysics. As he has accumulated the moments in that poem, he prepares the reader for a deepening aesthetic based on a collective ethos of cultural formulas and the realities of cultural empowerment that survived the migration of Africans and the transformations of America's aboriginals. Even the conqueror is affected, and the assumed significance of his civilization and knowledge degenerates into the world's proper balance. As he is literate in other languages, his work shows an appreciation for kindred spirits like the Cuban poet Nicolás Guillén, the Guyanese writer Wilson Harris and the Negritude poets, all of whom have rendered the tripartite continental nexus with provocative imagery and meditative rhythms and cadences. Wright's quality of line and phrase and his erudition promote the feeling that his poems were conceived in one or more other languages before being transformed into English.

Why then Jay Wright's obscure presence as a poet and the presumed difficulties his poems entail? This situation should be taken at least beyond cliché and established rhetoric. The poet whose language, style and treatment of subject matter show seemingly esoteric, even postmodernist referential proclivities, is increasingly at the disadvantageous mercies of a dysfunctionally literate audience; i.e., a segment of any audience will find the poet confusing and inaccessible if it cannot transfer elements and codes between literary poetic discourse and visual and aural popular culture. The mid-1920s reader of Eliot's *The Waste Land*, with the glossary Pound encouraged for it, represented an early twentieth-century type of audience distinction in that conceivably, disparate segments of that audience could easily identify with a few or perhaps many of the poem's references without relying on the glossary: the playful idea of the "Shakespearian rag"; the conversation in the pub; the metaphors of sex; the allusions to Greek myth and drama; and the quotations from Sanskrit. Applying 1990s standards of the visual and the aural to twenties culture connects us with an audience directly exposed to movies and passively contending with popular recordings of show music and performances, operatic solos, the new musics of jazz and blues, comedians and the like. These activities were at the time as new in cultural technology as the formats of music videos and musical presentation attractive to youth today. Technology altering public access to these media is the only substantial change.

In its broadest makeup, Wright's potential audience would equal Eliot's with the notable exception that Wright's suffers from the kind of attitude that imposes inaccessible status to his voice and his vision. Yet, contemporary youth as part of his audience to be are a "postmodern" aggregation justifying his poetry by sheer prevalence of their own multifaceted enjoyments: to wit, Wright's idea of poetic discourse fused imagery from history long before hip hop performers began grafting fifties rock and roll strains or hard-loop jazz elements into their performances, or before the rapid visual mixings produced for music television that are in fact created to reflect the changing imagery of memory and idea, and to respond directly to the shortened attention span. The potential audience for a poet like Jay Wright has more in common with his language, style, format and poetics governing presentation than it realizes.

The Heath Anthology of American Literature is one of the few academic survey anthologies containing any poems by Wright. The issue of race and ethnicity in the literature of the United States brought about more writers of color being included in these anthologies, which in turn fueled debates on canonical criteria and cultural diversity. Wright has gained little from either the debates or the opening doors in editorial offices. Jay Wright's name among (white) Americans who claim to know and teach poetry is likely to be heard as James Wright, another prolific and now canonized poet. Jay Wright is known to those institutions who award literary prizes, and since the sixties he has been awarded prestigious accolades abundantly, fellowships from the National Endowment for the Arts, Hodder-Princeton, Joseph Compton, Ingram Merrill, a Guggenheim, the American Academy and Institute of Arts and Letters, Oscar Williams and Gene Durwood, and a MacArthur. It is the greatest irony of our time that these awards for writing are incapable of supporting his reputation as deserving a wider audience or recognition by the academy.

Esoteric codes in subject matter affect several poets and their audiences, and a cadre of critics emerges ultimately to insure one's recognition. Reading Jay Wright easily determines him to be as simultaneously referential as Eliot or Pound and probably more historically and hemispherically expansive. It should be remembered that he is a later product of a vanishing era when educated Americans of color acknowledged both the canons of the academy and those of their own heritage, which they learned from their families and communities. These individuals from the first six decades of this century—the elders receiving the idealized "classical education"—had studied rhetoric and elocution, Greek, Latin and sometimes Hebrew, Egyptian culture and history, the Holy Roman Empire and the history of Europe; they knew something of colonial politics in Africa as they would relate to tribal practices; and they were substantially conversant about the destruction of New World civilizations because that experience involved their own presence as displaced Native Americans, as descendants of African slaves, as admixtures of two or three races.[1] Many individuals without college training were also capable of these articulations.

The poetics of Jay Wright, in inviting semiotic interpretations, are determined by a first-person identity within the multiple voices that move from singular to plural. Their immediacy of addressing a particular or unspecific person arrests reader sensibility because the style and tone are learned but casual as narratives. Personal origins and the metaphysics of place situate us at the core of his unfolding philosophy. Wright was born in 1935 in Albuquerque, New Mexico where his father, Mercer, also a native of the state, was a mechanic and jitney driver. His mother, Leona Daily Wright, was born in Virginia. The family moved to San Pedro, California where Jay finished high school, but his native state left deep impressions on him. The Southwestern landscape tends to dwarf personality and public and private gesture in ways that are not necessarily intimidating. This desert landscape is Wright's home, given the kind of alienation he feels in being cut off from an African ancestral homeland. Several early poems mention or are situated in Albuquerque or unspecified places in New Mexico. These places are both actual and ideal. In her critique of Wright's poetry, Vera Kutzinski concentrates on one passage from part two of *Dimensions of History* having to do with the alleged Seven Cities of Cíbola and the role and fate of Estabon in that region (111–122), close to 396 years to the day before Wright was born.

Critics overlook this New Mexico as Wright's own mythical and ontological point of departure. The site of Hawikúh, a Zuñi pueblo believed in Spanish thinking to be one of the cities of the legendary Cíbola, is 120 miles west of Albuquerque, and Estabon was the first non-New World person to arrive at its threshold. Estabon (Estavanico) was, by sixteenth-century Spanish standards, a Black Moor from Azamor, a coastal

city in Morocco. A slave, he was one of 301 men of an expedition led by
Paufilo Narvaez in 1528 that landed at Tampa Bay to explore the Florida
interior. Hampered by diseases and attacked by some aboriginal
communities while befriended by others, Estabon and only three others,
including Cabeza de Vaca and his master, ended an eight-year fifteen-
hundred mile ordeal throughout the present Southern states before
arriving in Mexico City. Despite this remarkable feat, Estabon remained a
slave until his death in early 1539, in the service of Fray Marcos de Niza,
himself an emissary of the Spanish Crown. Estabon's presence in the
unfolding drama in New Mexico is undoubtedly extraordinary for Jay
Wright. What comes together in this significant event in Wright's natal
region is an encounter involving a spiritual ancestor from Africa with what
Wright would appreciate as his own vague relations among Native
Americans transmuted to the Zuñi pueblo, and the Europeans who sought
the riches they believed Cíbola contained. Fabrications that Estabon's lack
of sexual discipline caused the Zuñi to slay him appear in some Spanish
and Anglo-American accounts, but these are contradicted by Fray
Marcos's *Relación*, itself a report with several inaccuracies and
contrivances.[2]

I suspect that the Estabon sojourn has direct bearing on the poet's
ideas about twins and the metaphysics of doubles or paired identities, and
to his treatment of invention and decomposition, death and rebirth,
process and initiation. Here and there in Wright's poems, his personae can
be viewed as amanuenses for Estabon and his shadow configurations,
recalling the rituals of his homeland, indulging in mystical practices that
are strange only in function. Estabon knows well the people to whom he
nominally and legally belongs as property, and he can read the meanings
of some of the signs belonging to the peoples of the Southwest.
Misreading and misapplying one of these signs in fact led to his death.

Kutzinski aligns Wright's use of Estabon with Benjamin Banneker:

[T]he mere fact that a black man was to discover the first "city"
on the North American continent is quite sufficient to accord
his story the status of a founding fable equal in importance to
Benjamin Banneker's participation in the founding of the
United States' capital. (116)

The collective personae in Wright's poems have assimilated the mythos of
Estabon and his coordinates, from the Egyptian god Thoth who would
prepare his burial to the poet's childhood in Albuquerque to the Bambara

candidate's preparations to reenact ceremonies that will reacquaint him with an historical and mythical self (*Dimensions of History* 27–29). In the cycle's poems culminating with the Komo initiation, the recurring imagery depicts the binary metaphysics of twins presented in an almost surreal fashion since their coexistence in a cosmic, imaginative and mystical relationship involves attributes of visibility and invisibility, and hence the shadow coordinates in the poems are prominent on a figurative level. Falling neatly into the poet's treatment of reality, the Estabon configuration provides him with two alter egos, one of himself (Estabon) and the other of Banneker; the Dogon and Bambara cosmologies affirm the twin relationships such as the initiate double, the teacher–initiate interaction, and the influence on these ceremonies of initiation by the dog star Sirius and its "invisible" twin star.

Either subconsciously or wittingly, Wright's poems embrace a subtle use of his birth sign, Gemini in late May, and contain the sign's popularly ascribed qualities of youthful vigor, love of language, mental agility, intellectual bent, and duality. By creating in the cycle a personal mythos as history, Wright appropriates his astrological identity for his personal aesthetic, his poetry cycle the obvious record of the meta-historical, the concrete and the arcane. Doing so, he may be the most outstanding example of a sophisticated American poet to deploy basic elements of a personal astrology in a way that avoids being trite yet offers a key to his poetic strategies. For all his construction of the mythos, however, the externalia of the sun sign is subordinate to his attraction to and reconciliation of opposites, dichotomies and ontological dualities consisting of the persona and its shadow realities. Risking a full immersion into astrological codes to identify Wright's aesthetic formulations is unnecessary and would be rather glib. Poets take dichotomy for granted as the basis for irony. Wright's strategies include centrifugal relationships between components of his pairs, and Kutzinski has identified a related quality in his poetics that is instructive here, his "attempt to separate truth from method." She finds such an impulse imbedded in anthropological concepts that assist our approach to and understanding for what she calls his "double intention"; as an anthropologist may "employ concepts without maintaining their truth-value," so the poet will employ Western languages that are burdened with "a predetermined set of metaphysical significances." This she advances as Wright's trope of exile (73), which can be explained as how he projects the truth of experiences that are historical, immediate and metaphysical through language and a method codified in a culture from which historical circumstances brought about alienation from a root experience and which his community and his readers likely find esoteric. Intellectually, the "double intention" Kutzinski locates in Wright's poetry derives from a scientific humanism, a focus that functions as a perceptual act, is momentary and tentative, not fully trusting the inevitable necessity for the separation yet resolving to employ it as a useful concept. Hence, the twin relationships in these poems assume countenances that to each other are both familiar and distracted.

So much of this, however, does not help us with "Entering New Mexico" (131 lines—an average length for a Jay Wright poem) from *Soothsayers and Omens* except to risk its most indirect associations as literal historical insights to truth (31–34). The Nommo principle, as Janheinz Jahn interpreted it from his readings on the Dogon, is "water and the glow of fire and seed and word in one ... a unity of spiritual physical fluidity giving life to everything, penetrating everything, causing everything" (Jahn 124). Rather well into the poem the travelers "stand like communicants" around their leader who tries to give them milk from a cactus, and who guides them into this new experience. "But that water will never be enough" in this "uneasy land." Indirect evocation of Estabon comes in the grandfather, the guide leader whose "weight on the land, / under a noble name, will frighten them." Ambiguity distinguishes how Wright treats the guide and alter-ego, urged into the New World following blood, not the quest itself, to affirm what the old ceremony should have taught the guide, the travelers, the narrator.

Twin and dual coordinates are not all there is to Jay Wright's poetry. Some of his recurring strategies and images that make these coordinates provocative include using nouns as verbs; expressing sometimes a musician's awareness of the phrase and line and the effectiveness of repetition and interpolation; a desirable woman with ringed eyes; a beloved yet distant sister; and the narrator being one of twins. Occasionally his personae assume the voices and identities of animals and plants. In the cycle his associations, through sensory and metaphysically inspired imagery, beg comparisons with Aimé Césaire's *Cahier d'un Retour au Pays Natal* (1935). Numerous in the long works and in the poems that make up *Elaine's Book* and *Boleros* are the surrealistic techniques André Breton hastily attributed to the Negritude poets, techniques Wright appears more accurately to have fulfilled—only Tchicaya U Tamsi of Negritude's second generation best anticipates Wright's achievement in tight linear control balanced by freer images. Ethnopoetics does not adequately describe or explain Wright's poetics either, especially as a method seeking in his work a foundation incantations. These vivid elucidations constituting his narrative voice achieve a meditative power where allusions to jazz or to Náhuatl culture make sense to his initiate. The poet allows himself to be open to the interconnectedness of a world community, compelling his readers to jettison their parochial notions of civilization and the mystical. His aesthetic suggests that who we are opposes the historical idea and the continuing sensation that we think and behave in some sort of spiritual and existential vacuum, or that history is something very far from the human spirit.

Prior to the publication of *The Homecoming Singer* (1971) by Corinth Books, Poets Press, one of the burgeoning independent small publishers of the 1960s, issued a chapbook of Jay Wright's poems, *Death As History* (1967). Wright does not view this as an "official" publication but as a pamphlet put together so he could share his poems with students during a tour of southern Black colleges. Eight of the poems from this slender volume reappear in *The Homecoming Singer*. The erstwhile title poem, "Death As History," features early rhetorical devices such as repetition, serial phrase elements, thematic recapitulation and summation of the central idea, and adjacent images of opposite conditions such as living and dying. In this personal narrative the speaker ruminates about how budding poet-scholars are charged by dancers to make for them another expressive realm of possibility, that being the perpetuity of renewal by death.

> And death is the reason
> to begin again, without letting go.
> And who can lament
> such historical necessity? (63)

Wright moves further to test probability in other poems of *The Homecoming Singer*, allowing his personae to be surprised in "An Invitation to Madison County," a poem recording his arrival in Mississippi and "The Baptism," which foreshadows his immersion into the Dogon and Bambara systems as "those confessed sinners, / who would leave another world / ... / who would take the terror in our eyes / to enter ours." The minister at the river comes along " ... detached, / seeming to be part of nothing / except the disordered day," and he does not calm the water in which he will bury "the stiffened bodies." Here the death and rebirth intrinsically a part of sectarian Christian immersion prevails among the initiates and their guide or teacher, and the invisible presence of Thoth resides as alter-ego Death's minister (8–10). Jazz compositions known to aficionados of the 1950s inspire "Wednesday Night Prayer Meeting" and "Billie's Blues"; the former was composed by Charles Mingus and its performance on the *Blues and Roots* album (Atlantic 1305) features various horns and piano in a holiness church testifying style. Coincidentally, Mingus played piano and string bass, an instrument Wright suggests a working knowledge of in "The End of An Ethnic Dream," and was himself born on the Arizona side of the border city of Nogales. "The Player at the Crossroads" and the three-part sequence "Variations on a Theme by LeRoi Jones" open with quotes from Baraka's "Poem for Willie Best," attesting to a shared perception of media use of African American actors as buffoons.[3] In the title poem the narrator arrives in Nashville for the festive campus weekend, dreaming of how one girl's touch and singing voice evoke Black folk culture; but this substance of expression is juxtaposed in the poem by a young halfback's uninhibited racing through this southern airport terminal scrutinized by the poster images of Mollie Bee. The poem illuminates the ironies of historical and cultural progress in the South while the narrator moves from observation of action to internalized response.

It is the two poems "Wednesday Night Prayer Meeting" and "The Baptism" on which Gerald Barrax's essay on Wright's first books turns. These poems encourage Barrax to designate Wright a "religious poet" looking ahead to the double invention as a synthesis of Christianity and the Dogon-Bambara cosmologies. These poems' constructs and associations with the Black church are not as ambiguous and inconclusive as Barrax states, for the ethos of these poems suggests the communicants have maintained allegiance to the ambiguity itself and the constancy of their uncertainty is ritual, their Africanizing of Christianity by means of a freedom they are "unwilling to change ... for a god" (*HS* 7; Barrax 85).

In *Soothsayers and Omens* (1976) Wright confronts feelings of alienation regarding his family and childhood in New Mexico. He invokes the mythos of Mexico through his familiarities with places there; and he devotes one entire section of the book to what becomes the beginning of his Dogon formulaic explorations. In this collection he establishes a shifting physical locus for his speaker amidst an unfolding narrative style that is anxious and introspective, conveying his perceptions of life's permutations in profuse detail.

It is in the fourth section where the distinct group of poems entitled "Second Conversations with Ogotemmêli" formally presents Wright's imaginative interpolations of texts attempting to elucidate the religious complexities of the Dogon: Marcel Griaule's *Dieu d'eau* (1948), translated as *Conversations with Ogotemmêli* in 1965; and Griaule's collaborations with

Germaine Dieterlen that produced *Le Renard pâle* (1965).[4] From this point on Wright's poems will exhibit his absorption of the particular West African systems even if from afar in much the same way Gerard Manley Hopkins's poems display a total assimilation of Christian ritual and scriptural symbols.

The eleven poems of "Second Conversations" can be read as paraphrases of significant information from *Dieu d'eau* in that they parallel Griaule's structure based on his day-by-day interviews with the Dogon sage. Throughout this section the persona is paraphraser and student, vacillating imperceptibly at times between who is the two roles, and it is the student who is engaging in the second group of talks to prepare for his initiation by circumcision. He designates himself the teacher's child: "I sit here with you, / and my hands learn the feel / of cloth and seeds and earth again" (78). "Ogotemmêli" gives us this blind teacher's gentle ruminative demeanor and the power of his wisdom as gleaned from Griaule's descriptions and the few photographs of him in the book (Ogotemmêli died on July 31, 1947). The third stanza brings the reader closer to the principles of the Nommo and the concepts related to the Digitaria, a tiny grain seed referred to by Griaule with its scientific name and interchangeable with the star Sirius's orbiting and virtually invisible twin that influences the world's unseen forces.

> Father, your eyes have turned
> from the tricks of our visible world
> to move within you,
> where God moves,
> where the seed moves,
> where we move,
> where the word moves among us,
> into this visible world
> and into its perfect order. (62)

At the section's midpoint is "The Smith," which would correspond to "La Forge" in *Dieu d'eau*, the thirteenth of thirty-three chapters. As Griaule reported earlier, "Ogotemmêli employant indifférrent les terms 'eau' et 'Nommo'" (*Dieu d'eau* 47), and indeed Wright follows this by referring casually to "Water Spirit" and "Master of Waters" in this poem. Note the apostrophe:

Nommo of the lake,
you swim sandalled in velvet;
you breathe the water awake.
I hear your twins chant dirges
    ....
Circumcised one,
God has put these pearls,
this water, into your hands. (69)

Two gods or spirits, Lébé and Binu, have individual poems also prefiguring their later appearances in the canon. Lébé, representing weavers and serpents, is to "protecteur des placenta, pourvoyeur de forces de vie" (*Dieu d'eau* 113) among his many responsibilities.

Now, here, the Hogon
holds the man and land in place,
holding his sweatless body
erect on my grandfather's back.
Though he is copper, sun and water,
he wears the moon,
the shell of an egg,
the ancestors' tombs,
the seed and soul of woman,
on his head. (72)

Binu, on the other hand, is profoundly abstract, but according to Griaule is as a term a contraction meaning to have gone and to return (95). It serves as a guide or connector between humans, animals, and earth, with special affinities to what Griaule (and Wright) refers to as a covenant stone or pierre d'alliance.

They go and come again
without knowing death.
They go and come again
when the seed is cast,
when the corn
is plucked from the ground.
    ... ...
I preen myself,
a dreamer,

too intimate with death,
going by night
over gorges, through marshes,
looking for the stone,
my own revelation,
my Binu.
My craft is the craft
of the word I say
you do not understand. (73)

The secretive and elusive fox recurs as an image in some of these poems with major emphasis in "Beginning" and "The Dead." In *Dieu d'eau* Griaule says nothing of the fox but speaks of the jackal as God's first—born who got into trouble—incest with his mother, among other transgressions-because of his loneliness (146). Wright turned to *Le Renard pâle* in order to utilize properly his fox imagery. *Le Renard pâle* is Dieterlen's exhaustive explication of additional Dogon formulas she co-investigated with Griaule, and it was not published until 1965, nine years after Griaule's death. Their joint article, "Un Système Soudanais de Sirius," first published in 1950 and translated especially for inclusion in Robert K. G. Temple's *The Sirius Mystery* (1976), also does not mention the fox but serves as otherwise an interesting precis to the later book. *Le Renard pâle* remains in its original French. Temple investigated the Dogon's knowledge of Sirius and confirmed Griaule's research that they have known of Sirius B, the Digitaria, the star of their Sigui ceremonies, for over 5,000 years and without the aid of a telescope.[5] The fox is Ogo, the disrupter of the Creation and the universe. He is "the imperfect, the meddler, the outcast. Ogo rebelled at his creation and remained unfinished." He is an equivalent to the Christian Lucifer. Nommo, acting as a monitor in the creation, continually resurrects himself to cleanse and purify those elements which Ogo defiles (Temple 32). Thus, in *Soothsayers and Omens* and especially its Ogotemmêli section, Jay Wright establishes the coordinates for subsequent works in the cycle.

After a publisher's interest in the manuscript of *Explications/ Interpretations* collapsed in 1976, the intact collection waited eight years to be issued (1984). Wright places it after *Soothsayers and Omens* in his canon and conceived of it as a unified group of poems. Textually it differs from his first two books without sacrificing his bent for a meditative rhetorical style to convey personal and cultural experience. The general texture of these poems is a smoother diction by which the poet avoids the profusion of commas that were so popular in the fifties. The settings for most of these poems are non-specific; however, some poems invoke Dogon concepts in a truly assimilated way, such as "Twin me in iron and weaving. / Binu, Lébé, my male hand / knows my woman's hardness" ("Love in the Iron and Loom" 60), or as in "The Continuing City: Spirit and Body" when he says: "If I accept the direction of the east, / a heavy star will seed me ... ." (16), and here the image of the "heavy star" is derived from Sirius B, the dog star's orbiting twin (Temple 12). In general, the collective sensibility of *Explications/Interpretations* leans toward Christian evocations, particularly in the dramatic sequence, "MacIntyre, the Captain and the Saints," perhaps the most thoroughly musical Jay Wright poem. Even here, Wright deftly brings about a fused association of Scottish history and Catholicism with Akan wisdom from another part of west Africa, and he describes this poem as "an attempt ... to claim this [Akan] knowledge as part of the continuing creative life of the Americas" as stimulated by reading *The Akan Doctrine of God* (1944) by the Ghanaian scholar, J. B. Danquah (83). Various Scots dialects lend a vivid quality to the conversations of Hugh MacDiarmid, the famed poet and lyricist, British philosopher David Hume, anthropologist R. S. Rattray, and Wright. Ideograms distinguish levels of meaning that are either internal, external, or mixed. Affected by their interactions, the personae in this sequence also pull away from each other despite their dialogues and their belief in the workings of one God. Each section of another poetic sequence, "Twenty-Two Tremblings of the Postulant," corresponds to parts of the body. Structurally the poem is made up of two choruses of twelve-measures *à la* the blues with sections 23 and 24 absent or tacit. Within the numbered sections Wright follows the I–IV–I–V–I harmonic progression common to many blues songs. The book as a whole may appear an anomaly by being published out of the poet's intended sequence. Because of its Christian allusions and the perambulations in "Polarity's," the first trio of poems that refers to various places and objects of the Americas, it ostensibly appears unrelated to the other three books. It anticipates *Elaine's Book* and *Boleros* quite effectively, and the reader can appreciate its place in Wright's canon as his initiate-candidate regrouping prior to the forthcoming vital stages.

The rich breadth provided by Wright's travels, observations, investigations, and quest for wholeness of identity contribute to the aesthetic triumph of *Dimensions of History* (1976). As a book-length sequence in three sections, *Dimensions of History* serves witness to Wright's ability to balance more or less simultaneously its composition with two other somewhat dissimilarly focused collections. As a tour de force

Dimensions of History teems with allusions and references to Pre-Columbian history and its cultural remnants in modern Latin America; New World Africanisms and practices; and references to the glory period of West African civilizations before the fifteenth century. As though to orient this poem in one metaphysical dimension, Wright uses symbols associated with Dogon Sigui (circumcision) ceremonies for the book's cover design and throughout the text. Ultimately this work adheres to a cyclical and synesthetic structure, forcefully evident in its middle section, "Modulations: the Aesthetic Dimension." Calvinism and New England lifeways coexist with the rhythms and religions of Brazil, Guyana, and Colombia; fruits and raw materials find reiteration; the African gazelle turns up in South America; the African origins of St. Augustine are considered. The mostly formal diction of the poem achieves a balance between occasional North American colloquialisms, bookish syntax, and words and phrases from Spanish and from African languages. In section one's "The Second Eye of the World," images of the historical Mali and Songhay mingle in Wright's meditations on the spirit of revolution in the history of the Americas. A significant aesthetic touchstone can be found in the imaginative use of Latin American song forms like the *son*, the *villancico*, and the *jaropa* (some of these having African origins), and various ceremonial and occasional percussion instruments and guitars. *Dimensions of History* succeeds in Jay Wright's poetic ambition to relate the panorama of effects lived and imagined from what essentially are multicultural sources.

Culminating Wright's philosophical inquiries into West African resources is *The Double Invention of Komo* (1980). Here his powers are at their strongest and his principal voice has discovered what he has been seeking. Where the Ogotemmêli section of *Soothsayers and Omens* and all of *Dimensions of History* exhibit the continuum of a personal process, *The Double Invention of Komo* takes poet and reader to the deepest realm of the spiritual quest for self-becoming as the initiate, into the Bambara (or Bamana) and to a lesser degree now the Dogon cultural systems, a complex group of fundamentals from which the persona has felt alienated. The text covers 106 pages and has nine sections; its postscript is essential reading although it does not explain the poem.

The emerging Jay Wright scholarship will come to grips with what he may consider of lesser significance about his poems, and that is what appears to be his shift after *Soothsayers and Omens* from the energies derived from the Dogon to those connected with the Bambara in *Double Invention*. Of the two peoples the Bambara are more westerly in Mali

toward Guinea and Senegal; their culture, art and artifacts do not receive
the popular attention in Western folklore as that of the Dogon. In broad
terms their rites and cosmologies have external similarities in male and
female initiation ceremonies involving circumcision and excision, and the
relationship of these rites to the influence of the dog star Sirius and its
orbiting twin. The Sirius system represents the foundation of knowledge
to the Bambara (Temple 48). Wright leaves the reader to ponder the shift
in cosmological focus; but the guesswork could prove unnecessarily time-
consuming given the systematic affinities. Rather, the Dogon influence
that sustained "Second Conversations with Ogotemmêli," the absorbed
points of view in *Explications/Interpretations,* and the applicable sensibility
and knowledge in *Dimensions of History* all characterize those books that
however coincidentally were to be available to readers in 1976, therefore
allowing a somewhat unified landscape to emerge. Readings in Dogon
philosophy preoccupied Wright up to the time of those compositions. The
shift to Bambara culture by no means indicates the poet having jettisoned
his Dogon readings or acquired knowledge. What seems feasible is that, as
Wright describes "the poem's first subject is history," the Komo cult
invokes

> a past, present, and future knowledge, one that comes from
> God and leads to God. Can we speak of a historical knowledge
> of the future? If we speak from the point-of-view of Western
> philosophy and history, obviously we cannot. From this point-
> of-view, the Bambara urge to go "beyond the pool," to
> understand the universe within which the human spirit
> "imbibes abstract things," or, as Dieterlen and Cissé (q.v.) put
> it, all knowledge is simply unscientific and has nothing to do
> with history or with knowledge. (112)

We can, therefore, acknowledge this transition between specific
African religious systems as integral to Wright's use of historical process
and personal process, and from these apply what guided him for
Dimensions of History from Wilson Harris's idea of "vision as historical
dimension" (Rowell 5) to *The Double Invention of Komo,* which is in turn
"an exploration of the fact of history" (111).

The poem sustains a cantatorial diction by means not of lyricism but
an even tone of rhetorical cadence. Phrase repetition here creates a strong
illusion of motion. The short line phrasings, carried over from the mid-
sixties, produce the texture of incantation.

Your own desire
declares that it is morning.
You awaken and arise
from your tomb-canoe bed.
Dry earth ripples,
under the sun's caress,
ready to embrace your boat. (6)

And in "The Opening of the Ceremony/the Coming Out of Komo," his
cadence recalls both Whitman and the Kiowa poet, N. Scott Momaday:

I am a heron bird,
with one leg in the pool.
Those who have seen my flight's curve,
see the strange glaze on my blue back.
I am the boy, with the shaved head
and crescent moon,
You know me, too,
as the rug-bearer and bead man
who hawks the eye of God. (69)

The personae include an omniscient observer, a predominating figure who
is to be initiated, and the teacher. Apprehension, fear, learning and deep
personal insight will characterize the initiate's experience as he seeks self-
definition in order to exist as a spiritual as well as a living force.
Metaphorically, the initiate is in the process of making the poem his quest,
and the poem in its way creates him and records both his progress and the
process he undergoes—the double invention. Ritual acts and degrees of
limitation, a complex codification of Bambara signs and symbols, and the
means to reconcile abstractions in the universe in terms of time past,
present and future are among the key elements offered by Komo. The
cosmological systems indigenous to Latin America find justifiable
acknowledgment here too in Wright's imaginative formulations. As the
initiate approaches Komo, memories of New Mexico and an intangible
memory of the reward heritage of the Western hemisphere reward his
total existence. He does not and cannot exist without them, and by
invoking their memory he actually reminds himself of how connected he
will always be to those places and materials he may feel he lacks relevance
with as he conversely feels alienated by history from his origins.

As he did with *Dimensions of History*, Wright in *Double Invention* pursues a loose and imaginative parallel of a text, Dieterlen's collaboration with Yousouff Cissé, *Les fondements de la société d'initiation du Komo* (1972), which describes the Komo cult, its 266 signs divided among the four elements of water, fire, air and earth, the thirty-three classes or categories for its initiates, and their particular ceremonies. The section "The Eleven Altars Dance in the Wood" early in the poem lists and meditates on the same Komo altars and their associated materials as given in *Les fondements* (19). As if reconstructing memories of wandering the streets of San Pedro and Los Angeles and the people and actions witnessed there, the Komo candidate realizes the power of the cult's mask, depicted in *Les fondements* as representing a very old hyena (48; Plates II and III):

> This large head upon my head
> conveys my power
> to commend the world's mask
> to my reason.
> Head under head,
> I determine what passion
> will lead me, endurable,
> under the body's endurable light.
> Even the mask upon my head
> is masked, my forehead
> haired for foresight. (30)

For the poem's seventh major section, as according to preparations for the actual Komo ceremony, the candidate for initiation must choose six of all the signs he adjudges to be significant to his name (*Les fondements* 79). Chosen by Wright's initiate are idiomatic terms with their ideograms: 1–*Sánú*: gold; 5–*Mámúrú-fla*: the rainbow; 8–*Mákó*: the abstracted leader, or as its persona in Wright describes himself: "I descend in the whirlwind, / ... / ... your initiate's agent on creation's knife" (54); 11–*Doó*: "la pierre de foudre" or Wright's "thunderstone" (55); 77–*Dyéé*: a sign of multiplication where union is realized through the star cluster Pleiades (and also the term that begins Wright's dedication of *Boleros* to his wife, Lois); and 165–*Kana ká*: the voice and language of birds (see *Les fondements* 84–154ff).

As the Bambara also recognize Sirius (*Sigi doolo*) according to a sixty-year cycle in their ritual calendar, they have in their cosmology for this star the figure Moussa Koroni, who is addressed in the poem as "keeper of the children of shame" (48) and referred to later as "foolish," having made for herself a "nest of misery and deception" (80). But Moussa Koroni, while she inaugurated the rituals of circumcision and excision, it must be understood, is the one chased by Faro, a twin creator of the earth and also the Sirius B star, because she refused excision for herself (*Les fondements* 263).

Brilliantly pulling together Bambara cosmology, the Western experience, and the parallel cognates of African and Christian beliefs, Wright presents the following stunning passage in the last section, "The Opening of the Ceremony ....":

> In the forest of the air,
> I have seen the dog star sniff
> and scurry to the bitch of existence.
> I move north.
> I move south.
> I arrive on these shores,
> where the star cuts earth's middle,
> and the rocks ridge me high, into memory's
> uneasiness and into my patience.
> I have in my care
> the memory of a passive saint's day
> and the saint's forgetfulness of my care. (73)

The teacher, seating him, can now address him amidst images of knives and cutting that recur throughout the poem:

> You become:
> children of the twins' star,
> children of the doubling star,
> children of the star of circumcision,
> children of the star of two eyes.
>   Doubled,
>   you grow,
> from stillness to sight,
>   into
>   vision and pain's power. (74–75)

In the two later collections, *Elaine's Book* and *Boleros*, one realizes that Wright's quest for metaphysically derived properties of truth have indeed been assimilated, so that their subtle incorporation into individual poems and shorter poem-sequences betrays nothing of pretense. *Elaine's Book* contains the thematically engaging "Zapata and the Egungun Mask," its longest poem, in which the famed Mexican revolutionary who was a campesino addresses the Yoruba ritual mask that represents the intermediation between forces living and nonliving. We are apt to find language in these two collections that is richer in metaphor than Wright's earlier poems, if that seems possible! He freely personifies inanimate objects and physical sensations: "No ruffled lace guitars clutch at the darkened windows" ("Madrid" 54); or the women who, knowing the autumnal flight of geese, "tell us that, if you listen, you can hear / their dove's voices ridge the air." Indeed, two of the book's short sequences, "Desire's Persistence"—whose "Winter" section contains the last example—and "The Anatomy of Resonance," are concerned with aural and visual perceptions. Several of the thirty-nine poems in *Boleros* lack titles outright, Wright preferring numbers to identify them instead. Spanish phrases, some idiomatically obscure, characterize many. Again, history, reality and myth blend without clear demarcations. Saints days, the Muses, New England, and a Moorish-Iberian point of reference that stimulates thoughts about the cultures of the Americas are its themes. Wright's use of colors is not as vivid as Wallace Stevens's, for example, but he responds to a symbolist's influence on the intellect and the senses without any lack of discipline in how he selects his images. The cover design of *Boleros* makes obvious Jay Wright's ideals of fusion and the kind of intellectual and metaphysical terrain he is willing to risk: a *bolero* is a Spanish dance at slow tempo; the figures depicted on the cover are a man and a woman in an African carving and they are playing a *balafon*, a precursor to the xylophone. Together constituting an image and impression on the senses, they demand that artist and public depend on an interactive freedom in order to attain a spiritual unity.

NOTES

1. Vera Kutzinski, acknowledging Wright's echoing a passage from W. E. B. DuBois's *The Souls of the Black Folk* ("I sit with Shakespeare and he winces not ... " [139]), triggers a personal memory of the assembly lectures at Lincoln University in Pennsylvania, at which attendance was mandatory until the practice ended in 1966. One lecture was given by Dr. Hildrus Poindexter, an alumnus of Lincoln's esteemed class of 1924 and a specialist in tropical diseases and medicines who taught at Howard University for several decades. I have long forgotten his topic; but he marveled undergraduates with his thorough command of far-reaching

references to Shakespeare, arcane Scriptures, Locke and Carlyle, African art, the civil rights movement, and other subjects which he used as analogies without intellectual pretension.

2. Among the reliable analyses of the Fray Marcos *Relación* is Frederick Webb Hodge's *History of Hawikúh, New Mexico: One of the So-Called Cities of Cíbola* (Los Angeles: The Southwest Museum, 1937) 20, which Cleve Hallenbeck relied heavily on for his *The Journey of Fray Marcos de Niza* (Dallas: Southern Methodist UP, 1987) 29. The friar, two or three days from Hawikúh, learned from an Indian in Estabon's party on May 21, 1539 that Estabon had been recently slain. Others agreeing that Fray Marcos fabricated specific details of what he claimed to have seen are Carl Sauer in *The Road to Cíbola* (Ibero-Americana No. 3, Berkeley: U California P, 1932) 28, and John Upton Terrell, *Estavanico the Black* (Los Angeles: Westernlore P, 1968) 111–15.

3. Willie Best played "Willie," an apartment custodian in the popular early-fifties television sit-com, *My Little Margie*, starring Gail Storm.

4. Wright informed the writer in June 1991 that he read the original French edition of *Dieu d'eau*.

5. Temple's book (New York: St. Martin's, 1976) was inspired by Erich von Daniken's *Chariots of the Gods* as a discussion of the speculated visit of extraterrestial life forms to earth over 5,000 years ago. While most of its content is unrelated to any concerns of Jay Wright's poetry, and while it possesses its own unique level of fascinating scholarship, parts of it may assist the reader curious about Dogon cosmology. Important to us here, and as Temple learned from Griaule and Dieterlen, is that Sirius B orbits the bigger star on a fifty-year elliptical path. This fifty-year cycle corresponds to the period of the Sigui, a major event in Dogon reckoning of chieftain succession; but the Dogon added ten years for holding the Sigui. The period of the orbit is counted as one hundred years consisting of five-day weeks, "so as to insist on the basic principle of twinness," the Sigui being conceived of as pairs of twins (41). Coincidentally, the second volume of Wright's quartet cycle, as the last to be published, appeared during his own forty-ninth year, in 1984!

WORKS CITED

Barrax, Gerald. "The Early Poetry of Jay Wright." *Callaloo* 19.6 (Fall 1983): 85–102.

Césaire, Aimé. *Cahier d'un Retour au Pays Natal* [Notebook of a Return to the Native Land]. 1939. Trans. Clayton Eshleman and Annette Smith. *The Collected Poetry of Aimé Césaire*. Berkeley: U of California P, 1983. 34–85.

Danquah, J. B. *The Akan Doctrine of God*. 1944. London: Frank Cass, 1968.

Dieterlen, Germaine, and Youssouff Cissé. *Les fondements de la société d'initiation du Komo*. Paris: Mouton, 1972.

Griaule, Marcel. *Dieu d'eau*. 1948. Paris: Librairie Artheme Fayard. 1966; Trans. Ralph Butler et al.

————. *Conversations with Ogotemmêli*. London: Oxford UP, 1965.

————, and Germaine Dieterlen. *Le Renard pâle*. Paris: Institut D'Ethnologie, 1965.

Hallenbeck, Cleve. *The Journey of Fray Marcos de Niza*. Dallas: Southern Methodist UP, 1987.

Hodge, Frederick Webb. *History of Hawikúh, New Mexico: One of the So-Called Cities of Cíbola*. Los Angeles: The Southwest Museum, 1937.

Jahn, Janheinz. *Muntu: An Outline of the New African Culture*. Trans. Marjorie Grene. New York: Grove, 1961.

Kutzinski, Vera M. *Against the American Grain: Myth and History in William Carlos Williams, Jay Wright, and Nicolás Guillén*. Baltimore: The Johns Hopkins UP, 1987. 45–130.

Lauter, Paul et al., eds. *The Heath Anthology of American Literature*. Vol 2. Lexington, MA: D. C. Heath, 1990. 2461–67.

Mingus, Charles. *Blues and Roots*. Atlantic 1305, 1959.

Rowell, Charles H. "'The Unraveling of the Egg': An Interview with Jay Wright." *Callaloo* 19.6 (Fall 1983): 3–15.

Sauer, Carl. *The Road to Cíbola*. Ibero-Americana No. 3. Berkeley: U of California P, 1932.

Temple, Robert K. G. *The Sirius Mystery*. New York: St. Martin's, 1976.

Terrell, John Upton. *Estavanico the Black*. Los Angeles: Westernlore, 1968.

Wright, Jay. *Boleros*. Princeton: Princeton UP, 1991.

————. "Desire's Design, Vision's Resonance: Black Poetry's Ritual and Historical Voice." *Callaloo* 30.10 (Winter 1987): 13–28.

————. *Dimensions of History*. Santa Cruz: Kayak, 1976.

————. *The Double Invention of Komo*. Austin: U of Texas P, 1980.

————. *Elaine's Book*. Charlottesville: UP of Virginia, 1986.

————. *Explications/Interpretations*. Charlottesville: UP of Virginia, 1984.

————. *The Homecoming Singer*. New York: Corinth, 1971.

————. *Soothsayers and Omens*. New York: Seven Woods, 1976.

PAUL CHRISTENSEN

Jay Wright:
Overview

Ever since Ezra Pound undertook his descent into the troubadour mind in the early twentieth century, American writers have been making pilgrimages to obscure cultures to bring back lore and insight in an effort to expand the visionary powers of the mind. Charles Olson made a trek to the Yucatán Peninsula to study Mayan culture in 1950, and the Beats scattered into Mexico, India, Japan, and North Africa in search of new ideas. Carlos Casteneda put his stamp on the 1960s with *The Teachings of Don Juan*, in which he became the willing initiate into the mysteries of a peyote cult among the Yaqui Indians of the southern Sonoran Desert. In Jay Wright's attempt to find a new source of religious ideas, he has plumbed the work of French anthropologists studying the Dogon and Bambara cultures of West Africa.

In *The Double Invention of Komo* Wright undertakes the task of imagining his own initiation into the rites of Komo as practiced by the Bambara, a people located on the upper Niger River and the subject of the book *Les fondements de la société d'initiation du Komo*, by the anthropologists Germaine Dieterlen and Yousouf Tata Cissé, on which Wright's poem is based. In an afterword to his poem Wright tells us that the initiate into the Komo religion attempts "to go 'beyond the pool,' to understand the universe within which the human spirit 'imbibes abstract things.'" Wright

From *Contemporary Poets*, 6th Edition, ed. Thomas Riggs. © 1996 by St. James Press.

has done this to bring about the "necessary transformation of an enhanced world of intransigent act"—to redeem us from our own errors and ignorance.

The claim Wright makes is familiar after a century of rebirths and conversions to other religions. This is one more piece in the jigsaw puzzle of twentieth-century art, in which Christianity's boundaries are scaled and other religions sympathetically explored. The goal is self-liberation, the transcendence of personal identity to gain the larger cosmos of nature and otherness. Here is some of the language of the poem's close:

> I forget my name;
> I forget my mother's and father's names.
> I am about to be born.
> I forget where I come from
> and where I am going.
> I cannot distinguish
> right from left, front from rear.
> Show me the way of my race
> and of my fathers ...
>
> You take me to kneel, forehead to earth, before Komo.
> You present me to sacred things.
> I am reborn into a new life.
> My eyes open to Komo.

The task is boldly undertaken, but there are structural and psychological problems posed here that the poem does not fully resolve. How is it that a poet of modern urban consciousness, with the whole range of English at his command, can hope to duplicate the modes of ritual descent as performed by rural Africans? The nature of ritual and of tribal cohesion depends upon body language, repeated gestures, grunts, mantras; yet this poem weighs in with a large dictionary to accomplish the same ends. The mind is here, but the body's powers to read signs and make meanings from gestures and animal noises is minimized. We have here a sort of orchestral transcription of the music from an African finger harp.

It simply does not work to bring such articulate skills to the person of a man who says that

> All day, I stub in my father's fields
> or whistle in the market over

my mother's pots, adept in the provisions
of belonging.
At night, I lodge
near the most familiar limbs.
On my bed,
I am fused to my brother's steel spine.
The wind's bugle covers my day's breath.

This language comes from a culture of self-consciousness. The diversity, density, and multiple layerings of the words used here attest to the autonomy and hypertrophy of the self that has arisen out of centuries of social evolution in the West. How can this weight of alien psychology be crammed into the mouth of a tribal youth who has no bearings in such a world?

Unhappily, the poem never moves beyond the paradox of its strategy. It strains to possess the feeling of the rituals underhand, but Wright keeps his personal identity out of the poem. The fact that he is himself an African-American might have helped to convince us of some innate, a priori resonance between his and the Bambara imagination. Perhaps not. In the end the poem seems to prove the reverse of its intention—that one cannot easily leap from one's own culture to grasp the reality of another's. The poem is stuck in its own metaphysical and linguistic provinciality, with much intelligent laboring exerted for a noble but unreached goal:

Down below the love bed,
the knit bones of the dead
cock their conch ears
to another soul's implosion.
My monody impels you to the shore,
where I enroll among the thorns
clutched in the rocks.
I will, by my heart's hunker-down
hazard, examine your twilight eyes
and will.

Boleros is a more effective use of Wright's powers. In it he keeps himself apart from the mythological landscape of Mexico, which he traces to Indian roots and from there to Asian Indian and Catholic European ideas. This is Wright country; he was born in New Mexico and raised there and in California. He has a passion for how the ritual mind works, and the ecumenical bent of Wright's thinking is put to good use here in threading together a world religious system from the faith of Mexico's southern indios. The plot of the book is a travel memoir of the poet and his wife moving from one world (Scotland, New England) to the other (Mexico), from Protestant rationality to the depths of the Mayan and Aztec worlds with their layerings of Spanish Catholicism and other New World elements.

Wright is buoyant and clearheaded in *Boleros*, and he stays out of the psychological traps of his earlier book. He enjoys his role as intelligent guide to both worlds:

> Here,
> as we stand in the Mayan evening,
> I know I should be able to say
> something simple,
> such as, it is the same moon,
> that the triad—moon, earth,
> and that star in Taurus—
> sounds right again.
> Where is my synodic certainty?
> I know less than the ancients
> who were accustomed to a late moon
> and its difficult omens.

"I am learning," he says later in the same poem. Indeed, Wright is a tireless worker in the quest to bring passion and sensuality to American belief. The story of religion in the twentieth century may one day be its central motif. Wright's early years in New York were spent among some of the brightest talents of the postmodern religious renaissance, and it is no accident that he should emerge as another of its principal voices.

JOHN HOLLANDER

Poems That Walk Anywhere

J ay Wright is a brilliant and original poet, difficult and allusive, beating his own unpredictable path through a variety of terrains. Never denying that he has been told much of how and where to go by great poets of the past, he also seems always to have known that their counsel—if it is to be taken at all—cannot be taken literally. This is one of the reasons that his poetry can be so powerfully concerned with roots—cultural, intellectual and spiritual—and with journeyings, both of which are often baleful cliches in so much contemporary verse. But a true poet's metaphor of the journey taken by his or her poetic work itself may have a much more complex and—ultimately—more universal tale to tell.

A widely and deeply read African-American from New Mexico, Wright took a graduate degree in comparative literature at Rutgers, where he studied with the critic and teacher—also originally from Albuquerque—Francis Fergusson. Wright taught for a while in Scotland, and also from time to time in universities in this country, but for the past 25 years has lived rather reclusively with his wife in rural New England. His poetry gives evidence of a bookish and extremely thoughtful life while encountering the forms and rituals of cultures without literatures—West African, Mexican and Central American—as well as the writers—Augustine, Goethe, Rilke, David Hume, Hugh MacDiarmid—whose

From *The New York Times* (January 28, 2001) © 2001 by *The New York Times*.

traces we find allusively placed throughout his work. Wright's poetic mythmaking derives as much from a purely American sort of engagement with major late Romantic poetry as it has to do with anthropologically framed story, song and ritual.

For the title of Wright's "Homecoming Singer" (1971) home is indeed New Mexico, but in the course of this immensely impressive first book we see it also as paradigmatic poetic ground, rather than merely a literal autobiographical locus. In the fine "Sketch for an Aesthetic Project" he speaks of "parchments of blood, / sunk where I cannot walk": this trope returns in a poem in a 1984 volume ("The Continuing City: Spirit and Body," from "Explications/Interpretations") as a bit of manifesto: "I take the earth beneath me / as parchment and intention, / memory and project of all / movement it contains." That the earth might be a document, or even a memory, is most Emersonian, but that it is an intention and a project is a very different kind of figure. "I await my completion in a strange house," the poem concludes, "my soul's rags falling in pride from its door." The earth beneath Wright's poems keeps moving about. A moment of light on Central Park Lake and Loch Lomond, or Cornelia Street in Greenwich Village calling up the story of the jewels of the Gracchi: all grounded in Wright's unfolding "parchment and intention."

In "Transfigurations," his monumental new complete collection, one can follow Wright's imaginative explorations of a variety of mythopoeic regions. This volume contains all his work, from the fascinating book-length poem called "The Double Invention of Komo"—only a small bit of which was in an earlier collection—to his most recent book and a good number of previously unpublished recent poems; only a few very early pieces from a 1967 chapbook are not included.

Wright's poetry cannot fit the most obvious sorts of generic categories in which popular cultural journalism might wish to place it, particularly under rubrics like "African-American poetry" or "poetry of the Southwest." If some things in it seem to have been shown their way— as the critic Robert Stepto has pointed out—by Robert Hayden, others, particularly in his earlier books, were profoundly engaged with the poetry of Hart Crane, both in their chastely forceful use of high diction and in their central quest for imaginative identity, as Harold Bloom has long recognized. At the end of a central poem in his first book called "Preparing to Leave Home," the speaker acknowledges, as he starts out on an imaginative quest, "I have not prepared. / I have gone too soon." But these stark lines, poetic in their allegorical reach rather than in their work and play with language, are preceded by a line of almost pure Crane, "The melancholy bells repeat themselves," referring to no literal bells present earlier in the poem. In a fine little poem on Crispus Attucks, the African-American killed in the Boston Massacre, the recollection is not only of a historical moment but of the continuing history and meaning of remembrance itself, a matter for Crane more than Whitman, say: "Now, we think of you, / when, through the sibilant streets, / another season drums / your intense, communal daring."

In Wright's later books he moves among lyric personae, having liberated himself, in his earlier work, from even the shadow of literal autobiography. In one of the odes of "Boleros," Art Tatum, the great blind jazz pianist, speaks of his improvisation:

> So I lay two notes in the bar ahead,
> diminish a major,
> tunnel through the dark
> of the brightest minor,
> and come out on the right side of the song.
> I pick the composer's pocket,
> and lay the hidden jewels out there.

This account suggests one of Browning's ventriloquistic musicians, talking as much about poetry as about musical composition. But the next lines bring all this home to Wright's characteristic imaginative concerns:

> Hammer and anvil guide the music of my
> house,
> smithy of the ear's anticipations, forge
> of the mind in what it denies
> and what it fulfills.

Throughout Wright's poetry, the speaker's body is central, and yet it is treated metaphorically in an array of different ways, all of them differing from anything Whitmanian or narcissistic. Bodily and mental partitionings, phases and elements of ritual, calendrical mappings— whether canonical saints' days or moments of remembered weather across two continents—all help name and shape parts of poetic structure for him. But language is as tactile for him as body, and the later "Desire's Persistence" and "The Anatomy of Resonance" are companion poems in their structural method. Each starts from an epigraph and then meditates on each of the substantive words therein. One epigraph is from a 1582

Spanish translation of Nahuatl poetry, the other is two lines from HRated PG-13lderlin. Even in the confrontation of these two precursor texts, the course of one of the paths taken by this remarkable singer, continuing to set out on various homecomings, becomes clear as the songs themselves become ever more vivid.

STEVEN MEYER

Transfigurations:
Collected Poems

J ay Wright is an unsung wonder of contemporary American poetry. To
be sure, he has received some choice acknowledgments: he's been a
MacArthur Fellow, a Guggenheim Fellow, and a Hodder Fellow, as well as
the recipient of awards from the Ingram-Merrill Foundation, the Lannan
Foundation, and the American Academy and Institute of Arts and Letters.
Still, each of his seven previous volumes has quickly gone out of print or,
due to the obscurity of the press, been all but impossible to find. As a
result, Wright has barely registered with the broader poetry audience. If
this means that most readers will experience *Transfigurations* as a first
book, then *what* a first book—displaying both the proverbial promise and
the astonishing fulfillment of that promise.

Volumes of collected poems like *Transfigurations* (more than thirty
years in the making) often force together earlier collections which cohere
only because they were written by the same person, not because of any
internal logic. With Wright, things are very different. In 1983—after he
had published five of the eight volumes included here—Wright said that
he had initially conceived of a series of volumes that would take the
dynamic form of "an octave progression." Having completed the first five
volumes, however, he realized that what he actually had was "a dominant
one" and that he was "working toward the tonic in a new progression."

From *Boston Review* (April/May 2002) © 2002 *Boston Review*.

Translated, this means that Wright's first book, *The Homecoming Singer*, set the basic tone for his eight-volume sequence; that the fifth volume, *The Double Invention of Komo*, stands in an especially close relationship to the first; and that the eighth volume, *Transformations*, which collects thirty-three new poems, returns at a higher pitch to the matter initially introduced by the tonic (even as, in conjunction with volumes six and seven of the sequence, *Elaine's Book* and *Boleros*, it resolves tensions introduced by the dominant).

Wright recalls having "discovered the pattern" of *The Homecoming Singer* "almost *a posteriori*. I had, as I looked at it, the record of my developing black African-American life in the United States, but I also saw that I had the beginning of forms to express lives that transcended that particular life." From early to late, Wright has been concerned to express "black people acting in history." As he put it memorably in "The Albuquerque Graveyard," in his second volume, *Soothsayers and Omens*,

> I am going back
> to the Black limbo,
> an unwritten history
> of our own tensions.
> The dead lie here
> in a hierarchy of small defeats.

These defeats ("small") match the triumphs ("small") he celebrated in "Wednesday Night Prayer Meeting," the poem that opened *The Homecoming Singer* and consequently opens *Transfigurations*, articulating

> the uncompromising
> need of old black men and women,
> who know that pain is what
> you carry in the mind,
> in the solemn memory of small triumphs,
> that you get, here,
> as the master of your pain.

So uncompromising are these adepts of "the insoluble / mysteries of being black / and sinned against, black / and sinning in the compliant cities," that Christ himself, who joins them, writhing "as if he would be black," is ignored. "He stands up to sing, / but a young girl, / getting up from the mourner's bench, / tosses her head in a wail." The poem concludes "This is the end of the night," and thus opens the way for the persistent questing of the poems still to come:

> and he has not come there yet,
> has not made it into the stillness
> of himself, or the flagrant uncertainty
> of all these other singers.
> They have taken his strangeness,
> and given it back, the way a lover
> will return the rings and letters
> of a lover who hurts him.
> They have closed their night
> with what certainty they could,
> unwilling to exchange their freedom for a god.

They are unwilling, that is, to compromise the small triumphs of self-mastery, the freedom that inheres in "the small, / imperceptible act" ("Benjamin Banneker Helps to Build a City"), for the sake of a "god / who chains us to this place"—a master enslaved to himself, "pitiable," "without grace, / without the sense of that small / beginning of movement, / where even the god / becomes another and not himself, / himself and not another." In place of *the* Transfiguration on Mount Tabor, we are presented, as we progress across Wright's octave, with many, many *transfigurations*, as Wright seeks to define in his poetry "a new and capable personality at home in the transformative and transformed world."

This last remark, closing his 1987 manifesto, "Desire's Design, Vision's Resonance: Black Poetry's Ritual and Historical Voice," designates the task that distinguishes "Afro-American poetry" from its African counterpart, even as "black experience in the Americas ... challenges the African world to examine itself." Although Wright meticulously reconstructs the initiation ceremonies of the Komo cult among the Bambara people of West Africa in *The Double Invention of Komo*, he does not do so in the spirit of returning to some putative origin. On the contrary, he aims to contribute to a New World "redefinition of the person" through the "formal juxtaposition" of "African, European, and American ... voices and persons" in the book-length poem.[1] Poetry's "extreme manipulative consciousness" fits this task of redefinition: because it "handles its 'facts'" with a certain "disdain" and "its spiritual domain" with a degree of "critical detachment," poetry is especially well suited to creating the sort of "awareness of differing and seemingly incompatible relationships" demanded by such redefinition, or transfiguration.

As Wright suggests, a pretty fair "record of [his] developing black African-American life in the United States" may be gleaned from the poems he chose to include in *The Homecoming Singer*. Born in Albuquerque, he was raised by guardians—see "The Hunting Trip Cook" as well as "The Faithful One" in *Soothsayers and Omens*—after his parents separated when he was three years old. At fourteen, he joined his father (who was light-skinned enough to pass for white) in the "naval city" of San Pedro, California. (See "Jason's One Command" and "A Non-Birthday Poem for my Father.") Poems about summer and winter jobs ("The Fisherman's Fiesta," "Two House Painters Take Stock of the Fog," "Track Cleaning") are concerned with a young man's growing awareness of what it means to be black in the United States at mid-century, as, more obviously, are "W. E. B. Du Bois at Harvard" and "Crispus Attucks." So, too, the poems about Mexico, where Wright taught in 1964 ("You come, black and bilingual, / to a passage of feeling, / to a hall of remembered tones, / to the acrylic colors of your own death"), about visiting New Hampshire ("I amble in this New England reticence, / cocksure of my blackness, / unsure of just how white / and afraid my neighbors are"), or about living in New York—where he moved in 1961 after three years in the army and three more as an older undergraduate at Berkeley ("I wait, here near the ocean, for the north wind, / and the waves breaking up on ships. / At this point, the slave ships would dock, / creeping up the shoreline, / with their bloody cargo intact ... ").

In his stunningly intransigent "Sketch for an Aesthetic Project," Wright says: "I have made a log for passage, / out there, where some still live, / and pluck my bones. / There are parchments of blood / sunk where I cannot walk. / But when there is silence here, / I hear a mythic shriek." In these lines, Wright sketches the shape of the "aesthetic project" he hears reverberating in that shriek. Call it *Transfigurations:* a work of neither fixed ends nor established beginnings, but of "passage" and "beginning again," as the title of *The Homecoming Singer*'s final poem has it. If the volumes collected in *Transfigurations* proceed rhythmically by means of rigorous renewals, in the end they form an astonishing New World epic—or anti-epic, since this is no tale of founding but of re-founding, of continuing re-creation, of creative juxtaposition. The victor may get the spoils, but the vanquished don't vanish. This multicultural engine—which Wright characterized in the early 1980s as "the fundamental process of human history"—has always been at work, even in the most isolated communities, but its recognition has been broadly resisted. For Wright (and he is surely not alone in this impression) the fact of an ever-widening community of humankind required the peculiar dynamics of the New World in order to be articulated and acknowledged. For this reason, "the African world," for instance, is challenged to self-examination by black experience in the Americas; and for this reason, *Transfigurations* may be viewed as a work of genuinely epic proportions and ambitions, albeit with a very different sort of hero: that "new and capable personality at home in the transformative and transformed world," seeking to understand what Wright refers to in the book-length poem *Dimensions of History* as "our life among ourselves."

Wright's progressive definition of this new personality may be charted in a series of poems that transfigure his basic device of "beginning again" in the terms and imagery of baptism. These include both "The Baptism" and "Baptism in the Lead Avenue Ditch" in his first two volumes, followed by the remarkable "MacIntyre, the Captain and the Saints" in *Explications/Interpretations*, in which Wright *elects* a Scottish heritage for himself; by "Landscapes: The Physical Dimension," suturing Mexico and the United States with Venezuela, Colombia, and Panama, in *Dimensions of History*; by "The Opening of the Ceremony / the Coming Out of Komo" ("I will be written in water, / measured in my body's curative syntax"); by "The Lake in Central Park" in *Elaine's Book* ("It should have a woman's name"); by "17 / [Melpomene <-> ba]" in *Boleros* ("When, tonight, under a new moon, / the soul's calendar turns another page, / I will go down, ash laden, and walk / the transforming light of Banaras," the great North India pilgrimage destination on the Ganges); and, in *Transformations*, by "The Anti-Fabliau of Saturnino Orestes 'Minnie' Miñoso" ("I had heard reports of a sanctified / woman in the town, one who could provide / hope in a dry season ... / But how could I bring myself to confide / in one who would bathe me in a flood tide / of improprieties ...").

Wright has always been exceptionally attentive to the formal possibilities of poetry, but he usually avoids traditional forms of versification. In *Transformations*, however, he embraces a broad range of rhyme and syllabic schemes. There are seguidillas and zejels, redondillas and sonnets, sextillas, dactylic hexameter, and a villancico to match the earlier "Villancico" in *Dimensions of History*, as well as the unique transformations that he works on a Keats ode ("The Navigation of Absences: An Ode on Method"), on the Spenserian stanza ("Intuition: Figure and Act"), on Donne's "Nocturnal upon S. Lucy's Day" ("Love's Augustine or, What's Done is Donne"), on blues rhythm ("The Healing Improvisation of Hair"), on both the Provençal retroencha ("The Hieroglyph of Irrational Force") and the dansa Provençal ("Lichens and

Oranges"), on the busy bees of Oulipo, the late-twentieth-century "workshop of potential literature" ("Coda V"), and on Thelonious Monk ("Coda VI"). These are *all* remarkable works, but no less remarkable is the way that Wright, by placing them at the close of so substantial a volume of intricate formal patterning, enables his readers to experience these formal schemes as *chosen* rather than imposed, emergent rather than imitated.

In 1969 Wright published an article in *Sports Illustrated* on baseball, the "diamond-bright art form." Partly autobiographical—Wright played minor-league ball in the St. Louis Cardinals organization after he graduated from high school—and partly analytic, the article ends with a commentary on a third-strike pitch to a close friend who was then home-run champion of the Mexican league:

> That pitch, more than any other, bothered me. It was such a blatant challenge, such a perverse reward for 15 years .... And at that moment I could think of baseball as the realization, the summit of a masculine esthetic—an esthetic, which, as in the highest art, summarizes a man's life, sets him in a historical context where he measures himself against the highest achievement and where he feels that he is perpetuating the spirit of the bst of his chosen work. Aggressive, at times mean, at times petty and foolish, the ballplayer still tries to transcend, by the perfection of his craft, the limitations that are inherent in it, and in himself .... Where we end is in the seemingly absurd realization that, for a good many, the game looks like life .... Our Yankee scout would say that is the American way. I would say it is something more, that baseball offers the ballplayer what any man can learn of art, and of his life as art.

In the thirty-odd years since he wrote these words, Jay Wright has written poetry in a similar spirit. He has composed an extraordinary epic of human transfiguration and transformation, of nothing less than the great work of art that is "our life among ourselves."

NOTE

1. This description comes from the "Afterword" appended to the original edition of *Double Invention;* unfortunately, like explanatory material in several of the volumes, it does not appear in the present edition.

Chronology

1935	Born on May 25 in Albuquerque, New Mexico.
1953	Finishes high school in San Pedro, California.
1954	Plays semiprofessional baseball in the Arizona/Texas and California State leagues. Joins the United States Army where he serves for three years.
1961	Earns a Bachelor's degree from the University of California, Berkeley.
1967	Earns a Master's degree in Comparative Literature from Rutger's University. Publishes first chapbook of poems, *Death as History*.
1968	Moves to Mexico. Awarded a Woodrow Wilson/National Endowment for the Arts Poets-in-Concert fellowship. Publishes the play *Balloons: A Comedy in One Act*.
1970	Granted a Hodder fellowship in playwrighting from Princeton University.
1971	Moves to Scotland; is the Fellow in Creative Writing at Dundee University. Publishes first major collection of poems, *The Homecoming Singer*.
1974	Receives Ingram Merrill Foundation award and a Guggenheim fellowship.
1975	Receives a Guggenheim fellowship. Starts teaching at Yale University where he stays until 1979.

1976   Publishes two volumes of poetry, *Soothsayers and Omens* and *Dimensions of History*.

1980   Publishes collection of poems, *The Double Invention of Komo*.

1984   Publishes collection of poems, *Explications/Interpretations*, in the *Callaloo* Poetry Series, Books on Demand.

1986   Receives a MacArthur fellowship (through 1991).

1987   Publishes *Selected Poems of Jay Wright*.

1988   Publishes *Elaine's Book*.

1991   Publishes *Boleros*.

1995   Named a Fellow of The Academy of American Poets.

2000   Publishes *Transfigurations: Collected Poems*. Receives the Lannan Literary Award for Poetry.

Contributors

HAROLD BLOOM is Sterling Professor of the Humanities at Yale University and Henry W. and Albert A. Berg Professor of English at the New York University Graduate School. He is the author of over 20 books, including *Shelley's Mythmaking* (1959), *The Visionary Company* (1961), *Blake's Apocalypse* (1963), *Yeats* (1970), *A Map of Misreading* (1975), *Kabbalah and Criticism* (1975), *Agon: Toward a Theory of Revisionism* (1982), *The American Religion* (1992), *The Western Canon* (1994), and *Omens of Millennium: The Gnosis of Angels, Dreams, and Resurrection* (1996). *The Anxiety of Influence* (1973) sets forth Professor Bloom's provocative theory of the literary relationships between the great writers and their predecessors. His most recent books include *Shakespeare: The Invention of the Human* (1998), a 1998 National Book Award finalist, *How to Read and Why* (2000), *Genius: A Mosaic of One Hundred Exemplary Creative Minds* (2002), and *Hamlet: Poem Unlimited* (2003). In 1999, Professor Bloom received the prestigious American Academy of Arts and Letters Gold Medal for Criticism, and in 2002 he received the Catalonia International Prize.

DARRYL PINCKNEY has worked as a novelist and literary critic. His essays and reviews have appeared in *New York Review of Books*, *New York Times Book Review* and *Parnassus*.

GERALD BARRAX is Professor Emeritus of English at North Carolina State University at Raleigh. In addition to scholarly essays, he has authored books of poetry including *Another Kind of Rain* (1970) and *An Audience of One* (1980).

ROBERT B. STEPTO is Professor of English, African-American Studies, and American Studies at Yale University. He is the author of *From Behind the Veil: A Study of Afro-American Narrative* (1991).

VERA M. KUTZINSKI is Professor of English, African-American Studies, and American Studies at Yale University. Her essays have appeared in *Black American Literature Forum, Modern Language Notes* and *Hambone*. She is the author of *Against the American Grain: Myth and History in William Carlos Williams, Jay Wright, and Nicolas Guillen* (1987).

CHARLES H. ROWELL has worked in the department of English at the University of Kentucky, and is editor of the journal *Callaloo*.

ROBERT B. SHAW has been a prolific literary critic and scholar. In addition to essays and reviews, he is the author of the book of poems *The Wonder of Seeing Double* (1988).

ISIDORE OKPEWHO is Professor of Africana Studies, Comparative Literature, and English at SUNY Binghamton. In addition to literary essays, he has authored novels, such as *The Last Duty* (1976), and scholarly volumes, such as *The Heritage of African Poetry* (1985).

RON WELBURN has been an essayist and scholar of West African and contemporary American poetry. His work has appeared in such journals as *MELUS*.

PAUL CHRISTENSEN has been an essayist and scholar of American poetry and literature. An essay of his was included in the volume *Contemporary Poets*.

JOHN HOLLANDER, distinguished Poet and Critic, is Sterling Prefessor Emeritus of English at Yale University. He has earned numerous fellowships and is a past chancellor of the Academy of American Poets. He has written seventeen volume sof poetry including *The Figurehead* (1999), *Tesserae* (1993), *Selected Poetry* (1993). His books of criticism include: *The Work of Poetry* (1997), *Melodious Guile* (1988), *The Figure of Echo* (1981),

Rhyme's Reason (1981), *Vision and Resonance* (1975), *Images of Voice* (1970), and *The Untuning of the Sky* (1961).

STEVEN MEYER teaches modern literature and contemporary literature at Washington University. His works include *Irresistible Dictation: Gertrude Stein and the Correlations of Writing and Science* (2001), "Ashbery: Poet for All Seasons," and "Critical Self-Critic (Gertrude Stein)."

Bibliography

Aasgaard, Elise Bordes. "'Weaving Speech into Spirit': Revisionism and Ritual in the Late Poetry of T.S. Eliot and Jay Wright." *Dissertation Abstracts International*, Section A: The Humanities and Social Sciences, 61:5 (November, 2000), 1834.

Barrax, Gerald. "The Early Poetry of Jay Wright." *Jay Wright: A Special Issue. Callaloo 19* vol. 6, no. 3 (Fall 1983): 85–101.

Benston, Kimberly W. "'I Yam What I Am': Naming and Unnaming in Afro-American Literature." *BALF* 16 (Spring 1982): 3–11.

Danquah, J.B. *The Akan Doctrine of God: A Fragment of Gold Coast Ethics and Religion*, 1944. London: Frank Cass Press, 1968.

Doreski, C.K. "Decolonizing the Spirits: History and Storytelling in Jay Wright's *Soothsayers and Omens*." *Reading Race in American Poetry: 'An Area of Act'*, ed. Aldon Lynn Nielson, Urbana: University of Illinois Press, 2000: 183–208.

Fortes, Meyer. *Religion, Morality and the Person: Essays on Tallensi Religion*. Cambridge: Cambridge University Press, 1987.

Gates, Henry Louis, J. *The Signifying Monkey: A Theory of Afro-American Literary Criticism*. New York: Oxford University Press, 1988.

Gilroy, Paul. *The Black Atlantic: Modernity and Double Consciousness*. Cambridge: Harvard University Press, 1993.

Hallenbeck, Cleve. *The Journey of Fray Marcos de Niza*. Dallas: Southern Methodist University Press, 1987.

Harris, Wilson. *The Womb of Space*. Westport: Greenwood Press, 1983.

Hodge, Frederick Webb. *History of Hawikuh, New Mexico: One of the So-Called Cities of Cibola*. Los Angeles: The Southwest Museum, 1937.

Hollander, John. "Tremors of Exactitude" [on *The Double Invention of Komo*]. *TLS*, 30 (January 1981): 115.

——. "Poetry in Review." *Yale Review* 74 (November 1984): 301–14.

Jahn, Janheinz. *Muntu: An Outline of the New African Culture*. Trans. Marjorie Grene. New York: Grove Press, 1961.

Kilson, Martin and Adelaide C. Hill, eds. *Apropos of Africa: Afro-American Leaders and the Romance of Africa*. Garden City: Anchor Press, 1971.

Kutzinski, Vera M. "The Descent of Nommo: Literacy as Method in Jay Wright's 'Benjamin Banneker Helps to Build a City.'" *Jay Wright: A Special Issue. Callaloo 19* vol. 6, no. 3 (Fall 1983): 103–19.

——. "Something Strange and Miraculous and Transforming." *Hambone 2* (Fall 1982): 129–34.

——. *Against the American Grain: Myth and History in William Carlos Williams, Jay Wright, and Nicolas Guillen*. Baltimore: The Johns Hopkins University Press, 1987.

Lauter, Paul et al., eds. *The Health Anthology of American Literature, Vol 2*. Lexington, MA: D.C. Heath, 1990: 2461–67.

Manson, Michael Tomasek. "The Clarity of Being Strange: Jay Wright's *The Double Invention of Komo*." *Black American Literature Forum*, 24:3 (Fall, 1990): 473–89.

Okpewho, Isidore. *The Epic in Africa: Toward a Poetics of the Oral Performance*. New York: Columbia University Press, 1979.

——. "From A Goat Path in Africa: An Approach to the Poetry of Jay Wright." *Callaloo* vol. 14, no. 3 (Summer 1991): 692–726

Pinckney, Darryl. "You're in the Army Now." *Parnassus: Poetry in Review* 9 (Spring–Summer 1981): 301–14.

Richard, Philip M. "Jay Wright." In *Dictionary of Literary Biography*, vol. 41: *Afro-American Poets Since 1955*. Eds. T. Harris and T.M. Davis. Detroit: Gale, 1985.

Rowell, Charles H. "The Unravelling of the Egg: An Interview with Jay Wright." *Jay Wright: A Special Issue. Callaloo 19* vol. 6, no. 3 (Fall 1983): 3–15.

Sauer, Carl. "The Road to Cibola." *Ibero-Americana* no. 3. Berkeley: University of California Press, 1932.

Soyinka, Wole. "The Fourth Stage." *Myth, Literature and the African World*. Cambridge: Cambridge University Press, 1976: 140–60.

Stepto, Robert B. "After Modernism, After Hibernation: Michael Harper, Robert Hayden, and Jay Wright." *Chant of Saints: A Gathering of Afro-American Art, Literature, and Scholarship*, edited by Michael S.

Harper and Robert B. Stepto. Urbana: University of Illinois Press, 1979: 470–86.

———. "'The Aching Prodigal': Jay Wright's Dutiful Poet." *Jay Wright: A Special Issue. Callaloo 19* vol. 6, no. 3 (Fall 1983): 103–19.

Temple, Robert K.G. *The Sirius Mystery.* New York: St. Martin's Press, 1976.

Terrell, John Upton. *Estavanico the Black.* Los Angeles: Westernlore, 1968.

Acknowledgments

"You're in the Army Now (Jay Wright, Etheridge Knight)" by Darryl Pinckney. From *Parnassus: Poetry in Review* (Fall/Winter 1981): 306–314–15. © 1983 by Darryl Pinckney. Reprinted by permission.

Barrax, Gerald. "The Early Poetry of Jay Wright." From *Jay Wright: A Special Issue. Callaloo 19*, vol. 6 no. 3 (Fall 1983): 85–101. © 1983 by Charles H. Rowell. Reprinted with permission of The Johns Hopkins University Press.

Stepto, Robert B. "'The Aching Prodigal': Jay Wright's Dutiful Poet." From *Jay Wright: A Special Issue. Callaloo 19*, vol. 6 no. 3 (Fall 1983): 76–84, © 1983 by Charles H. Rowell. Reprinted with permission of The Johns Hopkins University Press.

Kutzinski, Vera M. "The Descent of Nommo: Literacy as Method in Jay Wright's 'Benjamin Banneker Helps to Build a City.'" From *Jay Wright: A Special Issue. Callaloo 19*, vol. 6 no. 3 (Fall 1983): 102–119. © 1983 by Charles H. Rowell. Reprinted with permission of The Johns Hopkins University Press.

Rowell, Charles H. "'The Unraveling of the Egg': An Interview with Jay Wright." From *Jay Wright: A Special Issue. Callaloo 19*, vol. 6 no. 3 (Fall 1983): 3–15, © 1983 by Charles H. Rowell. Reprinted with permission of The Johns Hopkins University Press.

Kutzinski, Vera M. "Jay Wright's Mythology of Writing: The Black Limbo." From *Against the American Grain: Myth and History in William Carlos Williams, Jay Wright, and Nicolas Guillen.* © 1987 by The Johns Hopkins University Press. Reprinted with permission of The Johns Hopkins University Press.

"*Selected Poems of Jay Wright:* Review" by Robert B. Shaw. From *Poetry*, 152, no. 1 (April 1988): 45–47. © 1983 by *Poetry.* Reprinted by permission.

Okpewho, Isidore. "From A Goat Path in Africa: An Approach to the Poetry of Jay Wright." From *Callaloo* vol. 14, no. 3 (Summer 1991): 692–726, © 1991 by Charles H. Rowell. Reprinted by permission.

"Jay Wright's Poetics: An Appreciation" by Ron Welburn. From *MELUS* 18, no. 3 (Fall 1993): 51–70, © 1993 by *MELUS.* Reprinted by permission.

"Jay Wright: Overview" by Paul Christensen. From *Contemporary Poets, 6th Edition*, ed. Thomas Riggs. © 1996 by St. James Press. Reprinted by permission of The Gale Group.

"Poems That Walk Anywhere" by John Hollander. From *the New York Times* (January 28, 2001) © 2001 by *The New York Times.* Reprinted by permission.

"*Transfigurations: Collected Poems*" by Steven Meyer from *Boston Review* (April/May 2002) © 2002 by Steven Meyer. Reprinted by pemission.

Index